THE WESTMINSTER ABBEY SINGERS

Dean's Yard today: a painting by Donald C. Towner

THE
WESTMINSTER ABBEY
SINGERS

Edward Pine

London
DENNIS DOBSON

FIRST PUBLISHED IN GREAT BRITAIN IN MCMLIII
BY DENNIS DOBSON LTD., 12 PARK PLACE, ST JAMES'S, LONDON S.W.1
ALL RIGHTS RESERVED
PRINTED IN GREAT BRITAIN BY
THE CARLYLE PRESS, BIRMINGHAM, 6
331 R

To
EDWARD W. THOMPSON
for many reasons

CONTENTS

CONTENTS

PART TWO

HEARSAY

ILLUSTRATIONS

The jacket design shows the interior of the Abbey in 1753, and is taken from a contemporary print.

THE author of this book has broken new ground. The story of the Westminster Abbey Choir School has never before been told, for no one has been at pains to dig up the facts that lie embedded in old Chapter Minute Books, the Abbey Muniments and other documents in the Record Office, the British Museum and elsewhere.

Mr Pine has by long and diligent research unearthed much interesting information which he has woven into a story going back past the dissolution of the Monastery to the early Tudor days and beyond. He has also thrown new light on the confused period of the Commonwealth, when Westminster Abbey suffered the indignity of being turned into a Puritan preaching house. But at the Restoration daily worship in accordance with the Book of Common Prayer was revived, and from that day to this the choristers have handed on the fine tradition of Church Music for which Westminster Abbey has always been renowned.

The choristers, whose presence in Dean's Yard adds so much to the gaiety of the Abbey precincts, have every reason to thank Mr Pine for putting on record the annals of a Choir School in which all connected with Westminster Abbey take so legitimate a pride.

Alan C. Don
Dean

SETTING

HER MAJESTY THE Queen left the Abbey after the Maundy Service, the first official engagement of her reign, amid a roar from the crowds. Walton's *Crown Imperial* rode triumphantly to its close, as the scarlet-and-white robed figures moved silently out into the cloisters, across the ancient flagstones and into the Song School. The door closed and they were gone.

After a few minutes out came twenty-two boys between the ages of ten and fourteen, dressed in grey pullovers and corduroy shorts, grey shirts and stockings. A master took charge, and the boys went silently in twos under the stone arches and out into Dean's Yard where talking began.

They continued along the pavement to the entrance of their school and, on the five steps which led up to the door-way, grouped momentarily. A gong sounded, and they went clattering in to lunch.

Before following them in, let us pause a moment and look at the things they saw.

The entire length of the side opposite is composed of ancient buildings, some dating from the thirteenth century, some now part of Westminster School. The south side of the square is occupied by the mass of Church House, which has replaced Queen Anne houses: the north is of mock Gothic. The west, on which side the Choir School stands, is also unattractive architecturally, so that there is no doubt that

13

the choristers have the best view in Dean's Yard. The strange thing is that the first school building of which there is any record seems to have been only a few yards from the present site.

Here, if the eye had not been so busy looking at stones, it would certainly have noticed first the trees. Through their branches and high above them rises the Abbey, and there is probably no finer vantage point, unless it be from the very roof of the school, below which are seven lofty floors housing the thirty-six boys and the staff.

Immediately below the roof is a covered playground from which come in the evening the sounds of football and skating. Sometimes it is used for relay races, but only if it is wet outside and the juniors are in the gymnasium.

On the floor below are the sick rooms and the flat of the Headmaster, Mr E. W. Thompson, who came from Sherborne Preparatory School, when the school reopened in 1947 with thirty-three boys. Although thirteen of them had sung in the Temporary Choir, only three or four had been to a boarding school before. Under good organization, they settled down amazingly well.

Anyone coming into the buildings now would find little difference between the day-to-day existence of the boys here and those belonging to the ordinary preparatory schools of London. It is true that rehearsals and services take up time differently spent in other schools, but ingenuity provides games of football, athletics and cricket on many days of the week, and the list of fixtures with other teams is impressive. The long terms make amends, so that the syllabus does not suffer, and a keen eye is kept on the due proportion of games and work to music. The result is that when the boys come to leave, they find that they fit easily and successfully into their bigger schools.

This is very different from earlier days, for England has

always been cavalier towards her artists; but choristers are no longer boy players, no longer little madrigalists carted about by a Farrant or a Cooke. To the very vexed question of Choir School education, the Abbey seems today to have found an effective answer.

But what of the boys and men who sang at the coronations of the past, at the great occasions which the memorials recall? These, though expendable, left some traces behind. To follow the footsteps of these singers, whose existence flourished in flesh and blood, not in enduring stone, is the purpose of this book.

It could have begun with veiled references to the four centuries following the foundation by St Edward the Confessor, as there were certainly boys singing at the Abbey by 1388: and in 1392 a Brother Peter Cumbe bought clothes for one boy, possibly the Boy Bishop for that year; and 'a certain Nicholas' was paid 26s. 8d. for playing 'ad organa' in 1387-8. As he also appears in the Chapel Royal accounts he apparently provides a connection between the Abbey and the Chapel.

The year 1479 however has been taken as a starting point because that is the first time a separate Master of the Singing Boys is named. The research involved would have been impossible without the kind permission of the Dean and Chapter to examine and use the Chapter Minutes (which begin in 1542) and the 70,000 Abbey Muniments, whose Keeper, Mr Laurence E. Tanner, M.V.O., F.S.A., gave unrestricted access and valued encouragement.

PART ONE

DOCUMENTARY

'Mediaeval education began with the Song School: and although the universities and the other great seats of learning came to be much more than glorified choirs, they still retained certain traces of their humble origin.'

Sir E. K. Chambers,
THE MEDIAEVAL STAGE, i. 362-3

Chapter One

THE SUN IN SPLENDOUR

Tʜᴇ ʏᴇᴀʀ 1479-80 is a most important one because in that year for the first time there is given the name of the separate Master who taught the singing boys alone, though boys were singing at the Abbey long before. It appears to be a new appointment. His name was William Cornyshe, and the name at once arouses echoes in many books of reference.

It is worth noting that he was paid 13s. 4d. for teaching the singing boys, while the schoolmaster, unnamed, received 40s. Historians of Westminster School consider from the amounts spent on the cloth for the boys that those in the Grammar School numbered between twenty and thirty with a fairly stable number at twenty. There were forty of them after the Henrician dissolution of the Abbey when there were ten choristers on the foundation. Two of the forty are marked as 'late querister'. However, from 1486-7 until 1493 the Schoolmaster was paid only 26s. 8d. In 1493-4 the stipend returned to 40s. again.

Cornyshe's name is entered among the 'famuli' or servants of the Almonry; but then at the Marian restoration in 1556 the names 'Boorne, Cavall, VI choristars' are immediately followed in one draft by embroiderers and gardeners; though that was certainly not the position of the singers when Henry VIII's new College at Westminster was founded nor of William Grene their Master who in 1535 was described as: 'generosus'.

It seems most likely that the special favours shown to the Abbey in the 1470's were connected with the asylum which was given to Queen Elizabeth Woodville when she fled to the abbot for sanctuary on the Kingmaker's rebellion against her husband Edward IV in 1470-1. Her son and heir, the ill-fated Edward V, was born there and her daughter Elizabeth later married Henry VII whose proclamation of 1497 must have been of considerable assistance to the choral establishment of the Abbey.

The unpublished Accounts of St Margaret's parish seem to provide the thread that may lead out of the Cornyshe maze. There were obviously two Williams, as in the accounts for 1500-2 appears: 'for the knelle of Willm Cornysshe wt the grete belle vj*d* . . . for iiij torches for hym iiij*s*.' Soon afterwards is: '. . . at the moneth mynde of Willm Cornyssh for iiij tapres xvj*d* . . . for iiij torches iiij*s*' and: 'Itm Rd of Willm Cornyssh wyffe for the bequeste of hyr husband vj*s* viij*d*.' This means that he cannot be the William Cornyshe of the *Treatise between Trouthe and Informacion*. That was probably his son.

One other piece of evidence seems relevant and would appear to clear another difficulty, showing that Hawkins was right in assigning 'Hoyda, jolly ruttekin' to 'John Cornysh junior'. This is the will of 1474 made by John Cornyshe of St John Zacharie London. There he expressly begins: '. . . Ego Johannes Cornyssh senior . . .' and refers to his children John, Anne and William. He names also another son, Richard. To each he left twenty pounds sterling and other gifts.

There seems to have been a third generation as, in 1528-30, the churchwardens were still making payments to a Master Cornyshe, whereas William the impresario, composer and author died in 1524.

There was a William or John Cornish who set a carol for

20

the Queen in 1493. *The Cambridge History of English Literature* states that 'the elder William Cornish was master of the Song School at Westminster Abbey in 1479-80'. The Abbey Muniments, however, show that he was there not only then but received payments for teaching the singing boys until 1490-1 when he was paid a half year's salary and the name disappears from the Abbey Records; except for W.A.M. 33301 which has for 14 Henry VIII 'ffyrst in reward to Mast Cornysh on seynt Edwards day ao xiiij . . . Xs' On many occasions vestments were lent by him to the churchwardens of St Margaret's.

The details of the life of William Cornyshe junior have been discussed by Rimbault and others. His *Treatise between Trouthe and Informacion*, printed in the 1568 edition of Skelton's works, is worth studying for its references to music. Possibly it was written in collaboration with Skelton. Apparently trouble with Sir Richard Empsom, one of Henry VII's principal tax-gatherers, had landed Cornyshe in the Fleet Prison in 1504, but he was soon restored to favour and was a most popular pageant master.

One cannot help wondering whether it was Empsom the Minister or Empsom a singingman who was meant; and whether it was a quarrel between musicians, as an Empsom was connected with the Abbey Choir and was paid 20*d*. on the St Edward's Day 14 Henry VIII on which Cornyshe received ten shillings. Another Empsom was a chorister in 1540. Possibly they were poor relations of the Minister.

He is named amongst Fees and Annuities paid by the King in 1516 as 'W. Cornyshe Master of the Children of the Chapel . . . £26. 13*s*. 4*d*.' According to the Household Book of Henry VIII it seems that he himself composed at least some of the plays acted by the boys and the *Story of Troylus and Pandor* which was acted before Henry at Eltham at Christmas 1515 may have been his. Its title suggests a play rather than a pageant. At Christmas 1514 there was given *The triumpe of Love and Bewte wryten and presentyd by Mayster Cornyshe and oothers of the Chappell . . . and the Chyldern of the sayd Chapell.*

At the Field of the Cloth of Gold came, one imagines, his crowning triumph, when he had the devising of the pageants on the Sunday night. For that tremendous pageant the King borrowed the vestments given to the Abbey by his father Henry VII.

The Calendar of State Papers gives the directive:

The rich copes with the vestments given to the monastery by the late King are to be borrowed for this voyage, and afterwards returned. The clerk to the closet is to warn ten chaplains to accompany the King, and provide the closet with the best hangings, travers, jewels, images, altar cloths &c that the King has.

The Calendar also gives instructions for the meeting between Henry VIII and the Emperor Charles V.

'The garnishing of the church is committed to the dean of the chapel, the devising of pageants at the banquets to Cornish and the mummery is referred to the King's pleasure.' This is headed 'A memorial of things to be done at the meeting and interview of the King's highness and the emperor Charles at Gravelines.' Other items give Cornish's salary and 26s. 8d. for board wages for the children.

On the 5th of June 1522 the Emperor himself came on a visit and there is a detailed account of all things ordered and paid for in connection with 'a meskeler and revels devised by Wm. Kornyche, gentleman of the Chapel'. There are several payments to Mr Cornish for the children playing before the King, and 'for diets for 10 of the children during the King's voyage to Calais 62 days at 2d'.

He was also a man of much business, as in 1523, not long before his death, letters of protection were made to him as 'gentleman of the king's household, alias gentleman of the chapel, alias comptroller of the petty custom of the port of London, alias of London draper'. At various times also he was granted permission to import woad and wine, and to export beer, and to furnish five of the King's ships. On August 20, 1523, he was granted the Manor of Hylden in Kent. His will, made in January 1512, was executed on 14th October 1524.

It was a busy life for one man; but not at all impossible when one remembers the life of Geoffrey Chaucer, or of Cornish's contemporary and close neighbour, William Caxton. Of him Stow writes:

On the South side of the Gate House King Henry VII founded an Almshouse for thirteen poor man . . . near unto this house westward was an old chapel of St. Anne over against which the Lady Margaret, mother of King Henry VII erected an almshouse for poore women which is now turned into lodgings for the singing men of the College. The place wherein this Chapel and Almshouse stand was called the Eleemosynary or Almonry, now corruptly, the Ambry, for the Alms were here distributed to the poor.

And therein Islip, Abbot of Westminster, first practised and erected the first press of Book printing that ever was in England about the year of Christ 1471; W. Caxton, Citizen of London, Mercer, brought it unto London, and was the first that practised it in the said Abbey. [Islip was not Abbot but Prior at that time.]

It is thought that perhaps Caxton chose Westminster rather than London because he wanted to be near his parents. Amongst the Churchwarden's Accounts for St Margaret's Westminster A.D. 1474, is an 'Item the day of burying of William Caxton for ij torches and iiij tapers at a lowe masse xx d.' (In the same year is an item, 'the day of burying of a childe of the Amery for ij tapers ij d.')

In 1491-2 Caxton himself was buried, and in 1495-6 a Richard Caxton died.

In 1485 Caxton published in the same year as *The Morte d'Arthur* and the *Life of Charles the Great*, a romance called *Paris and Vienne*. It is not known why he chose to publish this rare example of the mediaeval French romances, but its story makes one wonder, especially in view of the fact that a play called *Paris and Vienna* was acted by the Children of Westminster in Elizabeth's day, and it was obviously based on Caxton's story. Its choice for performance by choristers is easily understood.

Vienne, daughter of the 'Doulphin of Viennoys' is a Provençal princess, beautiful and gifted. Paris, son of one of the lesser nobles of her father's court, first wins her attention by his skill in music in both voice and instrument.

In the end Paris captures her heart by winning the crystal shield and garland against all competitors in a tournament of song. Her father, angry at the young man's boldness, threatens his life if he remains at Court. For long years the lovers are separated. Then, after many adventures, Paris saves the dauphin's life by rescuing him from a Saracen prison. As a result the lovers are united.

There is one other possibility, and a most tantalizing one. If it could be proved, it would be a definite link with Caxton.

It appears in the 'Perquos of accompt of John Esteney, Warden of the New Work at Westminster, Michaelmas Day 22 Edward IV to Michaelmas Day I Richard III A.D. 1482-3, Item of a gift of 20s. from Otuel Fulle late Master of the Scholars at the Almonry by the Archdeacon's hands to the New Work.' Could he possibly have been 'the schoolmaster printer of St Albans?' Obviously one of the previous antiquaries at the Abbey has thought so. In 1480 Caxton published the Editio Princeps of *Chronicles of England*. In

1482 a second edition appeared under his imprint: and 1483 there was a third from 'the schoolmaster printer of St Albans'. Now the printing press was set up in 1479 approximately and this would accord with Otuel Fulle being late Master of the Scholars at the Almonry.

Also, a fact not generally known, there were two houses at the eastern end of the Abbey—near where the statue of King George V now stands. These were called 'Great St Albans' and 'Little St Albans'. Possibly this is the place and not the Abbey town as many have thought.

Among the members of the Chapel Royal attendant on the King the name of William Cornyssh Master of the Children is immediately followed by that of Robert Penne, who had been Master of the Singing Boys of Westminster until 1500. From 1494 until 1497 he received 6s. 8d. as a lay singer while a William Park received the 13s. 4d. for teaching the boys. In 1497-8 he received both the 13s. 4d. and the 6s. 8d., and in the following three years the 13s. 4d. when he was succeeded by a Thomas Watson.

Penne or Pen was a friend of John Skelton the poet laureate, as the only extant copy of Skelton's *Diodorus Siculus* was written out for him. In 1515-16 he is mistakenly put down as Sir Robert Penn under the misapprehension that he was in Orders. In that year he was a Gentleman of the Chapel Royal and was awarded an annuity of twenty marks out of the lordship of Denbigh in North Wales. He died in 1538, and certain clauses in his will suggest the character of a man who would be a friend of Skelton. It is dated September 26th and the reference to the Convent Seal is particularly interesting. One cannot help wondering whether the Mr Byrd who witnessed the will was the same as the William Byrd who signed the Dissolution Deed in 1540 and if he were related to Wyllyam Byrd the chorister (q.v.).

In the name of god amen I Robert Pen beyng in goode helth and memory make this my wyll ffirst I bequeth my soule to god the father & to Jhu crist his onely son and to the holy goost besechyng them that the blessed Mary ihu crists mother & vyrgyn wt all the saynts in heven may pray for me to them Also I make John my son and Anthony my son myne executors of all my goodes Also I gyve to Cecylly my doughter my Covent Seall of the Abbay of Westmr and xxti nobles of mony And a Ryng with a dyamond the which was hyr motheres And my best bedde and all that belongeth to ytt and my best courlett wt ytt Also I will that Elizabeth my doughtr haue xxs off money And hr doughter Anne a Ryall Also William my son the Bedde that he lyeth on All the Remayment of my goodes I gyve to John my son and to Anthony my son to be evenly devyded betwene them after my buriall where it shall please god to take me to hys mrcy Also I owe to mr ffysher iiijs but he saith that it is vjs but I confesse but iiijs And that ys all the detts that I owe in the worlde Also I will that mr Subdean of the Kyngs Chapell with all my ffelows haue eury man a penny that ys at my dirige or at my masse to drynk and to say god haue mrcy on my soule This will made the xxvj day of September in the xxxth yere of the reigne of or Sourayn lord kyng henry the viijth whome ihu prserve Amen qd Robert Pen Teste Mr Byrd Mr Barber Mr Radys Mr Bury Mr Colman Mr Raffe of the Vestry wt moo This will writen with mine hand the day abouesaid R Pen

[Probate was granted 16 October 1538]

In 1491-2 payment was made to William Park for teaching the singing boys, and he was succeeded, as has been shown, by Robert Penne who may have been a relation of the Peter Penne of whom mention will be made in Mary's reign.

Penne's appointment seems to have occurred at the same time as a proclamation of 13 Henry VII (1497) authorizing

26

the precentor or chanter to take boys from anywhere in England, except the Chapel Royal or any other place specially privileged, to sing in the Abbey.

PROCLAMATION IN ENGLISH

Henry by the grace of God &c to all archbishops, bishops, abbots, priors, and deans of cathedral churches and all other spiritual officers and ministers, and also to all manner mayors, sheriffs, constables, bailiffs and to all other our officers, whatsoever they be, being within franchises or without, as well as within this our realm of England, or of our principality of Wales, or of our lordship of Ireland these our letters to see or hear, greeting.

Forasmuch as the divine service of Almighty God 'owith' to be ministered and kept in our chapel of household as in other places of our foundation within this our realm and principality of Wales and also lordship of Ireland, 'specially' in our monastery of St. Peter in Westminster wherein resteth and remaineth the holy 'enunccion' and 'regalies' appertaining unto our 'trone' and royal coronation and kingly see, and also the blessed corse of St. Edward, our predecessor, there is shrined and with great devotion is worshipped, and other sepultures of our most noble progenitores kings of England to whom duly appertaineth after this temporal life there to have their sepulture, by whom holy privileges be granted and confirmed unto our said monastery of St Peter aforesaid; in consideration whereof we, of our most special grace, mere motion and favour which we bear not only to our said monastery but also to move and stir all manner of people well disposed, as well being our subjects as strangers hither coming, that they the rather to have more profit [and] devotion, have taken for us and our heirs and successors for evermore hereafter to come every person being a minister in divine service of our said monastery into the perpetual exemption and special protection of us and of our said heirs and successors for evermore; wherefore we will and straitly charge you and every of you that you 'ne take ne' withdraw out of our said monastery of St Peter of Westminster by force or otherwise by virtue of any our commissions heretofore unto you granted or hereafter to be granted, any singingmen or children, always our royal chapel of household to be except; yet nevertheless of our most abundant grace and mere motion by these our letters have given and granted for us and our said heirs and successors for evermore free licence and liberty unto the chanter of the said monastery of St Peter aforesaid for the time being, or his deputy to take any well singing men and children upon reasonable wages or exhibition wherewith they may be pleased, within this our realm except for our chapel aforesaid and other ministers, chapels, places or persons having our exemption and special protection in like wise. We therefore charging you and every of you in the most straitest wise that this our commandment you observe and keep, as you and every of you intend to avoid our most grevious displeasure and answer unto us at your uttermost peril.

Given at Westminster under our great seal 17 Dec the thirteenth year of our reign

[By the King]

In the year 1500 a Thomas Watson was paid for teaching the singing boys, and a John Kemp the 6s. 8d. In the following year John Kemp succeeded Watson and remained in the office until 1508 or 1509. From the year 1507-8 the sub-almoner received approximately £9 a year for the singing boys. In 1510 the salary was paid to a man of whom we know nothing except that his name was Jacobus. In the following year Roger Cretoff was responsible for them. After him things seem to have settled, as a John George was Master from 1513 until 1517 and a John Silvester from 1517 until 1531. Hawkins refers to the latter as an eminent musician who took his degree of Mus. Bac. at Cambridge in 1521. A John Silvester, obviously a man of substance, was buried in St Margaret's, Westminster 1516-17.

For the following two years the Master was a George Caxston, though in 1533-4 his name is coupled with a man named Mason. Nothing is known of any children of William Caxton and, in view of his final settlement of his affairs, it has always been presumed that he left no son. George however may have been some relation.

From 1535 to 1539 payments were made to William Grene, and he is the last Master before the Henrician dissolution in 1540, which he survived.

Plays and liturgical dramas continued to be performed during the first part of Henry VIII's reign. In 1521, with the visit of the Emperor Charles V, there is an item 'payd for wrytyng of plays V s.', and in 1524 'Item payd for wrytyng of a play for the chyldern xvj d.'

By a stroke of good fortune an account book of the period has survived (W.A.M. 33301) and this is worth quoting at considerable length as it gives us the most important thing of all—the names of some of the boys.

Only a very few years later, during the attacks on the monasteries in the years of spoliation, there was a complaint presented to Henry VIII in 1536 concerning *Seventy-eight Faults and Abuses of Religion* which declared 'the singing and saying of Mass, Matins, or Evensong, as but a roarying, howling, whistleying, mumming, conjuring, and jozelying and the playing of the organys a foolish vanitie'.

Chapter Two

W.A.M. 33301

A BOOK OF ACCOUNTS stained with damp and faded, but in some places excellently clear, gives many hints as to the life of the children in the earlier years of Henry VIII's reign. And it is a great pity for the present purpose that the sub-almoner William Fytte or Fyttz died during or immediately after his first year of office, as his accounts are clear and beautifully written in ink that seems scarcely to have faded at all. The book consists of twenty leaves but some of the pages are blank. Page 2a concerns the year 1512-13:

Here [begyn]nythe the booke of paym[ents of Dan Wyllyam] ffytte shaumer of Westmr from the day of his fyrst cmyng yn to the seyd offyce that ys to say the iiij day of November the yer of the reynge of K.h. viij

Imprmis the xth day for my costs to London to take too chyldren wt the comyssyon the tone called Richard Bemond the other callyd Wyllyam ffynnes		xijd
Itm gevyn to wyllyam ffynnes mastr lying seke by cause he had no body to help hym yn his sykenes	iijs	iiijd
Itm to the same w. ffynnes modr to have hyr good wylle		xijd
Itm to Richard Bemonds mastr by cause of hys good wyll		xxd
Itm for a russet cape for w. ffynnes		xijd

Itm a russet cape for Ric. Bemond			xij*d*
Itm spent of Ri Bemond ffadr & modr & W ffynnes modr when the came to Westmr to se the children			xij*d*
Itm the xxj day for my expencs to london to by fustyon & lynyng for the syngyng chyldren			xij*s*
Itm for my coste to london when y went to take petyr Best wt the comyssyon			vj*d*
Itm to the clarke of sent tolys master to the said petyr to haue his good wyll		ij*s*	vj*d*
Itm a russet cape for the same petr			xij*d*
Itm spent on w ffynnes modr & his syst(er) & the clarke of sent Botts			viij*d*
Itm for xx yards of blak lynyng for ther gowns			xv*s*
Itm delyvrd to symond volantyn yn tyme of his sykenes			iiij*d*
Sum	iiij*li*	xij*s*	j*d*

This is an example of the working of Henry VIIth's proclamation as the Chantor is going round 'finding' the boys from other churches. Presumably 'seynt tolys' is St Olave's of which there were several in the City of London; and St Olave's, Tooley St. is a clear survival of this corruption. 'St Botts' is probably one of the churches dedicated to St Botolph of which there was one at each of the City's gates.

The only mention of the Master of the Choristers at this date is unfortunately stained by damp, so that the entry reads: 'Itm to Jamys scolmast of the song scole iij*s* iiij*d*.'

The name of the Schoolmaster of the Grammar School is also missing. These entries are followed by items concerned with St Nicholas' Day. In December there were four singingmen to whom 4*s*. were paid in all; a shilling was spent in sweetmeats, a shilling for fur for the Boy Bishop's gown and 8*d*. for his offering to Our Lady of the Pew and at St Edward's Shrine. Three shillings were paid to a person named Grymshaw for 'mylke bred & other necessarys on sent Nicolas nyght', when 8*d*. was spent for malmsey wine ('mawmsey yn the vestry') and 2*d*. for bread there. Three-pence was spent on 'ij coms for w ffynnes & Bemod'.

In the same month shirts were bought for Peter Best and W. ffynnes while Grymshaw's wife was paid five shillings for doing washing and her husband received ten shillings for a gown.

Folio 3 also has an item 'for a pryksong boke of masses matens & other songs' price five shillings, and the sub-almoner put in a claim for 4*d*. for his expenses to London. Peter Best's father received 4*d*. and W. ffynnes mother 2*d*. Then follow payments for malmsey wine, to Jhan the barber, and to Grymshaw who provided 'bef & other neces-saryes for the chyldren'. There is an intriguing entry of 20 pence to the 'mynstrolls' and the same amount was 'spent yn the arshdekyns house'. There is one startling entry 'Itm loste yn gamyng at crystmas viij*s*.'

Dan William Fyttz or Fytte was defunctus 1512-13 and numbered 'inter mortuos' in 1513-14; and the accounts were taken over by John Bedford who is described as 'corderer' and 'sowthamner' which means Keeper of the Misericords and sub-almoner.

These accounts include yards of 'whyte coton' at 2½*d*. per yard and of 'blake' at the same price; and for making the gowns, coats, and doublets, for double and single gloves, for ribands and for many shoes and shirts.

Folio 6b deals with expenses in connection with the children in the twelfth year of Henry VIII's reign when Dan John ffulwell was in charge and again there is a reference to the Boy Bishop ceremonies. He records that he had received thirty shillings from the almoner for the children against St Nicholas' Day, and a further forty shillings for 'Saynt Nycolas nyght goyng wt the byshoppe'.

On 7a, the entries begin with similar payments.

ffyrst payde to Cristofer cordyn for shuys for the chyldern   viij*s*

payd for ij payr knitt hose   x*d*

payd to petrs wyffe for ij doz knyt hosyn for the chyldern a gaynst Seynt Nicolas day   x*s*

Itm payd to cristofer cordyn for shuys for the same day vz Seynt Nycolas   viij*s*

Itm payd for iij halffe pecs of ffustyan for the Syngyng chyldern at the same day   xxv*s* viij*d*

Other items include six purses, twelve girdles, six canopies; and six gowns for the 'Chyldern of the Chappell'. Eight shillings and fourpence was paid to the singingmen for accompanying the Boy Bishop on this occasion; and on the following page, folio 8a, Item to the barber 'for Rownding of the chyldern xij*d*.'

At this time the sub-almoner seems to have made equal payments to the two Schoolmasters.

In this particular book of accounts for several quarters the entries are the same, circa 12 Henry VIII:

'Itm payd to the scolle Mr of the gram' scolle . . . iij*s* iiij*d*.

'Itm to John Sylvestr scolle mastr of the song Scolle iij*s*. iiij*d*.'

In 12 Henry VIII, on folio 9a, there are signs of a well-provided table; for a 'barell of bere', a 'gylderkyn of ale', for white bread, for junkets, to the grocer for spice, for strawberries (iij*s* j*d*), for wafers, Ipocras wine (Keats's Hippocrene?), for rushes (which are a common item), more spice from the grocer, to the wax chandler—and more shirts for the children. Eightpence was spent in hiring vessels.

Another 40*s*. 11*d*. for the Boy Bishop in 1522-3. There is a definite number given to the singingmen as five of them

᠎᠎

were paid twenty pence each for going with him. There is a mistake in arithmetic soon afterwards, as the Schoolmaster of the Grammar and the Song Schools are each put down for 3s. 4d., yet the total is shown at 3s. 4d. Unfortunately the name of the Grammar Master does not appear, and for some unknown reason in 14 Henry VII for Michaelmas quarter he received the customary 3s. 4d. while Sylvester of the Song School received five shillings. The feast of the Nativity of John the Baptist was obviously an excuse for a feast as the expenses of the 'dryngyng' are listed including 2 lb. of sugar, 'comfetts', 'biskades', and 'strawberis'.

There is then a return, on folio 14a, to the year 1512-13 and the handwriting is that of the sub-almoner William Fytte who died in that year. It seems that W. ffynnes' sister mended the stockings of the boys as she received two shillings 'for yarne to mend hosyn'. Immediately following is an important entry 'Itm to Roberd Howe [or Hawe], for a peyr of clavycors vjs viijd'. This it would appear is the earliest mention of keyboard instruments at the Abbey and the name of Howe raises the possibility that he was connected with the Howe who mended the organs in later years.

On the next page, folio 14b, there is a receipt for the weekly dole 'for the chyldern of the amery and for other thyngs ther pteynyng to the subamn' offic'.

This was found partly in the singing of Masses, for the repose of the soul of Queen Eleanor which brought in 6s. 8d; on St Nicholas Night 39s. 6d.; 6s. 8d. from the Monk Bailiff in memory of Richard II; and 5s. for the repose of Henry VII. Then follows the first mention of Maundy Money, 6s. 6d. of which was received for the children, and there is another payment a year later. On folio 15a which deals with payments in 14 Henry VIII, from the 5th of October to Christmas, there is one of the most valuable pieces of information in the whole book, as it begins: 'ffyrst in

reward to Mast Cornysh on seynt Edwards day in October
anno xiiij . . . X*s*. . . .' This obviously refers to the great
Cornish of the Field of the Cloth of Gold and is almost
immediately followed by the names of the singingmen (led
by Sylvester the Master of the Children), who are Empson,
Coks and Rogr. Sylvester received 2*s*., the other three 20
pence each.

In the Churchwarden's Accounts of St Margaret's, Westminster, are the entries, during 1522-4, 'Payd to Petir Best
for a new surpleis xx*d*, and payd to Freman for pte of Petir
Best Indentures viij*d*'. So Peter Best continued his singing
in later life.

The entries which follow are similar to the earlier ones,
but they include 7*s*. 6*d*. for 'blak cappys for the syngyng
chyldern prce the pec xviij*d*' and one wonders whether it
could be argued that there were only five singing boys; but
it seems unlikely unless there was a sudden change as there
were ten in 1542 and in the Draft of the King's New
College after the Dissolution in 1540 ten are allowed for.

In the fourteenth year of Henry VIII's reign, on folio
15b, is an item for cloth for five 'sherts for the syngyng
chyldern vz S. More. J. Barwell. F. Wappys. W. Whygt.
J. Walker.' The total price was 6*s*. 8*d*. and there are five
names mentioned, not known to have been at the Abbey
apart from this book. Tenpence was paid for the making of
the said shirts.

Apparently Whyght's father was a medical man because
in the following year he was paid 'for his surgery & phisyk
in ye tyme of his sekness'; and we learn that More's name
was Symon as xiiij*d* was spent on a 'cappe' for him. Whygt
appears to have had a serious illness as eight shillings were
paid to 'Robert Medellam's wyffe for kepyng of W. Whygt
on of the syngyng chyldern viij weks at xij*d* th wek.' He
must have recovered however as later in the year there was

a shirt made for him, as well as for More, for J. Wappys and
for—a new name—B. Russell. In the previous quarter
shirts had been made for More and Whygt but Barwell had
two, so presumably that is why his name does not appear in
the later list.

As the book draws towards the end of its entries, and is
concerned with the fifteenth and sixteenth years of King
Henry's reign, Peter's wife is still being paid for hose, the
Grammar Master for some reason on two occasions received
3s. 4d. while the Scolle Mr of the Song Scolle received
6s. 8d., from the sub-almoner; another cape has been made
for S. More; 22s. 6d. has been paid for the drynkyng on
Saint John the Baptist's Day; and herrings continued as
part of the staple diet.

Apparently there was sickness again, but damp has caused
some of the important words to be unreadable, and especially
has affected the name of one of the boys.

Itm payed to the potycary for Edward ( ) tyne	vs	ijd
Itm payed to clarkson wyffe for kepyng of the seyd Edwarde	ijs	viijd
Itm payed for the kepyng of Wappys		xd

but apparently this sickness did not spoil all pleasures as the
next item is: 'Itm payed for wryttyng of a play for the
chyldern xvjd.'

This, in amount, is very different from the five shillings
spent two years earlier, at Christmas time 1522-3: 'Itm
payd for wrytyng of plays vs', a large sum.

Of the last leaf, 20b, the sub-almoner is still receiving,
on behalf of the children, 6s. 8d. for Queen Eleanor's and
Richard II's anniversaries.

Chapter Three

THE FIRST DISSOLUTION AND ERECTION

IN 1540 THE BLOW at last fell on the Abbey of St Peter in Westminster. On the 16th of January the Deed of Surrender was signed, the monastery dissolved, and the plundering began. The last Abbot, Boston, became the first Dean under presumably his family name of Benson. The King's order prescribed that the Abbey was to be governed by a Dean and Prebendaries. In 1541 it became a Cathedral, as the seat of a newly created Diocese of Middlesex and John Thirlby was appointed. It soon returned to the rule of the Dean however and in 1550 the Bishopric came to an end owing to the predatory Somerset faction, though the Abbey Church continued to be misnamed a Cathedral for two hundred years.

Benson wrote anxiously to Thomas Cromwell sending him:

thanks for your kind message to me this Saturday by Dr Peter. Please devise how I may be delivered from the governance of this house, and avoid the King's indignation. Through disease I shall have a very short, painful bodily life and also put my soul in danger. As for my pension, I pass not how little soever it be, so I may have the King's Highness my gracious lord.

In the King's new College at Westminster there were to be twelve Prebendaries to govern under the Dean. Some of them had already belonged 'to the house there', others were 'appointed pensions to depart the house'.

One of the things which particularly engaged the music-loving Henry was the singing. At Westminster on February 27, 1535 he had granted a Constat and Exemplification of his father's proclamation in 1497 concerning the Chantor's right to take up singing boys. It seems that the Abbey copy of this had been lost.

After rehearsing the Proclamation in English of 1497, the Constat and Exemplification continued in Latin, of which the following is a translation.

We however seeing that the aforesaid letters have by chance been lost as William Grene gentleman personally appearing in our chancellery has sworn that they are lost and that if ever it shall happen that he shall find those letters he will restore them into our aforesaid chancellery to be cancelled the tenor of the enrolment of these letters we at the request of our well beloved in Christ William Abbot of the Monastery of St Peter at Westminster have exemplified by these presents in testimony of which etc.

It will be noticed that William Grene continued in office as Master of the Choristers although he formally surrendered his Patent at the Dissolution. He made his will on January 14th 1546 and probate was granted on the 24th.

The xiiij day of January in the yere of our Lord god a Thousand fyve hundreth xlvjth And in the xxxviijth yere of the Reigne of our Soueraigne lorde henry theight by the grace of god king of Englande ffrance and Ireland defender of the faithe and in earthe of the Church of Englande and also of Ireland the Supreme headd I William Grene late of Whaplode in hollande in the Countie of Lincoln gentilman being of hole mynde and in good and pfite memorie (though sike in body) thanked be almightie god do make ordeyn and dclare this my pnt Testament and last will in maner and fourme folowing ffirst I geve my soul to my lord god my maker sauyor and oonly Redemer of the woorlde in whome and by whose merits deathe and passion I truste to be saved and to haue clene Remission of all my synnes I will my body shalbe buried in the Church of ffulham Item I geve to the high aulter there iijs iiijd Item I geve and bequeth to my derely beloued Annie Grene my doughter towarde her preferment in mariage by my executrix herin named And I will my said executrix shalhaue the custodye of the same Twentie pounds to be vsed and employed at hyr pleasure vntill the said full age or mariage of my said doughter Item I geue and bequeth to my welbeloued suster Katheryn Collage widowe ffourtie shillings and three paire of sheets Item I geve to my suster Agnes Coroburn Twentie shillings Item I geve to my suster Annable Blande xls And my dett of xxxiijs iiijd that one Stowe Talughchaundeler owith me Item I geve to my Cousyn Alice Grene doughter to my brother Hugh Grene vjs viijd Item I geve to my Cosin Katheryn Grene vjs viijd Item I geve to my Cosin Margery Grene vjs viijd Item I geve and bequeth to my doughtr Sybill Lynne asmoch of my householde stuffe at Whaplode as shall amounte to Sixe pounds xiijs viijd to be appoynted oute by twoo indifferent honest psones there inhabiting Item I geve and bequeth to my kynnesman and serunt Randall Grene and to my wyves kynneswooman ffortune Charley (whom the said Randall Grene intendith by godds grace to mary) all myn astate Lease interest possession and terme of yeres that I have yet to come of and in the messuage Inne and Tenement wt thappurtenncs callid the Sarazons hedd in Barly Stowe wthin the pishe of Whaplode aforesaid To haue and to holde to the same Randall and ffortune Immediatly after mariage bitwene them had and to their assigns during all the Residue of the terme of yeres yet to come in the same Inne wt thappurtenncs Also I geve and bequeth to the same Randall and ffortune twoo conuenent ffether bedds complete and the Compter and hangings being in the hall at Barly Stowe aforsaid Item I geve and bequeth to my Cosen and serunt James Grene Twentie shillings my Rydyng cote garded wt velwet my boots spurred and my three paire of hose my saddell and brydell and on conuenient horsse mare or geldyng Item I geve to my welbeloued brother Xrofer Doove my chamlet gowne furred with Sables tayles being at Whaplode Item I geve to my brother Hugh all myn apparell being in London Item I geve all myn other apparell being at Whaplode (not afore bequethed) to my twoo seruents Randall Grene and James Grene aforenamed indifferently bitwene them to be devided Item I geve to Sir Robert Kyrkham knight my five vyalls Item I geve to the prshe Church of Whaplode aforsaid my Regalls Item I geve to Edward Houghton my litill boye xxs and his appell which I will shalbe deliuered to Ball of ffoderinghey who may conuey the same boye into Lancashire to his frends Also I geve and bequeth to my said brother Hugh Grene all suche dett and money as is due and owyng vnto me by one Sir Garrett priest Item I geve and bequeth to the said Xrofer Dove and Hugh Grene all such detts and somes of money as is or shalbe due and owynge vnto me by one Mr Browne of the mydle Temple in london gent by vertue of his obligacon to me therof made and by one Nott of london by vertue of twoo seuerral Statuts willing and Requirenge myn Executrice aswell to make deliuerer to the same Xrofer and Hugh and to my suster Annable of the forsaid spialties bonds and statuts and euery of them as also sufficient lres of attorney and other assurancs in the Lawe to be sealed by myn executrix to euery of the same Xrofer Hugh and Annable for the Recoverye of the said detts and legacies to them seuerally given as is aforsaid with the full power and auctoritie of the same my Executrix in that behalf The Residue of all my goodes catalls detts plate Iuells Corne Implements and stuffe of housholde after my detts paide the costs of my buriall don and this my pnt Last Will in every thinge pfourmed and fulfilled I hooly gyve and bequeth to Rose my dere beloued wife whom I make and ordeyn my sole Executrix of this my last Will and Sponsours therof I make and ordeyn the said xrofer and hugh my welbeloued brethern And I geve to either of them

40

for their paynes to be susteyned herein ffourtie shillings a pece over and aboue the gifts and legacies to them seuerally gyven as aforsaid Thies being witnesses Bartilmewe Brokesby John Berkeley gentilman and William Beck singingman.

This last named, William Beck, was one of the singing-men of the Abbey Choir.

The preamble of this will is of interest when compared with that of Robert Pen of 1538 and of Robert White of 1574. Another tantalizing reference (amongst many) is to the property at Whaplode and his being domiciled there, because amongst his pupils when he retired in 1542-3 was a Wyllyam Byrd.

There are three drafts of the King's new College—at the Abbey, at the British Museum and at the Public Record Office. The British Museum copy is the earliest, as is proved by a point specially connected with the Choristers. Add. Mss. 40061 contains the names of 39 scholars at the Grammar School. None of these bears any comment. There are 12 pettycanons to sing in the quire but only ten are named. There are 12 laymen to sing in the quire but only seven are named. They are to receive viij*li* yearly. Amongst them is a Lewez Mogge, who may possibly have some connection with one of the choristers mentioned in the P.R.O. Draft. Also Randall Grene who was a poor relation of the Master of the Choristers, as appears from the foregoing will.

There are ten queresters of whom five are named.

Wyllyam Duffeld to have yerly for his wage	lxvj*s* viij*d*
Xrofer Breycoyte to have yerly for his wage	lxvj*s* viij*d*
Randalle Grene to have yerly	lxvj*s* viij*d*
Wyllyam Churche to have yerly	lxvj*s* viij*d*
John Wylton to have yerly	lxvj*s* viij*d*

In the Public Record Office and in the Abbey copies William Duffeld and Xrofer Breycott are amongst the scholars at the Grammar School and are further designated 'late querister'. Each grammar scholar received the same as each chorister. The Master of the Queristers is William Grene who surrendered his Patent. The five choristers already appointed are Randall Grene, William Churche and John Wilton as before; and Thomas Elys and Richard Moogge.

Amongst the twelve pettycanons singing in the choir was a Robert Grene 'one of the monks there'. Amongst the twelve laymen singers was Thomas Hethe who later became Master of the Choristers and a William ffoxe who may have been a relation of, or the same person as, the Robert ffoxe who succeeded William Grene in 34/35 Henry VIII.

There was also to be provision for 'twelve poore men decayde in the Kinges warres or in his Quire' who were to receive £6. 13s. 4d. each.

Of the two late queristers, Christopher Bryckett apparently became one of the twelve singingmen, and survived the changes under Edward VI, Mary and Elizabeth to appear for the last time in the Abbey accounts of 1596-7. The ramifications of this typically Abbey family spread through the departments of the College and are being charted by Mr J. B. Whitmore F.S.A. for the impending edition of *The Record of Old Westminsters*. A William Duffylde was buried September 13, 1544 according to the Records of St Margaret's Westminster. Another of the same name is in the same records as being married to Jone Henbury on January 17; and there is a curious anonymous song which begins 'Duffyld is my name' which may be a pun on the word 'Defiled'.

A William Churche was buried April 28, 1548 (St Margaret's Registers) and a Thomas Croppe whose name appears in the 1543-4 lists of choristers was buried 9 July 1548. A Thomas Elles is amongst the musicians to whom a livery was granted for the household for the coronation of Queen Elizabeth.

But the most interesting document concerning the choristers of this period is the one 'ffrom the ffeaste of Saynt Myghell th archangell in the xxxiiijth yere of the Reign of or Souergn lord kyng henry the viijth vnto the same ffeaste of Saynt myghell next ffollowynge ffor on yere complete.'

The Queresters for the quarter ending at the Nativity are as follows:

Thomas Gyles	Andrew Tysey
Wyllyam Monday	Wyllyam Marten
Symond Andrews	John Lockewood
Wyllyam Churche	Wyllyam Byrd
Wyllyam Atryk	John Bygynge

The Master of the Song Scole is still Wyllyam Grene, who received the same stipend as the Undermaster of the Grammar School.

It seems likely that the Thomas Gyles is the same person who was organist of St Paul's Cathedral from 1582 until 1590. In 1585 he was granted a commission by Elizabeth I to take choristers for the Cathedral. He was the father of Thomas Gyles and of Nathaniel Gyles, Organist of St George's Chapel, Windsor, and Master of the Children there. Another interesting point in connection with Westminster acting is that he succeeded Sebastian Westcote at St Paul's and continued the public performances by the 'Children of Paul's'. In the next payments (see the illustration) ending at the Annunciation, his name is crossed out, and William Monday stands at the head. In the third list, his name has disappeared, so presumably he left then. This coincided with the retirement of William Grene, the Master, as the second list has 'Wyllyam Grene ffox deputie' and in the third list Robert ffoxe is designated as 'Mr of the chyldern queresters'. It is important to note that his name has gone from the list of Vycars. From this, and from a Petition of Walter Porter, temp Charles I, it would seem that the two positions were

43

not held concurrently, although in earlier years they had not been considered incompatible.

The name of William Monday or Mundy seems to be evidence concerning his early musical education. His name is too well known to need comment here beyond the reminder that the composer was sworn a Gentleman of the Chapel Royal February 21, 1563-4, and died c. 1591, a Vicar Choral of St Paul's. His *O Lord the maker of all things*, is his most performed work today; and his son was the John Munday Doctor of Music who died in 1630, and who is included in the Fitzwilliam Virginal Book.

One cannot help wondering whether the Symond Andrewe was a member of the family of musicians named variously Dandre or Andrewe. A Nicholas Andrewe was awarded a livery amongst the musicians at the coronation of Edward VI on Feb. 20, 1546-7. In 1555 he figures as head of the players on the sackbuts, and appears several times, including the coronation of Queen Elizabeth. A Nicholas Dandre was a player on the Shackbuttes at the burial of Henry VIII, and a Henry Andrewe was a Childe of the Chapel Royal at Henry VII's funeral in 1509.

But the biggest query of all is raised by the name of William Byrd. Could he have been a relative of the great William Byrd? Was he related to the Gentleman of the Chapel Royal? There is no reason why the great Byrd could not have been organist at Lincoln for three years after he had become a Gentleman of the Chapel, but it has always been a cause of some surprise that the composer was still under twenty years of age when appointed organist of Lincoln. There may be a reason for the obscurity of information concerning Byrd in his known Papistry, and the one thing that really stands in the way of the identification with the Abbey chorister is his will in which he said he was 'in the 80th yeare of myne age'. And it is probably insurmountable as he would have been aged 2-3 at the time of this choir list unless his age was 90.

There may however be some connection between this chorister William Byrd and the William Birde alias Borne who figures in the *Diaries of Alleyn and Henslowe* between the years 1597 and 1603. He played women's or old men's parts, apparently combining this with the more masculine occupation of bear-keeper. This man was probably the Burne to whom Alleyn wrote in a letter full of exaggerated images asking for the hand of his daughter, whom he did not marry. A footnote asks Burne if his son John has the whelp he had promised Alleyn for the bear garden.

The reason for thinking that there may be some connection is that amongst the singingmen of the Abbey in Mary's reign is a Boorne or Borne and he continued to be a member under Elizabeth. The name of the Gospeller was John Allen or Alen. Perhaps there were connections through this older generation. There is also a William Byrd who on Sept. 7, 1583 was appointed 'Lord of the Tappes' at Sturbridge Fair. He was described as being recommended by several worshipful citizens of London and as 'a musitian and now servant and wayht of the University of Cambridge'.

Thomas Byrd received a livery for the coronation of Edward VI. A William Byrd was a signatory to the deed of surrender of the Abbey in 1540, while amongst the Almeysmen of the Abbey, 34 Henry VIII, is an Aymes Byrd, whose name is crossed out in that year and does not occur again. He may have been one of those who had decayed in the King's Choir.

Amongst the Vycars or Syngyngmen of these years—he first appears at the Abbey in 1543-4, and he was still a member under Philip and Mary—is a Robert Morley, whose name arouses the query whether he was related to the Thomas who was the composer, and who was so much associated with William Byrd. If Thomas Morley, born 1557 was a chorister at the Abbey, he would have been under John Taylor, so much associated with dramatic performances, and under the great Robert White.

At the end of Royal Music Library, B.M. 24. D. 2, 25 July 1591 is a lengthy poem of appalling doggerel by John Baldwin in which the following lines occur, concerning a store house of English musicians, which raises speculation when related to the Abbey lists.

I will begin with white, shepper, tye and tallis:
parsons, gyles, mundie th'oulde one of the queenes pallis:
mundie yonge th'oulde mans sonne:

The Chapter Minutes of this period have several references to the Choir; and for greater discipline, there was ordained a weekly Choir Chapter at which all those who had been guilty of neglect or misdemeanour were summoned to appear. Their names and fines were to be entered in a book of Perditions.

For the 25th of January 35 Henry VIII (1543-4), there is the entry concerning the Master of the Choristers' house, though he seems from a Chapter Act 13 Feb. 1545 to have lost it and had to 'dwell in the Allmyshowse'.

It is concluded yt fox the mr of the Choristars shall have the whole gourning of the Choristrs to rearse them, to prvide for meate & drink & to se them clenly and honestly apparailed in all things, & he to have the whole Stipend/ Also it is agreid, yt the said Mr of the Choristrs shall haue the howss our the gate going to the Allmery for hymself & the said Chorsts rent free, he repairing it sufficiently befor Estr next comyng. And because the howss is now in grett Ruyn, agreid yt the said fox shall only at this time have xls towards the charges of the said reparons.

On the next page dated Jan. 29 there is an order that

suggests a tightening up of discipline in religious worship. Fines were imposed of a penny for the principal services and $\frac{1}{2}d$. (an obolus) for the others.

29 Jan. It is cocludid that the Chantor shall have the ordryng of ye quere to chekke the prests & seculars absent and to multe theym as hath bene afore acustumdd and as was apointed by my Lorde of Westmr yt is for matens jd. masse jd. pryme & howrs eche of the(m) ob. Evensong jd. Also yt if any of the prestes or syngyngmen go forth of the quere and there tary forth any space wtout licence, then his negligence to be contid an absence although he cm in agayn afore the ende of the Svice.

The education of the children is clearly stated in a Chapter Minute of 1547:

This daye the VII daye of July was a specyall Chapiter apoynted at the whiche Chapiter was prsent Mr vyce Deane Mr Haynes Mr Keble Mr Bretten Mr Pekyns Mr Weston Mr Barnard Mr Carleton & Mr Reynolds yt was agred by the vyce Deane and the Chapiter wt ye consent of Mr Deane by reporte of Mr Keble fyrst yt ys concludyd and decrede yt Mr Deane shall have ye nomynacon & puttyng in of all ye querysters and of foure chylderne in ye gramer scole accordyng to a ball or lott wherin the namys of the sayd foure chyldern are coteyned And that euery prebendarye shall have the nominacon and puttyng in of the chylderne in the gram scole accordyng to a byll or lott callyd a ball wherein the names of ye sayd chyldern are wrytten & prvydyd yt ye seyd Deane & eury prbendary shall bryng in ther childerne to be so nominate by eny of theym before the Deane or vyce deane & the chapitr to be examyned by the Deane or vicedeane and the Scolemaister accordyng to ye statute of this Churche before they be admyttyd And yf eny childe so to be nomynatyd eyther by ye Deane or any prebendary shalbe found by the examenacon aforesaid to haue the qualities rehersyd in the statute that

47

then eny suche chyld nomynatyd or examyned to be forth-wythe admyttyd by the Deane or vicedeane and Scole-maister.

On the 20th February 1545 it was agreed 'by the vyce-deane & the chapter that the peticanos shalbe payd quarterly x*s* of their stipende vntyll the kings sbidye [subsidy] be fully payed And that the thesaurer shall paye of the remaining tresure the residue.'

On the same day:

Item that the chyldrn of the gramar skole/ the x queresters/ the fower bellringers. And the twoo subsextens shalbe divided into xiiij equall partes by balles. And Mr Deane to have the nomination & apoyntment of two partes and eury prbendary of one parte provided yt as well the Deane as evry prbendary shall bring his childe or scholar att euy vacacian into the Chapiter ther to be examined accor-dyng to the Statutes And furthermore that all Bfics [Benefices] & other prefermets within the church as the nominacion of the peticanos/clerkes/virgers/pisteler & gos-peller/ shalbe Lotted & appoynted after the same means.

Finally on July 6, 1547 a decision was reached concerning the distribution of the Granary and its contents, so im-portant a part of existence. It comes amongst a series of decisions headed:

Reformation of Statutes A.D. 1547

Item the seyd day & yere yt ys cocludyd and agreed yt ye hall buttrye & kytchyn for ye peticanons chorist' & schol-lers shalbe byldyd vppe this yere and the next wt ye resydue of the chabres necessarye for the quyer/ And yt the granr for wheat shalbe devyded in vij pts wherof Mr Deane shall have on pte seperate to hym selfe And the xij prbendaryes the other vj ptes ij & ij to have on pte to laye in theyr wheate the pticons to be made at ye Churche coste wt dores & locks.

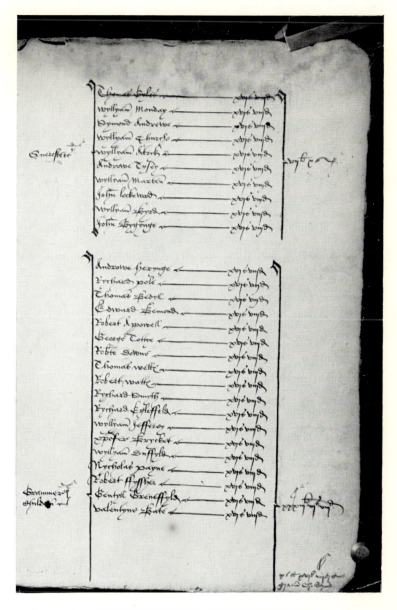

A page from WESTMINSTER ABBEY MUNIMENT 37045:
showing accounts in the Quarter ending at Ascension, 1543

It would appear from a note 13 Feb. 37 Henry VIII that Fox the Master of the Choristers was not particularly well treated:

It is also agreyd by the partes aforesayd yt fox Mr of the Quiresters shall dwell in the howse And the howse yt he lith in now tobe a howse for the audytt & to kepe the Evydence in.

It will be remembered he had been allowed 40s. towards the repairs of his ruinous house two years earlier.

Fortunately in the Dissolution Inventory there is a splendid description of the Boy Bishop's regalia. Some of the items seem to be either the same as the 1388 vestments or careful copies. Perhaps the most interesting item for the present purpose is the mention of the name 'John Cornyshe, monk'.

The vj myter for Seynt Nycholas bysshoppe the grounde therof of whyte sylk garnysshed complete with ffloures gret and small of sylver and gylte and stones complete in them with the scripture Ora pro nobis Sancte Nicholai embrodered theron in perll the sydes sylver and gylt and the toppys of sylver and gylt and enamelyd with ij labelles of the same and garnysshed in lyk maner and with viij long bells of sylver and gylt weying all together xxiij unces.

A marginal note records that the 5th and 6th mitres had been 'delyvered to the Treasorer to the Kynges use'.

The thyrd Crose for Seynt Nycholas bysshoppe the hed therof of sylver and gylt garnysshed with great perles and stonys haveyng therof an ymage of Seynt Peter and an other of Seynt Edward of sylver and gylt lackyng vij stonys and perlys the staff therof round of coper and tymber weying all together lx unces.

The viith chales with patent of sylver and gylt with the

Dowme enamyled in the myddest of the patent and the Crucifixe enamyled one of the fotte of the chales belongyng to Seynt Nycholas Alter xvij unces di.

a gret blew clothe with Kyngs on horsse bake for Saynt Nicholas cheyre

(Delivered to Mr Treasorer ut supra et postea d'no Regi deliberat.')

a nother albe with parells of grene velvet havyng oon ymage of Seynt Edw rd and a nother of Seynt Nicholas with iiij skouchyns all o₁ broth⸱red work of ye gyfte of John Cornyshe monke.

St Paul's Cathedral also at this time had a cloth with kings on horse-back.

On July 22nd 1541 a Royal Proclamation forbade the Boy Bishop ceremonies:

And whereas heretofore dyverse and many superstitious and childysshe observations have been usid, and yet to this day are observed and kept in many and sondry parties of this realm, as upon sainte Nicolas, sainte Catheryne, sainte Clement, the holye Innocentes, and such like; children be strangelye decked and apparelid to counterfaite priestes, bysshopps, and women; and so ledde with songes and daunces from house to house, blessing the people, and gatherynge of monye; and boyes doo singe masse, and preache in the pulpitt, with such other unfittinge and in-convenyent usages, rather to the derision than to any true glory of God, or to honour of his saints; the kyng's majestie therefore myndeth nothing so moche, as to avaunce the true glorye of God without vayne superstitition, willeth and commaundeth, that from henceforth all suche superstitions be loste and clyerlye extinguished throughowte all this his realmes and dominions forasmoche as the same doo re-semble rather the unlawfull superstition of gentilitie, than the pure and sincere religion of Christ.

Some faint hint of the magnificence of the Abbey can be

gained from the Inventory. The following entry tells its own story:

'Item for expenses the xvjth of Januar viz to the Bedell of the Goldsmythes in london wh iiij d for botehyre at which tyme Henry the vth tome was robbyd iiij s. viij d.' The tomb of the King had been covered with silver plates, and the head was of solid silver. The figures still lies headless on the perimeter of Edward the Confessor's chapel.

Nevertheless the schizophrenic Henry was still capable of having men hanged for eating meat on Friday, and there are references to the celebration of the Mass of the Holy Ghost in the reconstituted Abbey.

Chapter Four

THE FIRST PURITAN REIGN

O N THE CORONATION of King Edward VI, 1548 Archbishop Cranmer wrote:

After this his Grace was borne down to the High Altar in his chair and there sate bareheaded and all the noblest Peers of the Realme were about his Grace and my Ld of Canterbury Principall and there were certain prayers and Godly Psalms over his Grace and the Quire answered with goodly singing and organs playing and Trumpets blowing. . . .

Then my Ld protector D. of Somerset held the Crown in his hand a certain space and immediately after begun Te Deum with the Organs going and Quire singing and the Trumpets playing in the battlements of the Church then immediately after that was the Crown set on the Kings Majies head by them two and after that another crown and so his Gr was crowned wh 3 crowns. The Crown of England remaining on his head and the other two crowns on the Altar.

On the accession of Edward VI at the age of ten, and during his brief reign from 1547 until 1553, the Reforming party took charge and everywhere there was a taking down of altars. The Abbey seems to have been badly neglected, and the simplest proof is provided by the items of expenses incurred when Mary, his half sister, succeeded him. Windows had been broken, some of the new prebendaries had married. Service books containing the First Book of Common Prayer had been issued in 1549 in place of the Roman Missal, and action taken against the Catholic leaders.

The changing of names for ecclesiastical usage is demonstrated in the Churchwardens' Accounts of St Margaret's. In 1544-6 there appears: 'Also paid on Ascension-even for bread ale beer and wyne for the prebendaries and quyer of the mynster after mass was done js ijd.' In 1548-50 a similar entry reads 'Also paid for bread ale and wine for the gentlemen and children of the King's chapel for their panes in helping of the divine service at the blessed comunion on our Lady's day in Lent ijs xjd.' The entry 'Also paid to William Curlewe for mending divers pews that were broken when Dr Lattymer did preach xviijd' shows that the changes did not always go unchallenged.

On many occasions the Gentlemen and the Children of the Abbey Choir sang at St Margaret's. Under the year 1555, not long before Mary restored the monastic Abbey and appointed John de Feckenham as Abbot, the Churchwardens' Accounts read:

'Item paid for Bread Wine Bere & Ale for Mr Dean, the prebendaries & their choir when they came in procession to our church iijs viijd.'

Two years later under Mary the wording is significantly different: 'Item payde for breade Wyne Ale & beere a pon thassion evyn & day agaynst my lord Abbot & his Covent cam in procession and for strewyng erbes the same day vjs jd.'

'Thassion' is 'the Ascension', and the shortening of the word Covent still persists in Covent Garden.

A most valuable source of information—for much was destroyed by opposite sides during the perilous mid-century —is the partially burned manuscript diary put down by Henry Machyn a citizen and Merchant-Taylor of London.

Strype edited and published it and the brackets in the following extracts are supplied by him. But Strype was not always blameless in his transcripts and Machyn's diary as printed by the Camden Society and checked by Mr Tanner from the British Museum original has been used in the present volume.

The Chapter Acts of December 15th 1548-9 show the atmosphere at the Abbey:

Also yt is lykewyse determened that the tow lecterns of latten & candelstyks of latten wythe Amplls of copper & gylte & all other brasse latten bells mettell & brasse shalbe solde by Mr heynes Treasourer by cause they be monyments of Idolatre & Supsticyon and the monye therof cumyng to be receyvyd by the sayd Treasaurer for maykyng of the lybrary & bying of books for the same And it is also agreed that Mr pekyns & Mr Keble shall see the weyght of all the sayd metalle and that the lybrary shalbe fynsshed in the northe pte of the cloyster as sone as the money can be made of the prmisses.

Other plate was sold on the 24th of January following and in 1552 more was sold because of the late falling off of the money which was coming into the Abbey—certain plate and stuffs to pay the ministers and the officers' wages. This was on March 19th 1552.

The Dean Mr Heynes and Mr Perkyns had been authorized by the Chapter on Nov. 8th 1550 to sell 'certyn plate remaynyng in the Vestre' and devote it to be the alteration and removing of the Choir and for the Dark Entry and the College great gate.

It would appear that there was in 1552 a great shortage of money; because, besides the selling of the plate it would appear there was a danger of the prebendaries' being bribed to falsify the election to King's Scholarships. A Chapter Minute of April 8th states:

Yt ys decreed by Mr Deane and the Chapiter that yf at any tyme here after the deane or any of the prebendaries shall be proved to receyve any kynd of rewarde for the nominacon of any scoler to be admitted in to the scoole that then he shall loose the nomacon of his scolershipes for eur.

The last official robbery of the Abbey in Edward's reign took place on July 6, 1553, less than two months before his death. On the 20th May the Chapter entered in their Book and signed as witnesses the statement that on May 9th the King's Commissioners had taken away two cups with gilt covers, one white silver pot, three 'horse clothes', twelve cushions, seven 'carpetts for the table', eight 'staule clothes for the quyre', three 'pulpett clothes', a little 'carpett for Mr Deane's stall' and three 'tabull clothes'.

In 1549 Divine Service was ordered for 8 a.m.

Also it is agreed that from henceforth eruy Saterdaie in the yere the Deane & eruy prebendarie of this churche beyng in Westmr shall assemble in the Chaptre howse imediatly after mattens whiche shalbegynne dayly at viij of the clocke to comun and determyn things for the prfit & quietness of this howse vpon payne eruy of theym beyng at home for lackyng there to forfett xijd to be imploied to the comon dividint except he be lawfully letted.

Also the Chaunter yerely when he is chosen shall take an othe to marke bothe the absence of syngyngmen from the quyer and Also of the Deane and eruy prbendarye and further to note the dayes of their residence truly wtoute prayallete [partiality] & prsent the defaults at eruy wekys ende in the Chapit howse accordyng to this order taken.

In the same year one of the former choristers became a singingman. This is the Christopher Bryckett or Brickhead who went from the choir and was one of the original King's Scholars after the Dissolution in 1540. He seems to have taken the religious changes in his stride as he sang under

Edward, Mary and Elizabeth and was living in Tothill Street in 1585, leaving the choir in 1596. His colleague Thomas Sandland was presumably a relation of the Sandland who appears amongst the boys of Mary's reign and may well have been in the Choir in Edward's.

The Chapel Minutes record:

Vpon fryday the eyght daye of noveber in the thirde yere of the reigne of or sourygne lorde Edward the Sixt by the grace of god kyng of England ffrance &c. was admitted by Mr Deane & the Chapit ij syngyngmen whos names are Xrofer Bryckett & Thoms Sandland That is to saye the sayd Xrofer Bryckett in the Rome of Willm Atherston And the sayd Thoms Sandland in the Rome of Thoms Roo late decesed.

From another Chapter Minute it appears that the house of Thomas Roo was appropriated for the Usher of the Grammar School for ever. On November 23rd another singingman's house was given up to a prebendary: 'Rychard Elyot syngyngman was cotentyd that Mr Keble shall have his howse.' The house was situated in the Close and four men were chosen by the two sides to assess the amount of the repairs Elyot had done to the house, and bound themselves to abide by the award. So the encroachments on the rights of the choir went on and continued in all ecclesiastical establishments until it began to abate towards the end of the nineteenth century.

In August 1551 there was trouble in the choir, though whether the cause was personal or religious is not known:

The deane in the prsens of Mr pkyns & the hole companye of the quyre have dyscharged John Markcant of his Rome of a Syngyngman wtin this church by cause he hathe used him self busely raylyngly & sediciously by castyng of bylls agaynst Scorse & slanderyng of Roche.

On the death of her half-brother Edward VI, Mary acted

as a true daughter of Henry VIII and Catherine of Aragon,
and was seated firmly on the throne before Northumberland's attempt against her could succeed.

At the funeral of Edward, Cranmer was allowed to take
part and Bishop Day was permitted to preach the sermon
and survived to preach at Elizabeth's coronation; but everywhere there was a setting up of altars, paschal candles and
Easter sepulchres and statues.

But first Edward was buried in the Abbey, and Machyn
describes the scene:

The viij day of August was bered the nobull kyng Edward
the vj and vij yere of ys rayne; and at ys bere[ing was] the
grettest mone mad for hym of ys deth [as ever] was hard or
sene, boyth of all sorts of pepull; wepyng and lamentyng;
and furst of alle whent a grett company of chylderyn in ther
surples, and clarkes syngyng, and then ys father['s] bedmen
and then ij harolds, and then a standard with a dragon, and
then a grett nombur of ys servants in blake, and then
anodur standard with a whyt greyhond, and then after a
grett nombur of ys of[ficers], and after them comys mo
harolds, and then a standard with the hed offesars of ys
howse; and then harolds, Norey bare the elmett and the
crest on horsbake, and then ys grett baner of armes in-
brodery, and with dyvers odur baners, and then cam rydnyg
maister Clarenssuhs with ys target, with ys garter and ys
sword, gorgyusly and ryche, and after Garter with ys cotte
armur in brodery, and then mor [harolds] of armes; and
then cam the charett with grett horsses trapyd with velvet
to the grond, and hevere horse havyng [a man] on ys bake
in blake, and ever on beyryng a banar-roll [of] dyvers
kynges armes, and with schochyon[s] on ther horses, and
then the charett kovered with cloth of gold, and on the
[charett] lay on a pycture lyeng recheussly [pitifully or
religiously?] with a crown of gold, and a grett coler, and ys
septur in ys hand, lyheng in ys robes [and the garter about

his leg, and a coat of embroidery of gold; about the corps
were borne four banners, a banner of the order, another of
the red rose, another of Queen Jane [Seymour], another of
the queen's mother. After him went a goodly horse, covered
with cloth of gold unto the ground, and the master of the
horse, with a man of arms in armour, [which] was offered,
boyth the man and the horsse. [There was set up a go]odly
hersse in Westmynster abbay with banar [-rolls] and pen-
sells, and honge with velvet a-bowt.

Chapter Five

MARY, MARY, QUITE CONTRARY?

THE PANIC IN ecclesiastical establishments was great. Amongst the Abbey Muniments is a bill: 'Item for my botehyre the last day of marche when I went in hast for waxchaundlers to trym the fote of the pascall agaynst the Quenes grace came to ye holy gost masse.'

On March 21st the Council ordered country gentlemen to erect altars in their churches within a fortnight on pain of a fine of £100. At the Abbey Hugh Weston, favouring the old religion, was installed as Dean on September 18th.

On Rogation Day Mary attended in state the churches of St Giles in the Fields and St Martin in the Fields and proceeded to the Abbey accompanied by four Bishops wearing their mitres. There are bills for books for the choir and for the altars; for the Rood screen with the Virgin Mary and St John £18; for a silver pyx for the sacrament. There is an 'Item for goodwyffe Wyllet & mother syllybarne for makyng cleane King Henry the vijth wth sope & warme watr ij days ijs.' Another is for 'washing of the kings'.

Most tell-tale of all, before the coronation ceremony, is 'Item for a pounde of gunpowder to destroye the pigions in the churche viijd', and 'Item for owlde shaftes to shote at the pigions ijd'. The expenses at that time amounted in all to £374. 5s. 4d., a considerable sum. Grants were made to a John Howe for putting the organs in order, though whether he can in any sense be called an organist, as has been thought, is very doubtful.

The bill and allowances paid to John Howe in 1553-4 specify the organs: 'The lyttill orgaynes in the newe Chapell . . . called King Henry the seventh's Chapel . . .' and 'the greate woodde orgaynes in the loft over the greate quere in the bodye of the church'.

On November 11th, 1554, at the opening of Parliament, Philip and Mary went on horseback in great magnificence and with a sword of state carried before each of them. The Dean of Westminster, Dr Weston, composed a prayer to be said daily for the Queen's safe delivery of a child, and directed that it was to be said in the School also. The replica of her body, severely spoiled by water after bomb damage in the 1939-45 war, still shows the swelling which the pathetic woman imagined was the visible sign of childbirth.

Mary did all she could to restore the ancient worship. The Easter Sepulchre was returned and there are many instances of re-decoration such as: 'Itm the Roodes Marye and John with the ffoure evangelists gyldyng and all wyll cost xiij*li* vj*s* viij*d*.'

There is a grim note in an Abbey document giving the allowance for diet for the Lord Chancellor when he came 'for the deprivacion of the prebendaries being maried within the church'. This is the Commission referred to in the *Calendar of Patent Rolls* for 29 March, 1554.

Commission to Stephen bishop of Winchester and chancellor of England, that, because it is notorious that many of the canons and prebendaries of the cathedral church of Westminster have contracted marriage with certain women and have cohabited with them as their wives, he is to summon the same before him and without any noise or figure of judgment, when the fact shall be established by summary examination, he is to exclude them for ever from their canonries and prebends and enjoin upon them salutary and summary penance.

The Chapter Minutes have the names of the new Chapter, with pencilled remarks in a later hand—the same which wrote the remarks concerning the 1556 Dissolution.

New Prebendaries of the Romish persuasion installed 12 May 1554	George Gryffts	} turn coats
	Thomas Raynolds	
	Francys Malet	vice John Perkins
	Henry Cole	vice Sandiforth
	G. L. Pye	vice Birkhead
	Joanes Ramys	vice Alvey
	Joannes Ricard	vice Nowell } fled
	Joannes Moreman	vice Grindall
	A de Salinas	vice Humphry Perkins

Humphry Pkins, Richard Alvey and Alexander Nowell were restored in 1560.

An indication of the status of the various office holders at the Abbey is given by a list of fees payable to the Chapter Clerk. It is dated Saturday the 23rd September, in the first year of the reign of Queen Mary.

It is decreed by Mr Deane and the Chapiter that William Browne Chapter Clarke and his successors for the tyme beyng shall have towards the better mayntennce of his and their lyvyng for the regestryng & doyng thoffyce of chapitr clarkshipe at thinstallacion or admission as well of eny deane and prebendarye as all other mynistres almesmen and children of the fondacyon of this Cathedrall Churche, all suche ffees as hathe byn hertofore accustomed. That is to saye for eny deane o--xs for eny prbendarye o--vs for eny Scolemaster of the gramer scole o--iijs iiijd of eny peticanon gospeler & pystoler --xijd of eny ussher of the gramer scole & scolemaster of the querysters --xijd of eny clarke & other officer belongyng to this churche --viijd of eny almesman --viijd of eny of the quenes scollers & querysters --iiijd of eny payre of Indentures wryting & regesteryng xxvjs viijd of eny patent xxs and for eny Saynctuary man that shalbe pryuelegyd wythin this Saynctuary xiijs iiijd.

By great good fortune some of the Treasurer's Accounts of Mary's reign give the names of the boys. One may assume by the first list ending Michaelmas 1553, that the choir was that of Edward VI's reign as he had died on July 6th. The fact that there are only eight seems another indication of the Edwardian neglect. The names are: Hawclyffe, Holden, Blomefeld, Lewez, Sandeland, Bleayer, Bryfeld, Massye.

The Master of the Songe Scole is Thomas Heath. The Vicars are Thomas Askewe, Roger Empson, John Wynston, Richard Elythorne, Robert Morley, Richard Elyott, Thomas Cavell, John Marshall, Thomas Sandland, Xrofer Bryckett, John Wood, Thomas Damport.

There are no Christian names given to the boys but there is only one Hawclyffe in the St Margaret's Registers—a Richard Hawclyffe who was christened on September 12, 1539, which would accord excellently as regards age. Curiously he is still head of the list in the fourth year of Mary's reign when he is paid for two quarters, W.A.M. 37714. In the other two lists, 37713, Michaelmas 1556 and 37709 Christmas 1556, he does not appear. This also applies to Sandland who may well have been a relation of the Thomas Sandland who is amongst the singingmen but has gone by 1556. It is perhaps worth stating that a Thomas Sandland married an Alyce Atykns—the only one in St Margaret's Registers—and that a Thomas Atkyns was one of the choristers in 1543-4.

These for the quarters ending at Michaelmas and Christmas, 3 Philip and 4 Mary, are identical with each other. Thomas Heathe is still Master of the Songe Scole.

Thomas Lewys, Thomas Burffelde, John Massye, John Baker, William Lovell, Samuell Becke, Ambrose Hollande, Danyell Browne, Thomas Morgan, John Rysse, are the boys.

'Morgayne butler' appears amongst the names of my lorde Abbat's men under Abbot Feckenham, but Morgan or Morgayne and Rysse have as Welsh a lilt as Lewis and are equally difficult to identify.

An Ambrose Holland, christened on April 5th, 1547, was possibly the same Ambrose Holland who was married to Anne Rydstone on August 20th, 1571 also at St Margaret's: their son Abraham being christened there on February 4th, 1573. A Thomas Holland was the senior of the two cooks.

A Lewys was one of four scholars admitted to West-minster as King's Scholars on July 28th, 1553 and a Hakenett de Lewez was granted a livery 'for the household' for the funeral of Henry VII and was Head of the Musicians at the coronation of Edward VI.

A William Lovell who might well be this chorister of 1556-7 was christened on August 26, 1542, although another of the same name was also christened at St Margaret's on March 12, 1539, but if the latter were he, then his age might preclude him from the choristers. A Thomas Lovell or Lovewell is the first of four of 'the monkes there' who were retained amongst the 'xij Petycanones to syng in the Quere' and to have ten pounds a year when Henry erected his new College after the Dissolution.

The forty Grammar Children include a Massye, a Penne, a Lowell and a Byrkehed.

The singingmen are of considerable interest and reference will be made to John Wood in a moment. Head of the list in 1556 is Roger Empsom who must surely be one of the same family as he who sang with Master Cornish in 1522-3 and the William Empsom who was a chorister in 1542-3.

John Smythe raises a big query for the present writer because the back of the Treasurer's Accounts for 1530 has a scribble and some doodles including the name of John Smythe. This would be of no interest were it not for the fact that the scribble is: 'Dame Elynor Rumyng by her hummyng sunyng Itm paid to John Smythe.' 'Smythe' then proceeds to doodle and has several attempts at the initial letter of his surname. The interpretation of the word 'hummyng' is very doubtful and 'm' or 'n' is uncertain. As is well known Skelton, the poet laureate, tutor of Henry VIII before his accession, lived from 1523 in Westminster and remained in Sanctuary there until his death in 1529—the year of Wolsey's fall. Yet this scribble is on the Treasurer's Account for the following year. There seems no reason whatever why John Smythe should have written it twenty-five years later, yet there is no list of the men for 1530. Possibly he was elderly by 1556, and he has gone from the choir by 1560, so that it is not impossible that he wrote the scribble which is of particular importance if it can provide another link between Skelton, Cornysh and the choir.

The name of Robert Morley, which has appeared amongst the singingmen in 1553, and who may have joined them any time after 1544, makes one wonder whether he was related to the madrigalist Thomas Morley whose birth is assigned to 1557. This same document raises again the question of William Byrd the chorister of 1543, as the man in Henslowe's and Alleyn's Diaries of 1597-1603 is continually referred to as 'Bird alias Borne'. Amongst these singingmen of 1556 is 'Borne' who of all the singingmen has no surname. In W.A.M. 37713 Michaelmas, a John Marshall's name has been crossed out and Borne's name substituted, but in the margin is written 'borne his wyffe'. This apparently does not mean his decease as his name appears for the Christmas quarter. Perhaps he was ill. Possibly the family changed its name; but the presence in the establishment of a Thomas Tarleton, a John Allyn, a Robert Morley and this Borne raises queries which may be settled hereafter.

Four Choristers, the Sergeant Porter and the Sergeant of the Vestry: an illustration from Sandford's CORONATION OF JAMES II

Amongst the rewards separate from stipends are ten shillings to Heath the Master of the Song School and two shillings to 'the organ keaper'. This is for Christmas quarter. In the previous quarter Willm Howe is entered as 'custos organ' and is paid for three quarters. Amongst the rewards for this quarter are payments to 'pulsatores campan' . . . 'penycote, holand and hawclyff' each of whom receive £3. 10s. for three quarters of the year. The last two sound remarkably like two of the choristers. Thomas Heathe received thirty shillings in reward for the three quarters. Penycote, or John Pennicott is presumably the bellringer who was appointed at the request of the 'Lady Elizabeth daughter of our Sovereign Lord the King'—when Elizabeth was only thirteen—on November 5, 1544.

Machyn's Diary recounts some of the events in Westminster, though he seems, as were many of his contemporaries, rather hazy as to the justice or injustice of dogmatic persecution in his own times.

[1555]. The xxiiij day of Aprell was the sam man cared to Westmynster that dyd hurt the prest, and had ys hand stryken of at the post, and after he was bornyd aganst sant Margett chyrche withowt the cherche-yerde.

The xxvj day of Aprell was cared from the Marselsee in a care thrugh London unto Charyng-crosse to the galows, and ther hangyd, iij men for robyng of serten Spaneardes of tresur of gold owt of the abbay of Vestmynster.

The xxix day of Aprell was cutte downe of the galows a man that was hangyd the xxvj day of Aprell, a pulter['s] servant that was one of them that dyd robed the Spaneard with-in Westmynster Abbay, and he hangyd in a gowne of towny fryse and a dobelet of twonny taffata and a payre of fyne hose lynyd with sarsenet, and after bered undur the galaus, rayllyng a-ganst the pope and the masse, and hangyd iiij days.

Railing was not excluded from the Abbey precincts as is shown by the Chapter Minute of:

17 January, 1555.

Also it is decreyd the same tyme that if any of the petycanones scolemasters or any other of the clarks or other-wyse in the comons aboue the adge of xviij yrs shall calle any of those before namyd in the comnes foole knave or any other contumelius or slanderous worde shall paye for every suche defaulte xij*d* . . . the comnes the whiche shalbe set on by the chanter if he be ther or in his absens by the stewarde of the comnes . . . & that whereas edmond hamonde pryste dyd breake John Wodes heade being one of the clarkes wt a pote he was comadyd to ye gate howse for ye space of iij dayes by Mr deanes comandment and payde to Jon wode for the healing of his heade xl*s* by the decree of Mr deane and the chapiter.

Edmund Hamond and William Hamond both appear amongst the Petycanons. John Wood is one of the singing-men or Cantatores in choro, and all were still among the officers of the Abbey in the following year so the fracas seems to have been lived down.

There is a gap in the Chapter Minutes from the 24th of September 1556 until the 5th of July 1560. Written in pencil by a later hand are the words:

Sept. 27 1556. The Dean and Chapter were forced to surrender soon after this time, and the Church was again changed into a Monastery.

John Howman called John de Feckenham was brought from the Deanery of St Paul's and made Abbot of West-minster of which he and fourteen Monks took possession 21 November 1556.

Weston the retiring Dean and Feckenham the incoming Abbot seem to have been men of very different character. This is how Holinshed writes of the former:

Doctor Weston being (as you have heard before) prolo-
cutor of the convocation house, was at this time in displeasure with cardinall Poole, and other bishops: because he
was unwilling to resigne his deanrie of Westminster vnto
the queene whose purpose was to place there (as in old time
before) the religion of monks, whome in deed he fauored
not, although in all other things he stood with the church of
Rome. Neuerthelesse, by verie importunate sute, or rather
compulsion, he with his colleagues resigned the deanrie of
Westminster. In recompense wherof he was made deane of
Windsor, where not long after he was taken in adulterie,
and for that fact was by the cardinall depriued of all his
spirituall liuing, from whose sentence he appealed vnto the
court of Rome. For the following of which appeale he
sought secretlie to depart the realme: but he was appre-
hended by the waie, and was committed to the tower of
London, where he remained prisoner, vntill (by the death of
queene Marie) queene Elizabeth came vnto the crowne, by
whome he was set at libertie, and foorthwith fell sicke and
died.

. . .

This Weston was ghostly father to the Duke of Suffolk at
his execution but Suffolk did not want him, and there was
some unseemly pushing at the scaffold. At the execution of
Wyatt he tried to make Wyatt inculpate Elizabeth, but was
unsuccessful. When the Lord Mayor of London was told of
this he remarked, 'Said Weston so? In sooth I never took
him otherwise but for a knave.'

Machyn's Diary is useful concerning the ceremonies
connected with the revived monastery.

[1556 21st of November]. The sam day was ye new abbott
of Westmynster putt in, docthur Fecknam, latt dene of
Powlles, and xiiij moo monkes shorne in; and the morow
after ye lord abbott with ys coventt whentt a prossessyon
after the old fassyon in ther monkes wede, in collys of blake
say, with ij vargers carehyng ij sylver rodes in ther handes,

67

and at evyngsong tyme the vergers whent thrugh ye clostur to ye abbott; and so whentt in-to the churche affor ye he auter, and ther my lord knellyd downe and ys coventt and after ys praer mad was browtt in-to the qwyre with the vergers and so in-to ys plasse, and contenentt he be-gane evyngsong--xxij day of the sam monyth, that was santt Clementt evyn last.

.　　.　　.

The xxix day of November was my lord abbott consecratyd at Westmynster abbay; and ther was grett compene and he was mad abbott, and dyd wher a myter; and my lord cardenall was ther, and mony byshopes, and my lord chanseler dyd syng masse, and ye abbott mad ye sermon, and my lord tressore was [there].

.　　.　　.

The vj day of December the abbot of Westminster went a procession with his convent; before him went [all the] santuary men with crosse keys apon [their garments, and] after whent iij for murder; on was the lord [Dacres so] ne of the Northe was wypyd with a shett a-bowt [him, for] kyllyng of on master West sqwyre dwellyng be-syd [torn here] and anodur theyff that dyd long to one of master comtroller [. . .]dyd kylle Recherd Eggyllston the comtroller ['s] tayller, and k[illed him in] the Long Acurs, the bak-syd Charyngcrosse; and a b[oy that] kyld a byge boye yt sold papers and pryntyd bok [es with] horlyng of a stone and yt hym under the ere i[n W]estmynster Hall ye boy was one of ye chylderyn that w[as at the] sckoll in ye abbey the boy ys a hossear sune a-boyff London-stone.

From this it is difficult to say whether this Westminster boy flung, or was killed by, the stone. Perhaps if he were the guilty party he would find Sanctuary safer than the other boy would have done amongst the Westminster boys had he been responsible.

Amongst the publications of the Catholic Record Society

are the *Memorials of Father Augustine Baker*, *O.S.B.* who, writing of Fr. Sigebert Buckley, O.S.B., says:

And accordingly he then learned somewhat therein, under a certain old priest that was yet remaining of those of Queen Maries dayes. But what he then learnt, he being then but so young and being not afterwards exercised, as he was not, he forgot, and so it all vanished and came to nothing. Neither was he ever afterwards put to learn singing, albeit there was alwaies, till our man attained to mans estate, for the most part in the same town, a very expert teacher of singing who had been a chorister of Westminster; whose name was P e t e r   P e n n e, and mostly resorted for singings sake to our young mans fathers home.

This was in or about the year 1570, and the Father Sigebert Buckley, to whom it refers, was the sole survivor of the monks installed by Queen Mary, and it was he who preserved the Benedictine succession down to the present day. After centuries abroad they have now returned to England and have their headquarters at Ampleforth Abbey and College, in Yorkshire.

It would seem possible that this Peter Penne was a relative of the Pennes or Pendes of fifty years before, who figure in the Abbey and Chapel Royal accounts.

Father Augustine Baker, writing of the information he gained from Fr. Sigebert Buckley, says that

his abbot Mr Fecknam, had not insisted much upon monastic regularities, at what time he was restored to the Abby at Westminster, but contented himselfe to have sett up there a disciplin much like that which he saw observed in cathedrall churches, as for the Divine Office; and as for other manner of government of his monks and monastry in dyet and other things, he brought them to the laws and customs of colleges and inns of court.

He continues:

I yet remember that he [Buckley] told me, that they rose at midnight, that they did eate flesh, that at refection in the refectory they satt face to face on both sides the table being fowre to every messe as they do in the innes of court; that at supper they had so in common between every fowre, first a dish of cold sliced powdred beefe, and next after a sholder of mutton rosted. I do not remember what postpast they had, but it is likely they had cheese and perhaps allso an apple or two, or a peare. I do not remember what they had at dinner, but remembered what they had at supper, because it seemed a fare somewhat heavy for digestion to them that rise at midnight to me, who had lately before only experienced the monastick fare of Italy, where they so rise at midnight and never eate flesh; their habit for coole and hood appeareth by pictures in Westminster church not unlike our habit; though for Abbot Fecnam I have heard there is a picture of him in England with a cornered cappe on his head, and some furre appearinge at the end of his cassock sleeve at the wrist.

One of the Queen's dearest wishes was the re-interment of St Edward the Confessor and, after great preparation, on March 20, 1557 she was present when this was accomplished. Machyn's Diary 1557:

The xx day of Marche was taken up at Westm[ynster] agayn wt a hondered lyghtes kyng Edward ye confessor in ye sam plasse wher ys shyrne was and ytt shalle be sett up agayne as fast as my lord abbott can have ytt don for yt was a godly shyte to have se[en] yt how reverently he was cared from ye plasse yt he was taken up wher he was led when yt the abbay was spowlyd and robyd and so he was cared and goodly syngyng and senssyng as has bene sene and masse song.

. . .

The xxvij day of May, the wyche was the Assensyon day, the Kynges and the Quen['s] grace rod unto Westmynster with all the lords and knyghtes and gentyllmen, and ther

ther graces whent a prossessyon abowt the clowster, and so thay hard masse.

It seems that not all was well at the Abbey as there is this surprising note in Machyn's Diary (1557) after Anne of Cleves' funeral.

The xxij day of August was the herse (of my lade Anne of Cleves) taken downe at Westmynster, the wyche the monkes (by night had spoiled of) all welvett cloth, armes, baners penselles, of all the (majesty and) valans, the wyche was never sene a-fore so done.

When Mary died those who owed their positions to the Old Religion wondered what would happen. The following letter from John Moulton, Receiver General of the Abbey, gives his feelings as he writes to the Auditor who lived safely in the country.

Mr Audytor I commende me vnto you and my lorde Abbot wellyd me to wryte to you to be here at Westmr with all spede for he lokyth euery daye ffor the house to be desoluyd praying you to bryng with you suche bokes as ye thynke conuenyent. I would ffayne ffor my parte to be in the contrey but I can not awaye I pray you fayle not to come for yt ys mete ffor vs bothe nowe attend And thus fare yo well with my hartye commendacions to Mtres Bolland Scrybelyd in hast this mornyng the xixth day of June.

To my vearey louyng   by yor assured louyng ffrend John
ffrend Mr Humfrey Boll-   moulton receyuer there
and audytor at Westmr be
this delyuyred at his house
in Essex with spede

Chapter Six

ELIZABETHA FUNDATRIX

The xv day was the crounasyon of quen Elsabeth at Westymynster abbay, and theyr all the trumpettes, and knyghtes, and lordes, and haroldes of armes in ther cotte armurs; and after all they in ther skarlett, and all the bysshopes in skarlett, and the Quen, and all the fottmen waytyng a-pone the quene, to Westmynster hall; ther mett all the byshoppes, and all the chapell with iij crosses, and in ther copes, the byshops mytered, and syngyng, Salve festa dyes; and all the strett led with gravell, and bluw cloth unto the abbay, and raylled on evere syd, and so to the abbay to masse, and ther her grasse crounyd; and evere offeser rede against she shud go to dener to Westmynster hall, and evere offeser to take ys offes at serves a-pone ther landes; and my lord mare and the althermen.

So Machyn in his Diary; although he must have been mistaken, as the whole bench of Bishops was absent with the single exception of Oglethorpe, Bishop of Carlisle, and Dean of the Chapel Royal, who consented to act. The detestable Bonner, Bishop of London, was in prison. The See of Canterbury was vacant: the Archbishop of York objected to the English Litany. The rest of the Bishops, unwilling to acknowledge her disputed accession and also objecting to the English Litany, and to the reading of the Gospel and Epistle in Latin and in English, refused to be present. Oglethorpe carried through the ceremony and according to Burnet died of remorse. The anointing oil was of grease and

72

smelt horrible. The omens were unfavourable. So much for omens, when the person in question is Elizabeth Tudor.

Ten days later the Queen attended High Mass before going to open her first Parliament.

Then a Bill was passed dissolving all monasteries and the Feast of the Nativity of St John the Baptist was made the last day for taking the oath of allegiance. Feckenham was silent: and on July 12th the monastery was dissolved and the constitution was in abeyance for the best part of a year. At last on May 12, 1560, there was granted a Charter of Foundation.

Meanwhile the Chapter decreed that every Saturday there was to be a Choir Chapter at which there must be present one prebendary before whom all the choir were to appear for the redressing of any faults in the previous week. Two years later it was re-enacted that one of the prebendaries residentiary or his deputy was to keep the Choir Chapter every Saturday upon pain of a fine of 4d. for every day so omitted; and on the 23rd of March 1562-3 it was decreed that every one of the clerks who was at home and in health was to be present at the services from the beginning until the end on the Sundays upon pain of 7d. for every default therein, and the chantor was ordered to mark and account their absence.

Examination was being made of the financial situation within the College. Amongst the Abbey Muniments undated but apparently belonging to the first year of the reign is an account of 'The Overchardge of the College of Westm aboue the allowed pporton.'

There is a section concerning the scholars of the Grammar School, amounting in all to £34. 5s. Then follows:

The 10 Choristers

Gownes. They haue aboue theire allowed pporton wch is iijs viijd a peece yearely x gownes wch doe stand the house in xiijs iiijd a peece the whole is vili xiijs iiijd

Gaudye dayes. Item they haue x gaudedayes in the College wch comes to xxd the day the sume is xvj*s* viij*d*.

Breade. Item they haue aboue their allowance a bushell of wheat eury weeke wch comes in the yeare to x*li* xiij*s* at iiij*s* the bushel. The totall of the Choristers chargd is xvij*li* xviij*s*.

The totall that the Schollers Choristers Servants Petycannons and Clarkes do charge the howse is ccc*li* xiij*s*.

The Choristers were housed separately and there has survived a bill for 'ye Queristers House. Item 10 foote of new glass iij hall windows x*s*. Item for putting vij foote of glass in ye upper chamber ij*s*.' This is about the year 1561.

A bill for a Queen's Scholar named William Goodwyn provides an inventory of the schoolboy's clothes of the time. It consists of a gown, doublet of 'sake clothe' lined with canvas, 'a payre of scabylouyans' (pantaloons), 'hamsher carsey uper hoose', a hat which cost 18*d*. and a pair of shoes which cost 10*d*. but had to be renewed every month. He also had a 'tallowe candell to boorne in the scole' (wax being provided in church), 'a quyer of papre and ynke, a booke called Xinifon or tullis epystles'.

The choristers were an official part of Westminster School until the 1840's and names there might have been numerous: but, as the compilers of the *Record of Old Westminsters* state in their Preface:

At no time in the past do the Head Masters' Admission books appear to have been kept with any great care, and the names are omitted of several boys who should have been entered, and are known from other sources to have been at the School. On the other hand, there are a number of names in the School lists for whom no admission can be found. These probably in many cases refer to Choristers of the Abbey, who under the Statutes received a free education at the School until 1848, and were not regarded as being of sufficient interest to have their names formally entered.

ELIZABETHA FUNDATRIX

The Elizabethan statutes for the school within the framework of the Collegiate Church of St Peter Westminster has the following clauses concerning the choristers, and it has been suggested that they contemplated a good deal of interrelation between the choir school and the grammar school.

There were to be *clerici duodecim*, of whom one was to be *choristarum doctor*. He was to be a Doctor or a Bachelor of Music and a person of good repute, godly life, sincere religion and practised in singing and performing musical instruments. There was no position for an organist as such.

There were to be *decem pueri symphoniaci sive choristae*. These continued the line of the old singing boys.

There were to be two preceptors for the purpose of teaching the young, and there were forty grammar pupils.

A section stated that as well as certain Abbey tenants the choristers were to have a preference in elections to the Grammar School. These boys were to be of tender age and of well-sounding voices suitable for singing: but the Public Schools Commission in their Report of 1864, i. 159, state that there was no reason to believe that the preference of election was ever attended to.

Sargeaunt in his *Annals of Westminster School* says 'the choristers were to attend lessons during two hours on each weekday. Before this they were to have received a preparatory training in grammar.'

Strype states 'The Master of the Singing Boys hath his House, and other due Allowances for himself and Ten Children, whom he is charged to bring up in Song, for the daily Service of the Church.'

The Elizabethan injunctions also decreed an hour twice a week was to be given to music with the choirmaster around middle day. This was continuing the mediaeval position of music in education.

And so the choristers became scholastically a part of

75

Westminster School. That they were members to a varying degree is true but even as late as 1844 the Precentor's Book has the entry against a boy's name 'Took advantage of his statutable right of admission to Westminster School'.

Perhaps the fates would have been kinder if Dean Goodman, who has been hailed as the second Founder of the Abbey and who allowed his nephew to be a chorister, had insisted that the two schools should be separate, as Dean Colet at St Paul's in 1509 founded an entirely independent school, leaving the ancient Cathedral Choir School a continuing and distinctive entity.

This is not to derogate the greatness of Westminster School, which sprang to full height in Elizabeth's reign and flourished exceedingly until a temporary decline at the beginning of Victoria's. No school which included Sheridan, Warren Hastings, Locke, Prior, Atterbury, Bentham, Bagot, Cowper, Wren, George Herbert, Dryden, Gibbon and Ben Jonson, to name but a handful, could be other than great: but the school that catered for a great percentage of the peerage and gentry and provided a line of proconsuls and whole Benches of Bishops, so that it is almost impossible to turn a single page of the *Record of Old Westminsters* without coming upon a distinguished family, was bound also to regard with condescension—the word is pregnant with the eighteenth century—the choristers who came to the Abbey (their School Chapel), and vicariously into their school merely because of their voices and the original intention of their Royal Foundress. In the age of religious apostasy this was likely to degenerate into contempt, for boys know little of pity, and the break in the 1840's when the numbers of Westminster School had shrunk to no more than 85 in all, was both timely and beneficial.

The historians of Westminster School have been many and zealous and none more than Mr Lawrence E. Tanner,

M.V.O., himself an Old Westminster. In his books on the
school he has reminded his readers that under the Elizabethan foundation meals in Hall—commons—were accompanied by Bible reading and that the Muniments contain a
dispensation to eat meat on Wednesdays. It had been forbidden, not for religious reasons but to help the fishermen:

Dispensation from Matthew Archbishop of Canterbury
to the Dean and Chapter of Westminster for the Undermaster, pupils in the Grammar School, and the boys serving
in the choir, and other boys having their victuals together in
hall within their College to eat meat each Wednesday; in
gratitude whereof the college shall every Easter Eve bestow
6s. 8d. in alms on the poor of the parish next their College
Dat. 1 Sept. A.D. 1570.

On the reverse is:

My lord of Canterburys license for the scholars of Westm
to eate Flesshe vppon the Wednesdaye and also for the
Vssher and Schollers of the Songe Scoole. For this lycense
ther is yerely to be payde to the poore of St Margarettes
church on Easter Eve vjs viijd.

Every minute of the day was organized and the boys
had certain places or stations in which they had to be at
set times of day. The school was almost in the country
but although the water was good and a spring in the yard
was fed from the high ground, the situation was too damp
to be healthy.

The brook which ran into the Thames determined the
line of Great Smith Street and Great College Street and the
bridge over it has been seen within living memory during
reconstruction work. It also flushed the cesspools, though not
always adequately, as was discovered in Victorian times.

Plague devilled Westminster in Elizabeth's reign and in
1562-3 on the 23rd March the Chapter Acts record:

It is decreed that if any sickness happen, the children of the gramer schole shalbe by the discretion of Mr Dean and others which shall happen to be resident at that tyme, removed to Whethampsted or to any other convenient place, there to abide during the time of suche sicknes, and that one of the prebendarys having thallowance of xxs by weke being bound for the tyme to be resident, shalbe there with them.

Two years later on the 23rd June in the Chapter Acts appears:

It is decreed the daie and yeare above said that the scholemr and the ussher wt the childer of the gramer schole shall xiiij days after thelechen next be past go to putney there to remaiyn vntill Michaelmas next if it shall not in the meane tyme be otherwyse thought good And that thone half of the prbendarys comons shall be there & thother half here at Westm during there continuance there.

The chance survival of a Bill for boarding the ten choristers had led to the preservation of some of the boys' names. Mrs Perryn with whom they stayed was the widow of one of the lay vicars whose name appears in earlier Treasurers' Accounts.

the 19 days of decembr 1569
Wyddowe perrins byll for the boorde of x skollers
Itm of mr porye the 29 daye of Septembr 1569 Sum iij*li*
Itm more of hyll ye porter ye 26 daye of novembr 1569
Sum xl*s*
　　　　Sum all is vij*li*
Itm for iij monthes boorde of x boyes　Sum vijli
I moste be a lowyd for one of the boyes wch is gon a waye
for iij wekks boorde　Sum iij*s* vj*d*
more for his washing & bedding for those iij weks Sum vj*d*
more I most be a lowyd for hose and showes, bedding
washing for x boyes, for this xij weks

Itm to browne ij payre of showes	Sum xvj*d*
Itm to francys a payre of showes	Sum viij*d*
Itm to henlye a payre of showes	Sum viij*d*
Itm to harrye a payre of showes	Sum viij*d*
Itm to baker a payre of showes	Sum viij*d*
Itm to james a payre of showes	Sum viij*d*
Sum iiij*s* viij*d*	
Itm to francys a payre of hose	Sum xiiij*d*
Itm to james ij payre of hose	Sum ij*s* iiij*d*
Itm to francys a nother payre of hose	Sum xiiij*d*
Itm to browne a payre of hose	Sum xiiij*d*
Itm to edwards a payre of hose [or edwarde]	Sum xiiij*d*

Itm to henlye a payre of hose Sum xij*d* [Possibly they
Itm to harye a payre of hose Sum xij*d* were smaller
Sum ix*s* boys]

Itm for washing of thes x boyes this xij weks
of ther clothes the (Sum) x*s*
Itm more for lodgin for them (Sum) x*s*

So there dothe Remayne unto me of this byll wch I have
layd oute of my owne monye the Sum of j*li* xvij*s* viij*d*
(In a different hand)
pd all this and receyved her xxiij*s* iiij*d*
Total of this qtr viij*li* xvij*s* viij*d*

On the other side is:—
Mres peryns Bill
for the Boyes
charge
Itm pd her moer for v weeks bourdyng at xij*d* the wk for x
quiristers viij*s* iiij*d*
Itm pd her moer for theyr lodging after j*d* a wek iiij*s*
Itm moer for theyr washing as hr byll iiij*s*
Itm moer for viij payr of showes v*s* iiij*d*
Sums total iij*li* xij*s*
wherof she hath receyved ij*s* iij*d*
And so ther is still due to her xix*s* viij*d*
Itm pd her moer for viij wek bourdyng of the sayd x

79

queristers at xiiij*d* pr wek endyng the xxth sept 1569
iiij*li* xiiij*s* iiij*d*

Itm moer for theyr lodgyng and washyng xiij*s* iiij*d*

Itm moer for ij payers of showes and the makyng of ij over
for ij queristers iij*s* j*d*

Mrs Peryns the late Choristers wyffs byll

Chapter Seven

DRAMATIC INTERLUDE

IN ACCORDANCE WITH the injunction in the Elizabethan statutes that they were to act a play in English or pay a fine of ten shillings, the choristers seem at the beginning to have fully discharged their obligation; but the plague and the inopportune death of the leading spirits seem together to have produced a lacuna, and the tradition was not continued. In order properly to understand this, it is necessary to remember the incidence of plague.

1563. Brought by troops from Havre

1568. Precautions taken in City and Westminster.

1569-74. Plague general.

1574. Lord Mayor's Feast suppressed. Plays restrained. 15 November, Robert White, Master of the Choristers died, also his wife, daughter of Christopher Tye, and three daughters, all in 1574.

1575. Plague in Westminster: apparently none in City. There is no evidence of plays or pageants after 1573.

There were other bad years especially 1592-3. The year 1606 was bad and it is possible that Henry Leeve died of plague. He was Master of the Choristers, and organist from 1575 until 1606, but little is known of him except his position at the Abbey during those years. He seems to have been Master of the Choristers only from 1575 until 1585 when Edmund Hooper was appointed, but he was the organist for more than thirty years. There is a beautifully written bill of his for 'Suche Books and Songs for the Quier Collected and Prickte By me Henry Leve Mr of the Children'. But we know little or nothing about him at present.

John Taylor, who was Master of the Choristers at the Abbey by 1561, had been Master of the Singing Children at the hospital of St Mary Woolnoth, as he features there on the 8th September 1557. He appears to have been something of an impresario.

The expenses of the Merchant Taylors' for their pageant on Lord Mayor's Day, 1561, include:

Item to John Tayllour, master of the children of the late monastere of Westminster, for his children that sang and played in the pageant.

Item to John Holt momer in reward for attendance given of the children in the pageant.

In 1562 'the choristers of Westminster performed a goodly play' before the Society of Parish Clerks after their annual dinner.

In 1564 when the *Miles Gloriosus* was given before the Queen by the scholars of Westminster, there was 'Geuen to Mr Holte yeoman of the reuells xs' and a payment to Mr Taylor's man.

Included in the Abbey Muniments, and printed by Mr Tanner in his *Westminster School*, is the expense account of a play acted before the Council on January 17, 1565-6, by the scholars and choristers of Westminster.

It will be remembered that John Taylor was Master of the Choristers. The play was *Sapientia Salomonis* so the presence of the woman and the real live baby will be understood. Elizabeth herself was present. Some of the items are as follows:

Item geuen to Mr Vssher for colors and gold foyle bestowed

in coloring the children faces and in gylting the garlandes
for the prologes   vj*d*

Item geuen for an instrument called a payre of peaces
occupied of one of the plaiers   iiij*d*

Item for twoo yardes of brode saye for the Queen of Saba hir
heade   xij*d*

Item for pines to pinne upp the canapee   iij*d*

Item for perfumes for the chambre   viij*d*

Item for greate pines to pinne upp the Lettres   ij*d*

Item for a thousand of small pinnes   vij*d*

Item for ij boxes of dredge to cleare the children   xvj*d*

Item geuen for botehier for the conveiance of thapparell
from the reuelles vnto Westminster and from thence vnto
the reuelles again   xx*d*

Item geuen to thofficers of the reuelles   xiij*s* viij*d*

Item geuen to a tayler for making fytt the childrens attyre
attending vppon theim one hole daye   ij*s*

Item geuen to Mr Tayler his man for his botehyer to and
fro conueying his Masters apparell and instrumentes from
London vnto Westminster and for his paines taken
therein   xij*d*

Item geuen to a Trompeter   vij*s*

Item geuen to a woman that brawght hir childe to the
stadge and there attended vppon itt   xij*d*

Item geuen to a painter for drawing the cytee and temple of
Jerusalem and for paynting towres   v*s*

Summa Lij*s* -x*d*

pd to Mr Brown

Gabriell Goodman

The item for 'ij boxes of dredge to cleare the children
xvj*d*', which is obviously a preventive or cure against
hoarseness, would perhaps more especially apply to the
choristers.

In 1566 payments were made to John Taylor as 'Mr of
the quirysters' for the performance of the children in the
Ironmongers' Pageant.

In 1566-7, for the services of the children at Shrovetide 9-11 February, John Taylor Master of the Children at Westminster was paid £6. 13s. 4d.

At the same season Sebastian Westcote, Master of the Children of 'Powles', and Richard Farrant, Master of the Children of 'Windsore' also presented entertainments, Westcote's acting two plays.

The plague seriously threatened the Collegiate Church of Westminster, and Dean Goodman who held the prebendal stall of Chiswick arranged a *pied-à-terre* there, so that the school could copy the example of its royal foundress and go on a progress. Previous to this the Collegiate School had moved to Wheathampstead and to Putney. At the latter in 1567 a play was presented before Grindal, Bishop of London, who had in his custody the former Abbot John de Feckenham. The Abbey Muniments supply the details:

Thexpenses of a plaie sett forthe att Putneie before my L. of London and other by the children of the grammer schoole Septemb. 4. 1567.

Imprimis for the conueiance of Mr Tailer his attyre fro London to puttneie and from thence to London againe by water   ijs

Item for the conueiance of attyre from the Reuelles unto Putneie and from thence to ye Reuelles again   ijs

Item geuen to Mr Holtes man attending vppon thattyre att Puttneie and healping to make the same fytt for ye children   vs

Item geuen to his other man receauing thattyre againe   xijd

Item geuen to the trompeter   ijs

Item to the baggpype plaier   xijd

Item for ij whistles   jd

Item for frankincence   jd

Item for packthredd to make whreathes and garlands of yvie   iiijd

Item for whight threade to sowe yvie Leaves on the childrens surplesses   vj*d*

Item geuen for the conueniance of diuerse parcelles borrowed att London as basons iauelinges etc.   xx*d*

    Summam xvj*s* (vj*d*) ij*d*

      Per me Thomam Broune

        Paedotri

This paid by me George Burden by Mr Deanes Appointment.

At Christmas 1567-8 John Tailer as Master of the Children of Westminster received £6. 13*s*. 4*d*. under a Warrant of the 10th January. In the Revels Accounts their pageant or play is named inextricably with two plays by 'The Lord Ryches Plaiers', two by 'Sebastian Westcote and the children of Powles', and two at Shrovetide 29th Feb. to 2nd March, one by 'William Hunnys Master of the children of the Quenes Mates chappell' and the other by 'Richarde Farrante Master of the children of Windsore'.

The list is as follows:

their plays Tragides and Maskes . . . viz. . . . seuen playes, the firste namede as playne as canne be, The seconde the paynfull plillgrimage, The thirde Iacke and Iyll, The forthe sixe fooles, The fiveth callede witte and will, The sixte callede prodigallitie, The sevoenth of Orestes and a Tragedie of the Kinge of Scottes.

In 1569 this producer Master of the Choristers, John Taylor, died, and the next time they are heard of is in the Revels Accounts of 1571-2.

'19 Feb. Payee John Billingesley Amount £13. 6*s*. 8*d*. Warrant 22 Feb. (W); D. Viii. 71. *Paris and Vienna* showen at Shrovetewsdaie at Nighte by the Children of Westminster.'

A Court Calendar 1570-2 has 'Westminster (*Paris and Vienna*, with tourney and barriers.)' According to the Privy

Council Acts the payee is described as Master of the Children of Westminster, and he appears in the Treasurer's Accounts as a Minor Canon (Pettycanon). Sir E. K. Chambers in his *Elizabethan Stage* adds 'in the triumph (where parris wan the Christall sheelde for vienna at the Turneye and Barryers)', which at once brings Caxton's book to mind.

For the first of January 1573-4 the Revels Accounts has the entry 'Truth, ffayth, & Mercye, playde by the Children of Westminster for Elderton vpon New Yeares daye'. The Chamber Accounts state that the payee was William Elderton and the amount was £6. 13s. 4d. (Warrant 10 Jan. (W); D. viii. 178.)

The Court Calendar for 1572-4 adds: 'Mask (Foresters and Wild Men)'.

The same sources state that in the previous year, 6th January, 1572-3 an entertainment was given by 'Elderton and the Children of Eyton' for which he received £6. 13s. 4d. This is presumably the occasion when on Twelfth Night the children of Eton gave a performance before the Queen at Hampton Court.

Unfortunately Taylor's successor, Robert White, Organist and Master of the Choristers and a composer of outstanding ability whose name has been coupled with the greatest of the Elizabethans, died in 1574, in the time of the plague and this presumably had some connection with the fact that the choristers do not appear after the beginning of 1574.

In the year 1570 Robert White was appointed Master of the Choristers. He is now recognized as a composer who has been unduly neglected. It is likely that he was the son of a Robert White who was an organ builder, as that name is found in contemporary payments. In 1553 the Parish of St Andrew's, Holborn, paid 'young Whyte vli for ye great orgaynes wh his father made for ye church'. This organ was sold in 1572 to 'Robert White, gentleman of Westminster' and to John Thomas. Possibly they were related to the W. Whygt, chorister in 1524.

White became a graduate of Cambridge University on December 13, 1560 after studying music for ten years. He was ordered to compose a Communion Service to be sung in St Mary's Church on Commencement Day on penalty of a 40 shilling fine.

By Michaelmas 1562 he was Master of the Choristers at Ely Cathedral, having succeeded Christopher Tye. He apparently went to Chester Cathedral, as it was from there he was appointed to Westminster, where he was allowed as Master of the Choristers, in accordance with Elizabeth's foundation, a house, £10 salary, £4 in regard or reward, and 'iij*li* vj*s* viij*d* for euery of the tenne Queresters, besydes a yerely lyverey to each one, and a bushel of wheate weekely.'

Between 1570 and 1573 three daughters were baptized at St Margaret's, Westminster, but all apparently died of the pestilence in 1574 and were buried in the Churchyard of St Margaret. On the 7th November White, still under 40 years of age, made his will as follows:

I Robert White bacheler of mvsicke and master of the queristers of the Cathedrall Churche of St Peters in the Cittie of Westm in the countie of middx beinge sicke in bodie but of psent remebrance Laude and prayse be giuen to almightie god do ordaine and make therin my Last will in manner and fforme followinge

ffyrste and principallye I recomend my sowle into the hands of almightie god my maker Creator and redemer and my bodie to be buried in the prishe Churchyard of St Margaretts in westm nere vnto my Children, I giue and Bequeathe to Ellin White my wyfe all that in messuage lands wodes medowes and pastures sett lyenge and Beinge in the prishe of Nuthurst in the Countie Sussex for and duringe her naturall lyfe wthout anie Impeachmente. . . .

Item I give and bequethe to margery white my daughter six syluer spones and a mazer wch was her late granndmothers, Item I giue and bequethe to Ann White my other daughter one salt of syluer Itm I giue and bequethe to prudent my other daughter on boule of syluer and parcell gilte to be deliuered to them and eche of them at the daye of their mariage of thage of xviij yeres whether of them first happen. . . . Item I will and bequethe to my wellbeloued father Robert White the some of three pounds of Lawfull money of England and all suche his househoulestufe and goodes wch he did bringe vnto me at or before his cominge to me Item I will and bequethe to Mr Crawell my Spanishe blacke cloke Item I will and bequeth to Catherin my svant my gowne with a sashe of budge Itm I will and bequethe to Margaret Michell my other svante my gowne laced with blacke coney Item I will to euery of my skollers to eche of them iiij*d*.

The residue of all his goods and chattels movable and immovable after his debts had been paid and the funeral expenses discharged he left to his wife who survived him only by a few weeks. In her will she refers to her well beloved mother Catherine Tye who has generally been supposed to be the wife of the composer Christopher Tye, which in view of their connection with Ely where White succeeded Tye as organist is more than reasonable.

White directed that he should be laid beside them, and was buried on the 11th. On the 21st his wife made her will and did not long survive him, as letters of administration were taken out for both wills on the 8th December. Two daughters, Margery and Anne, survived.

He was of great reputation amongst his contemporaries, and Baldwin begins his list of great composers with his name. Morley said that he was 'nothing inferior' to the Continental masters. One wonders whether by any chance Morley had a very special reason for knowing. A Robert

Morley was a Member of the Abbey Choir when Thomas Morley was born in 1557. Unfortunately there is no list of the choristers for these years, 1558 onwards. Thomas Morley would have been 13 years of age when White came to the Abbey. It is a most tantalizing possibility because, if Thomas Morley were a chorister at the Abbey when White came, it would seem that he had been one there in the days of the John Taylor, who was so interested in acting, and would help to explain, perhaps too easily, why Morley later set some of Shakespeare's songs—the only contemporary ones we know.

At Christ Church Oxford there are some part-books which contain a couplet to Robert White:

> *Maxima musarum nostrarum gloria White*
> *Tu peris: aeternum sed tua musa manet.*

which may be roughly translated:

> *O greatest glory of the Muses, White.*
> *Thou diest: but thy Muse for aye remains.*

Amongst the Elizabethan injunctions to the Church of which she became Supreme Governor and not Supreme Head, was that 'in the beginning or in the end of Common Prayer there may be sung an hymn . . . in the best sort of melody and music that may be conveniently devised'. This is the source from which have come the hymns which have proved so popular with the British people.

The Puritans were attacking again. In the year 1586 there was a petition to Parliament asking—demanding would be a better word—

that all cathedral churches may be put down, where the service of God is generally abused by piping of organs, singing, and trowling of psalms from one side of the choir to the other, with the squeaking of chanting choristers, disguised (as are all the rest) in white surplices: some in corner caps and silly capes, imitating the fashion and manner of Antichrist, the Pope, that man of sin and child of perdition.

On December 3, 1588 a Patent was granted to 'Edmond Hoop of the Mrshipp of the Children for tearme of his life', and of him there is a good deal of information.

His most distinguished pupil was Godfrey Goodman (1583-1656) Bishop of Gloucester who was a nephew of the Dean who reigned from 1561-1601. The Rev. Geoffrey Soden's book published recently by the S.P.C.K. makes supererogatory any analysis of him here and Goodman was far too interesting a person to dismiss briefly. Instead he is represented by a quotation from one of his books, *The Court of King James*, as it shows the great Queen in the Armada year. In the same book he makes a curious reference to Raleigh: 'No man doth honour the memory of Sir Walter Raleigh and his excellent parts more than myself; and in token thereof I know where his skull is kept to this day, and I have kissed it.'

In the year '88, I did then live at the upper end of the Strand near St Clement's Church, when suddenly there came a report unto us (it was in December, much about five of the clock at night, very dark) that the Queen was gone to council, and if you will see the Queen you must come quickly. Then we all ran; when the Court gates were set open, and no man did hinder us from coming in. There we came where there was a far greater company than was usually at Lenten sermons; and when we had staid there an hour and that the Yard was full, there being a number of torches, the Queen came out in great state. Then we cried, 'God save your majesty! God save your majesty!' Then the Queen turned unto us and said, 'God bless you all, my good people!' Then we cried again, 'God save your majesty! God save your majesty!' Then the Queen said again unto us, 'You may well have a greater prince, but you shall never have a more loving prince:' and so looking one upon another while the Queen departed. This wrought such an impression upon us, for shows and pageants are ever best seen by torch-light, that all the way long we did nothing but talk what an admirable queen she was, and how we would adventure our lives to do her service. Now this was in the year when she had most enemies, and how easily might they have gotten into the crowd and multitude to have done her a mischief! But here we were to come in at the Court gates, and there was all the danger of searching.

Take her then in her yearly journeys at her coming to London, where you must understand that she did desire to be seen and to be magnified; but in her old age she had not only wrinkles, but she had a goggle throat, as her grand-father Henry the Seventh is ever painted withal; for in young people the glandels being shrunk, the gullet doth make a little deformity. And truly there was then a report that the ladies had gotten false looking-glasses, that the Queen might not see her own wrinkles; for having been exceedingly beautiful and fair in her youth, such beauties are ever aptest for wrinkles in old age.

Godfrey Goodman, Bishop of Gloucester.

Chapter Eight

JACOBEAN HEY-DAY

FORTUNATELY, AS THERE is no list amongst the Abbey Muniments, the Lord Chamberlain's Accounts give the names of those to whom an allowance of mourning was granted for the funeral of Queen Elizabeth. It can be assumed that these men and boys were identical or almost identical with those who sang at the coronation of King James the Sixth and First.

The Quiristers of Westminster

John Hoop	Marmaduke Feild
Walter Porter	John Clarke
Richard Warren	Richard Hutchins
Samuel Brown	William Chambers
Thomas Pee	Thomas Case

The Singingmen of Westminster

Matthew Holmes	Thomas Godinge
Richard Baker	Robert Forrest
John Searell	John Gregorie
John Thorogood	Henry Northedge
William Murrey	Richard Bently
William White	James Hoop
William Heather	John Estey
John Stone	

It is possible to add some information about a few of the boys on this list, also of their Masters.

John Hooper, presumably the senior chorister, was

christened the son of Edmond Hooper on November 8, 1590, which would make him in his thirteenth year. Edmond Hooper had been Master of the Choristers since 1585 and was to be in 1606 the first properly constituted organist of the Abbey. On March 1, 1603 he had been admitted a Gentleman of the Chapel Royal, but that year of 1603 seems to have been a difficult one for him. Two days after the coronation of James, the college broke up on the 27th of July until the 7th of October, a thing unprecedented, as modern holidays were undreamed of and previously the move had been made to Chiswick. The reason was plague, and a Chapter Minute of 3rd October 1603 decrees that if the cause of the dissolution of the College 'wch is ye visitation of God by ye plague' should continue 'in so great measure as it doth viz 2000 a week' the dissolution is to continue. Commons, the eating of meals together in Hall, was discontinued until the end of the year. Lancelot Andrewes, at this time Dean, insisted however on the senior boys who were Major Candidates (for the Universities) being brought back into residence with the Headmaster or one or two of the prebendaries, and five servants were retained to look after them.

On December 3rd the fourth item of the Chapter Minutes reads:

Itm that sithence there are many disorders in the Choristers, Mr Deane and the Prebendaries present then shall, in what tyme they think good take order for the reformation of them & the maner of their keping both in what sort and by whom. . . .
5. Itm that Mr Deane and the Prebendaries present shall call before them Mr Hooper both for the shewing of his Patent, & also the lease wch he claymes of the Vicarige of St Margarets & to order the same lease according to the right intendment in equity.

6. Itm that the K. Schollars shall have present notice to repayre hether agaigne & meete at the schoole on ye Monday next after the Twelfth day if the Sickness increase not.   Signed Lancelot Andrewes etc.

Another of Hooper's difficulties appears from the following document to have been financial:

To the ryght hoble Mr Doctor Andrewes Dean of Westminster.

In most humble wise do complane vnto yor wor wee whose names are subscribed, That wheras Mr Hooper shold have paid vs our Dividents for the whole yere at midsomer last, to the ministers 32*l* a peece and to the laymen 17*l* a peece instead of 32 he hath paid 20 and us 17.12. Our humble sute vnto yor wor is that you will geve order now against the pay day that wee may be payd oute of his wages And wee (as our duty is) will duly pray for yr wor helth and prosperity long to continew

Mat: Holmes   William White
John Serle   Willm Hether
Rich: Baker   Tho: Godwin
Willm Murrey   Peter Hopkins
John Thurgood

Endorsement in the hand of Lancelot Andrewes:

I think it convenient yt Mr Threasarer doe make stay in his hands, of so much of Mr Hoops wages as doth amount to this sume vntill Mr Hoops answer be heard concerning this demand, wch if it be not lyked, then may they receive their severall sumes according to their desires.

Lancol: Andrewes

This is undated but must be prior to November 3, 1605 because on that day Lancelot Andrewes was consecrated Bishop of Chichester.

His last Chapter Minute as Dean is dated 30 Aprilis 1605. It is of the utmost importance for the present purpose.

It is decreed that from the feast of the nativitie of St John Baptist next ensuing the tenne Queristers shall have their Comons in the Hall as the Kinges Schollers have, and shall all of them goe to the Gramer Schoole at suche tymes as the are not attending the service of the Churche, and are not Learning to singe And shalbe at the appointing & choyse of Mr Deane.

Lancel: Andrewes

The Chapter Minutes dated May 29, 1606 have the entry: 'Patent to Edmond Hooper 10th, 16*li* fee as organist of ye church.'

It is obvious also that there was a radical improvement in his fortunes, from the Minute dated 7 May, 1610:

Memorandum that, vpon due consideration of the good service wch Mr Hooper our Organist hath and doth continually performe in the Service of the Church it is decreed by vs that the sayed Mr Hooper shall peacably inioye that part of the house alotted for the Mr of the Queresters and the children themselves the saied Queresters wch he now dwelleth in and inioyeth, howsoeuer the now Mr of the Queresters or anie other shall impugne the same hereafter and there being some defect in the sayed Mr Hoopers patent as Organist sealed in the 4th yeare of his Mties reighne there was this day a new patent sealed to his vse as Organist wth a fee of xvj*li*.

James, his second son, was a singingman at the Abbey, dying in 1651, and his grandson William was a petticanon who lived from 1611 until 1663 and is generally considered to have been the Hooper who took Samuel Pepys into the choir on the 29th of December 1661 where he 'sang with them their service'.

It was the first time that the Coronation Service was in English when James I was crowned and in contrast to Elizabeth's single representative, the whole Bench of Bishops was present.

95

The boy whose name appears second on the list of quiristers is Walter Porter who later became Master of the Choristers in 1639, following in that office another old chorister, James Trye, but of them more will be heard later.

Thomas Pee, fifth on the list, probably was the Thomas Peers, Peirs, Pearce who is the first named of the singing-men at the funeral of James I, immediately following the Chantor and Orlando Gibbons. The first bass in the list of those appointed to wait upon his Majesty King Charles on his Scottish journey is a Thomas Piers senior, and Rimbault says that he was a member of the Abbey Choir before his admission into the Chapel Royal. He seems also to have been related to the Edmund Pearce who was Master of the Choristers at St Paul's. He contributed to John Hilton's *Catch as Catch Can*, 1652, and died on August 10, 1666. Both he and John Harding (chorister at James I's funeral in 1625) sang at the coronation of Charles II on April 23, 1661. On December 10, 1663, he was second on the list of Gentle-men of His Majesty's Chappell Royal exempted from pay-ment of subsidies granted to his Majesty by Parliament, 8th May, 1661.

Marmaduke Feild, sixth of the quiristers of Westminster at Elizabeth's funeral was in his twelfth year, having been christened according to the Registers of St Margaret's West-minster on July 11, 1591, the son of Edward Feild.

John Clarke may be the same as the last of the singing-men of Westminster at James's funeral in 1625. If this is correct then he was a Gentleman of the Chapel Royal at the time of the funeral of Anne of Denmark in 1618 and was another of those appointed to wait upon Charles I on his Scottish journey in 1633. Yet another chorister-contem-porary, Walter Porter, was with him and Porter and Clarke are two of the four tenors, Thomas Pee or Piers being a bass.

A William Chambers was buried on October 5, 1609,

having died of the plague and on the previous day the Registers of St Margaret's also show the burial of a Jane Chambers who had died of the plague. Thomas Case, the last named of the ten, may have been the Thomas Case, son of Robert christened on July 11, 1589 (St Margaret's Registers, which also record the burial of a Thomas Case August 20, 1645—a child who died of the plague.)

It is perhaps worth noting the scale of funeral charges at this time:

A note of the chardges for the buriall of the ho Henrie Seamor beinge wthout funerall buried the II day of Januarie 1606.

Item to the organist	vj*s* viij*d*
To the Mr of the Choristers	vj*s* viij*d*
To the schoolmaster	vj*s* viij*d*
XIJ Singingmen	Ix*s*
XI Schollers	xI*s*
X Choristers	x*s*

For the funeral of the Earl of Devonshire May 7, 1606 the payments were the same except that the Master of the Choristers and the Schoolmaster each received x*s*.

The only thing known about John Gibbs, who was Master of the Choristers from 1605 until 1613, is in an Abbey Muniment dated 26th November 1608 which records a delivery of 'Mault to Mr Gibbes' for allowances as Master of the Choristers from 22 February 1607-8 to 1st May 1609.

Not always was there peace and quiet about the Abbey in James's reign. On April 14, 1614, the *Calendar of State Papers* records of Parliament. 'The whole house is to receive the communion not at Westminster Abbey for fear of copes and wafer cakes but at St Margaret's where absentees are to be noted.' In April 1616 took place the pompous funeral of one of Sir George Villiers' favourites in Westminster Abbey; whereupon the butchers of King Street buried a dog in Tothill Fields ridiculing the Abbey ostentation, saying that the soul of a dog was as good as that of a Scot. Several of them were arrested and were sentenced to be whipped. At the same time the communion cloth, two copes and Prince Henry's robes were stolen from the Abbey Church.

On September 7, 1621 John Parsons was granted a Patent during his life to be 'Organist, and Mr of the Choristers Fee £16' and for teaching and finding the children 'Thirty six pownds, thirteen shillings four pence a quarter'.

Parsons, who thus succeeded Hooper, may have been the son of Robert Parsons with whom he has often been confused. He was elected organist and a parish clerk of St Margaret's, on the recommendation of the Dean, but received the double appointment as Organist and Magister Choristarum on the death of Hooper. As a musician he was much appreciated, and a burial service of his was used by Purcell at the funeral of Charles II. William Camden wrote of him:

> Death, passing by and hearing Parsons play,
> Stood much amazed at his depth of skill,
> And said, 'This artist must with me away,'
> (For death bereaves us of the better still),
> But let the quire, while he keeps time, sing on,
> For Parsons rests, his service being done.

After two years at the Abbey he died, being survived by his wife Jane and by three children, William, Dorothy and Thomasine. There is no reference to him in the Chapter Minutes other than the Patent; and not one single mention of Orlando Gibbons by whom he was succeeded, and who held the office an equally short time. Unfortunately Gibbons, one of the greatest musicians of Stuart times, was at the Abbey only from 1623-5, but he coincided with Dean Williams, and the result musically was most happy. We are told by Bishop Hacket in his Life of Williams:

98

JACOBEAN HEYDAY

That God might be praised with a cheerful noise in his sanctuary, he procured the sweetest music both for the organ and for the voices in all parts that ever was heard in an English choir. In those days the Abbey and the Jerusalem Chamber where he gave entertainment to his friends were the votaries of the greatest singers that the land has bred.

It was Williams who appointed John Parsons on the death of Hooper and, on Parsons' sudden death, Orlando Gibbons.

A great occasion occurred when the French Ambassador and his suite came to a service in the Abbey while the engagement between Prince Charles and Henrietta Maria was being considered. The proposed Spanish marriage had been a fiasco for the Prince and for Buckingham, and the French were given special service books which they examined and followed, all except the Ambassador who behaved with contumely and left his unopened book behind while the rest took theirs away.

Williams's enemies were constantly attacking him, and in 1623 some Hymns set by Orlando Gibbons were described as 'Popish, superstitious, obscure, and unfit to keep company with David's Psalms'. It was the same seam which had showed itself under Henry VIII, Edward VI and Elizabeth; but now it was much nearer the surface.

Westminster School was very royalist and William Camden and the boys roundly denounced the Percies Treason, the bloudy Gowries Plot and the great Gunpowder Conspiracy of November 5, 1605. There is a John Catesbie in the list of singingmen for 1604 and only in that year. He also had a son born in that year.

In 1605 two Prayer Books were bought for the Abbey containing the Special Thanksgiving for the escape from the Percies Treason. 'For two prayer books touchinge thanks gevinge for the escape from the late most horrible treason viij*d*.'

99

The Abbey Muniments record the expenses incurred 'to set up a place for the mewsick in Jerusalem Chamber'. Amongst the fees during 1623-4 there is one for canopy and copes when the King came on the first day of Parliament, which sounds as though the charges of 'Popery' had some outward foundation; and it is worth remembering the doctrinal position of that ex-chorister of the Abbey Godfrey Goodman, who became Bishop of Gloucester. Some of the singingmen from 1540 onwards fished in very dangerous waters, and in 1610 the Headmaster of Westminster submitted to the Roman Church.

Gibbons does not seem to have been over-generous in his dealings with subordinates if we can judge from a note of his concerning repairs done by John Burrard to the organ which cost a little over £20. Orlando Gibbons to Mr Ireland:

'Mr Ireland: I know this bill to be very reasonable because I have already cut him off ten shillings, therefore I pray despatch him, for he hath delt honestly wth ye church soe shall I rest yr servant

Orlando Gibbons'

At this same time, in 1621-2, there is other evidence of the influence of Dean Williams. 'Item paed to Mr Batten for pricking Mr Weekes his Service and Mr Talles his Magnificat & nunc dimittis as also Mr Tomkins service xxxs.' This is the Adrian Batten, a member of the choir, who became organist of St Paul's Cathedral and made a priceless Organ Book containing in some cases the only copies of music by his contemporaries and by the Elizabethans. But for his book much superlative work would have been lost to the iconoclasts.

Frequently at the Abbey there have been robberies. The most sensational had been perpetrated from the inside, when the Treasury of England was systematically looted in the reign of Edward I; and one recalls the robbing of Henry V's tomb, and Machyn's record of the hanging of some men who had robbed Spaniards while they were in the Abbey during Mary's reign.

In 1615-16 there was paid 'to William Ireland for his chardges in pursuinge the Theeves that robbed the Church' 56s. 6d., and in 1620 an 'Item for seekinge ye bible that was stolne out of ye Church'; while in 1631-2 a payment was made to a certain Thomas for keeping the cloisters free from loose people in the time of the danger from infection xxxs.

There is particular interest in the fact that when William Camden founded the History Professorship at Oxford, he asked the University to confer the musical degrees of Doctor of Music upon Heather the first professor and on Gibbons. According to Rimbault, Heather had been a chorister at Westminster, but the term at this period sometimes seems to refer to an adult singer. Another instance is of Lancelot Coborne who called himself Quirister of Westminster when his daughter was christened in 1619.

In April 1625 Gibbons conducted the funeral of James I; and composed music for Charles I in honour of Henrietta Maria on her first coming from France. He was summoned to Canterbury, but died of an apoplectic fit and was buried in the Cathedral.

The Lord Chamberlain's Accounts give fortunately the names of the Westminster Choir that sang at James I's funeral. The whole list is headed 'The Chamber of our late Sovereign Lord King James'.

Choristers of Westminster

George Heath	Abraham Laugton Langton or Laughton
Owen Adamson	Andrew Scriven
James Trie	Thomas Kealish
John Harding	Thomas Finch
John Jewill	Hercules Geeringe

John Frost is Chanter; Orlando Gibbons Organist; Thomas Day Master of the Choristers; the singingmen include Thomas Petrie, James Hooper, Richard Giles, Adrian Batten, John Clarke, Two Shagbutts and Two Cornitors.

Of these choristers at least one died of the plague in the very same year. Hercules Geeringe was buried November 11, 1625 and against his name in the Registers of St Margaret's, Westminster is the note: 'child. plague'. On August 18th an Abraham Laughton, probably the Abraham Langton, was buried, his name being accompanied in the registers by: 'child. plague'. The plague raged in Westminster from June 10, 1625 to February 2, 1626 a duration of 33 weeks and 5 days during which out of 2,080 burials, 1462 were due to plague; a percentage of 70.2. A George Heath was buried on February 15, 1627 (St Margaret's Registers), but the name is not an unusual one.

John Harding may be the John Hardinge who was one of the musicians for the violins in the royal band of Charles I, December 20, 1625. He was sworn a Gentleman of the Chapel Royal in 1638 and the cheque book also has the entry 'M. John Harding Gent of his Maties Chappel Royall, departed thes life the 7th day of November 1684'. He sang at the coronation of Charles II, and was buried in the Abbey cloisters.

James Trie became Master of the Choristers in 1637 and two years later was succeeded by Walter Porter. The Registers of St Margaret's record the christening of a Richard Trye on December 2, 1639 the son of James and Jane, and an Amis Trye was buried August 24, 1638. There is also a Chapter Minute dated December 22, 1638 when

It was then also ordered and agreed uppon that ye Treasurer for ye yeer ensuing should pay to Mr Dean of Bangor ye sume of xij*li* xvj*s* vj*d* being by him paid unto Mr Trie Master of the Chorasters for ye diett of ye children

in ye two first yeeres of his stewardship & not allowed by
Chapter in ye former accompt; & that Mr Trye should be
paid by ye said Master Treasurer the sume of eight pounds
for money by him laied out in ye last yeere of his stewardship of ye said Deane of Bangor; And that this allowance
should be in lieu of all former demands made or to be made
for ye time past by the said Mr Trie And it was also then
agreed on that for ye time to come the Chorasters should be
allowed Comons on these festivalls following; that is to say,
All Saints, Novemb 5, Christmas day & ye three holydaies,
Newyeers day, twelfe day, Candlemasse day, March 25 & 27
Easter day and ye two holydaies, Ascension day, Whitsonday
and ye two holydaies elecon Sunday & ye Monday following
yff ye elecon be solemnely kept, & on S. Peters day, & no
other, and that the said Mr Trye for every of ye said daies
shall receive of ye Steward for ye time being the sume of
iiij*s* onely, except uppon the holledayes, on wch he shall be
allowed five shillings for the said Comons.

The other reference is the appeal of his widow which tells
its own sad tale and, taken with Walter Porter's and other
petitions, shows the misery that fell upon those who so short
a time before had made the sweetest music that ever was
heard in an English choir.

To the right honble the Comittee of Lords and Comons
for the Colledge of Westm.
The humble petiton of Jane Try widdow
Sheweth
That Mr William Hutton late deceased, one of the singingmen of the Collegiate Church of Westmr was iustly
indebted unto yor petr in ye some of ffower pounds wch
hath bene a long time due: And for payment thereof the
said Mr Hutton gave yor petr an Assignemt vnder his hand
for her to receive ye same out of such monye as should be
due unto him for his wages and dinner money at Midsomer
next As by the said Assignemt appeareth.

fforasmuch as yr petr late husband James Try who was Master of the Children of the said Church depted this life about 4 yeares since, leaving her a most disconsolate widdow, with 4 small children, and no meanes of livelyhood wherewith to maintaine them. So that shee and they are now exposed to much distresse and misery.

Yr pets humble suite therefore is That this honble Comittee wilbe pleaseid to give order That shee may forthwith receive the said 4li so long since justly due, To releive her and her Children prsent necessitiee.

And shee and they shalbe ever obliged to pray &c.

12 August 1648 (1648-9)

[Endorsed] It is this Day Ordered that this Petitonr be Referred to Mr Arthur Squibb to Examine and to testifie what money was due vnto Mr Hutton (late one of the Singingmen) before his Decease.

Thomas Day became Organist and Master of the Choristers in 1625 on the death of Orlando Gibbons. He had been one of the musicians in the service of that Henry Prince of Wales, who would have been king if he had lived. When Charles I came to the throne he appointed Thomas Day to a similar capacity; and Day carried through his part of the coronation of Charles, which was marked by omens. In particular it was noted that the King was crowned in white.

In 1632 Day left the Abbey, becoming Master of the Children of the Chapel Royal in 1637, and is believed to have died in 1654.

At the Abbey he was succeeded in 1633 by Richard Portman, who had been a pupil of Orlando Gibbons, was made a Gentleman of the Chapel Royal in 1648, and died just before the Restoration in November 1659. Like Walter Porter, who was Master of the Choristers, he lost his post in 1644 and became a teacher of music.

An important Chapter Minute, dated 7 December 1626,

concerns a deal with that Duke of Buckingham who bears such a heavy responsibility for Stuart disasters:

Whereas ther is now at this Chapter one hundred pounds per annum or therabouts, of Mannors, Lands, tithes or tenements for euer to be conueied to this church of St Peter from the Lord Duke of Buckingham his Grace, by way of fyne, for the lease of diuers Mannors, and Lordships &c in Worcestershire and Gloucestershire, graunted to John Browne Esquire, by the Assignment of the said Duke: And that ther lies a bond of Mr Thomas Fotherleyes to the Deane and chapter of three Thousand pounds for the performance of the same. Now therfore the Deane and chapter of one unanimous Consent and assent, haue alotted for euer out of the said lands forty pounds per annum therof, to be paied by the Treasurer of the church for the tyme being, quarterly to the Pettycanons, and singingmen of this church, together wth the Organist if he haue not a singingman of Petticannons place; and twenty pownds also yearly of the same to be by the same Treasurer to the Mr of the Coristers, for the bettering of the apparrell and diet of the said Coristers, as shall be approued by the Treasurer of the said Collegiat church for the tyme being.

Apparently moves were made for the better housing of the singingmen as a Chapter Minute dated 23 May 1631 states:

Memorandum that one of the Tenements and back yards in the Almery late in the possession of Abraham Beck, and now purchased of him by the Colledge, is assigned ouer unto Mr Thomas Day, one of the singingmen of our church and his successors. So as all the 16 singingmen ar now by the Care and charges of the Deane and chapter prouided of houses.

By the year 1631, although the Headmasters of Westminster School seem to have remained bachelors in accordance to the statute of their foundress until 1695, many of the clergy had married and the vexed question of 'Commons' or communal meals in Hall, came to a head. On the 11th January, the following appeared in the Chapter Acts:

Forasmuch as the College at this present is destitute of means to keep Commons together, according as they have done heretofore, and the most part of our Society being married men have families of their own and live here in residence, we have agreed that while the said Commons raised out of our means and stipends is so discontinued, the Scholars, Choristers and Poor being provided according to the usual proportion of their allowances, and the servants allowed board wages one full third part of wheat, malt and other provisions shall be delivered to the Lord Bishop of Lincoln, our Dean, and the other two parts shall be divided among the twelve Prebendaries according to the term of their several residences and housekeeping in this place, and according to such orders as they shall make among themselves with the consent of the Dean.

Finally, when the great storm was about to break on England, a Chapter Minute records a recrudescence of a lesser quarrel:

25 Jan. 1640-1

Whereas there was a difference between the Organist and the Master of the Coristers about a stipend of ten pounds per annum to whether of them it should be paid & It appeerd to us that the Organist hath bene in possession of the said Stipend for many yeeres together, but that the right was & is in the Master of the Coristers. It is therfore thought fitt and orderd by the Deane and Chapter, that in rispect of bothe their interests and paines, that the said ten pounds shall be continued to the Organist and that ten pounds more shall be paid by the Treasurer to the Master of the Choristers yeerly.

It is agreed that ye Choristers gownes shall be made at the charge of the College.

Chapter Nine

THE BREAD OF CAREFULNESS

THE ABBEY MUNIMENTS have a number of petitions from the disbanded choral establishment, and Goodman's later years are typical both of those who died during the Civil War and the Commonwealth and of those who were lucky enough to survive into the Restoration and cluster round an impecunious King.

The Abbey had many troubles of its own. At the turn of the year 1642 there was an 'Item given to certayne Captaynes by Mr Deans appointment for defending the Church Cs. Item paid to Mr White and Mr Smyth for powdr and shott lxiij*s*.' Other items were paid to a Company of the 'Trayne bands lxxiij*s*', while the purchase of muskets, pikes and pistols came to £35. 6*s*. 6*d*.

In 1643, as everyone knows, the Roundhead soldiers broke down the organ pipes and sold them at several ale houses for pots of ale. The services were discontinued and an act was passed in 1644, which recalls Edward VI's time, for the removal of superstitious monuments. This included organs. Any music was unaccompanied and the congregation sang metrical psalms.

It is a matter of conjecture as to what happened to the choristers between the opening of the Civil War and the Restoration. Obviously, after the break-up of the choral establishment in 1644-5, no more boys came into the choir and thence into Westminster School, and there were none available until 1661. Presumably there were none at the funeral of Archbishop Ussher in 1656, the only occasion when the English liturgy was permitted in Commonwealth times. Documents at Cambridge show there was provision for choristers until 1643.

Another possible pointer has survived in the Report of Arthur Squibb, which is undated but can be placed between 1646 and 1660. The 25th of January 1648 to which he refers should be 25th of January 1640-1.

May it please this right ho:ble Comittee

According to yor order of the 13th August last, I have made a search in the accompts belonging to the Colledge concerning the Allowance heretofore made for the Choristers and doe find the sume to be as followeth

To the Mr of the Choristers for x Choristers at lxvis viiid a peece } xxxiii*li* vis viii*d*

More to the Mr of the Choristers for dividend and augmentacon for the Choristers } xx*li*

In toto   liii*li*   vis   viii*d*

more for diner mony v*li*

There was alsoe an allowance yearly made unto the Choristers of wheat

And an allowance yearly of maulte

And also a yearly allowance for gownes   iii   vi

There was alsoe an allowance in the Treasurer's accompt yearly to the Mr of the Choristers of ten pounds wch though it went in the name of the Mr of the Choristers, yet the same had for a long time bin paid to the Organist w:ch being in dispute betweene them before the Deane and Chapter, upon the 25th of January 1648 And was then ordered In regard the *sd* stipend of x*li* p annum had long bin in possession of the Organist that it should still be continued unto the said Organist. But in regard the right was in the Mr of the Choristers the Deane and Chapter

Ordered that x*li* more should yearly be paid by the Treasurer to the Mr of the Choristers wch was accordingly paid.
All wch I humbly submitt to this rt ho:ble Comittee

Arthur Squibb

On December 26, 1641, there occurred a celebrated attack
on the Abbey which Fuller describes in his *Church History*.

Eyewitnesses have thus informed me of the manner
thereof. Of those apprentices who coming up to the Parliament cried, 'No bishops! No bishops!' some, rudely rushing
into the Abbey church, were reproved by a verger for their
irreverent behaviour therein. Afterwards quitting the
church, the doors thereof, by command from the Dean, were
shut up, to secure the organs and monuments therein against
the return of the apprentices. For though others could not
foretell the intentions of such a tumult, who could not
certainly tell their own, yet the suspicion was probable, by
what was uttered amongst them. The multitude presently
assault the church (under pretence that some of their party
were detained therein), and force a panel out of the north
door, but are beaten back by the officers and scholars of the
College. Here an unhappy tile was cast by an unknown
hand, from the leads or battlements of the church, which so
bruised Sir Richard Wiseman, conductor of the apprentices,
that he died thereof, and so ended that day's distemper.

Dean Williams had on December 4th been elevated by
the King to the See of York. Fuller's narrative continues:
'After an hour's dispute, when the multitude had been well
pelted from aloft, a few of the Archbishop's Train opened a
Door, and rush'd out with swords drawn, and drove them
before them like fearful Hares.'

It was a time of desperate uproar. Anyone who had an
axe to grind or a grudge to repay went to Parliament. All
the loafers and lechers cried for justice, and the drunkards
and thieves called for honest, sober government.

A few days before the execution of Archbishop Laud, the Assembly of Divines at Westminster on January 4, 1645, resolved that *The Book of Common Prayer* should be set aside, that the form of divine worship hitherto observed should be abolished and a new form substituted. This was framed by the Assembly and consisted of a creed, a catechism and the outline of the Presbyterian constitution of the Church. The creed in point of fact was strict Calvinism, and especially stressed pre-destination. Crosses, altars, confessions of the sick were all abolished, and it was decreed

Nobody shall write or preach against the new ordinances; he who shall in future use the old common prayer book either in the church or in public places, nay, even in his own house and family, shall pay for the first offence £5, and for the second £10, and for the third be imprisoned for a year, and not allowed to give bail. The church having the right of the keys, may, through its priests, classes, and synods, censure, remove, depose and excommunicate.

But while the Presbyterians rejoiced at their victory, it was to be Pyrrhic as their power was passing to the Independents. The House of Commons did not confirm their resolutions and the people did not willingly carry them into effect. It was only a matter of time for the sects and warring Saints such as the Levellers and the Erastians to quarrel amongst themselves, and on the death of Cromwell the whole edifice fell to pieces. But until then England was to be dictated to by fanatics. *The Flying Eagle* of 24 December 1652, reporting on affairs in Parliament, shows the state of mind of those in authority:

The House spent much time this day about the business of the Navy, for settling the affairs at sea, and before they rose were presented with a terrible remonstrance against Christmas Day, grounded upon divine Scriptures, 2 Cor. v. 16; 1 Cor. xv. 14, 17; and in honour of the Lord's day, grounded upon these Scriptures; John xx. I; Rev i, 10; Psalms cxviii, 24; Lev xxiii. 7, 11; Mark xv. 8; Psalms lxxxiv. 10; in which Christmas is call Anti-Christ's masse, and those Masse-mongers and Papists who observe it, etc. In consequence of which Parliament spent some time in consultation about the abolition of Christmas day, passed orders to that effect, and resolved to sit on the following day, which was commonly called Christmas day.

How detestably petty it all seems now. As childishly petulant as John Vicars, the Puritan divine, who in 1646 published his *God's Ark over-topping the World's Waves*, in which he rejoiced over the new worship at Westminster. The present writer owes the reference to the Rev. Dr Jocelyn Perkins.

. . . a most rare and strange alteration in the face of things in the Cathedrall Church at Westminster. Namely, that whereas there was wont to be heard nothing almost but Roaring-Boyes, tooting and squeaking Organ-Pipes and the Cathedrall-Catches of Morley, and I know not what trash; now the Popish Altar is quite taken away, the bellowing Organs are demolish'd and pulled down, the treble or rather, trouble and base singers, Chanters or Inchanters driven out —and instead thereof, there is now set up a most blessed Orthodox Preaching Ministry . . . O our God what a rich and rare alteration! What a strange change is this indeed.

Meanwhile in November 1645 an Ordinance of the Lords and Commons entrusted the government of Westminster School to a joint committee of thirty-three, eleven from the Lords. This was Presbyterian in bias, and suspended from office all who did not take the Covenant. It had not been known what the Headmaster of Westminster, the great Richard Busby, had done in answer to the order. Of recent years, however, Mr Tanner found amongst the Muniments of the Abbey notes on the whereabouts of the members of the College; whether they had taken the Covenant, or who occupied their houses. Against the names of Dr Moore and Dr Weames is written 'sculks up and doune'. Doctors Wilson, Killigrew, Lanye and Steward are 'at Oxford'; Dr Haward 'in prison'. Against Dr Busby's name is written 'sickly'. It seems the commissioners, realizing Busby's worth, left it at that.

The Committee in 1645-6 or thereabouts, recommended that Mr Busby be continued in his office and that the 10s. for diet and 10s. for tutoring paid quarterly by the scholars be remitted, the Committee esteeming it a dishonour to the Parliament 'that those poore boyes should be att that charge'.

Amongst the petitions is one from the former organist, Portman, who is stated to have fled overseas before 1648. This is obviously untrue from the following document:

To the right honoble the Gouernors of the Schoole and Almeshouses of Westmr

The humble Peticon of Richard Portman and Robert Willis of the late Quire of Westmr

Humbly sheweth

That yor peticors haue enioyed the benefit of a tenement in the great Almery westmr by vertue of their places about eight and twenty yeares, and in the yeare 1640 on mr James Church had a Lease of the said Tenement from the Deane and Chapter of the said Church of westmr for the terme of forty yeares, he paying eight pound per anum to the receiver of the Colledge for yor peticors vse, and the said receiuer paid the foresaid rent to yor peticors. That in the yeare 1645 the said James Church sould his right tittle and interest of the said Tenement to yor peticors, soe that yor peticors enioyed the full possession of the said Tenement. That about Christyde Last and neuer before, yor honors receiuer demanded rent for the said Tenement of yor peticors, but by reason of the Losse of yor peticors Liuely-hoods they are no way able to satisfie yor honors for the

112

arreares of rent except it be by perpetuall Imprisonment of their crazie bodies. That in regard Mr James Church sould his interest of the said Tenement to yor peticors before the Parliaments Act for selling the Colledge Land and houses, yor peticors conceiue he is not Liable to satisfie for the arreares of rent, That yor peticors are obldged in a bond to saue him harmlesse, therefore if he should be compelled to pay the said arreares of rent he will endeauor to recouer satisfaction of yor peticos to their vtter vndoeing.

may it therefore please yor honors to comisserate the sad condicon of yor peticors hauing lost their Liuelyhoods and hauing each of them a wife to maintaine being in want, to voutsafe them the benefit of the said Tenement as formerly or to take the house into yor honors hands and to grant yor order to acquit and discharge them from paying any arreares of rent for the time past

And yor peticors shall euer pray &c

On the left side of the document and written at right angles are the words: 'This Peticon referred to a Comittee who are to sitt on fryday next att 4 of the clock in the Afternoone.'

On the right hand side, also at right angles, is written: 'That Portman be heerd on this day sennight Thursday the 9 of ffeb 54. This peticon referred to ye Rec:rs Mr Bemroe & Mr Broune who are to report their opinions thereof.'

On the back is: 'Recvd seal Aug. 5. 54.'

A petition to Cromwell's Council of State dated February 29, 1656 speaks of Portman as recently deceased.

To the ho:ble Comittee of Lords & Comons for the Colledge of Westmr
The humble Petiton of all those resident in Towne that were of the late Chore in Westmr Abby
Sheweth
That (by reason they haue not recd their divident

Augmentacon monies &c for ye space of 2 yeares & up-
wards, beeing a great part of their Livelihood) the Petrs are
nowe exposed to extreame necessitie & want.

wherefore they most humblie implore this ho:ble Cmittee
to take their sadd Condition inter consideraton, and so Order
the paym:t of one quarters stipend due to each of them at
Christide last for their present releife. As also to take such
further Order touching the arrears aforesaid due to y:e
Pet:rs as to yo:r wisdomes shall seeme meet.

And (as in dutie bound) the Pet:rs shall daylie praie &c.

Edm: Nelham	Walter Gibbs
Ric: Portman	Chr: Chapman
Will: Hutton	Jo: Harding
Robte Willis	Robte Smith
James Hooper	Walter Porter
Jo: Lawes	

There is also an undated petition from Stephen Strong,
John Eastman and John Hill,

3 of ye Sackbutts & Cornets belonging to ye Quire of the
said Church

Sheweth

That they were admitted to their places by ye Deane and
Chapter & had a stipend of 4*l* p annm & 40*s* for their dyett

That they have had noe pay since ye Annuncacon last
was 12 moneth Now in regard they have wifes, Children &
families to mayntayne. . . .

One cannot help regretting that both petitions are undated; and particularly that of all the Choir who were in
town, as the list contains the names of several of whom
more is known.

On December 17, 1649 payment was made to the soldiers
'that shall attend in ye Abbey Church Westmr on the Lords
Daie to restraine the noise that is made in the time of
Divine Service, 1*s.* each'.

114

Dated the 26th is a letter from a Captain James Straghen asking for payment:

I was comanded be my mayor on the Last Lords day to send myn musketeers and an ofischer from seven a clock in the morning untill the afternoon sermon was endid and to helpe the peopell from meking distirbance in sermon time: and if aney did make aney to bring them to the maine gaurd at white hall.

Robberies, as was to be expected, were also taking place. There is the note of a theft of lead by one Nicholas Asaby 'having not the feare of God before his Eyes'. The middle of the twentieth century has seen a return of this lead stealing.

The Commonwealth might be strong while Cromwell lived, but it was with the strength of an occupying power. Dated February 21, 1656-7 is the Order:

. . . And as an expedient for redressing of the unlawful meetings of idle persons at night in the Abbey we conceive it fit for the officers of the Church to take a Constable two nights in the week and upon examination of such suspicious persons as they shall there finde to carry them before a Justice of Peace to be proceeded against according to law. And this we conceive fitting to be continued for a month.

Some of the former dependents of the Abbey must have been in a sad case to judge from the petition of the composer and former Master of the Choristers, Walter Porter, who was himself an ex-chorister. Baptie had considered he was born in 1595; but Porter died in 1659 and in this undated petition he states that he is over seventy years of age:

To the Honble Governors of ye Schoole and Almesmen
The Humble Petition of Walter Porter
Sheweth
That yor Petiton:r was herttofore one of the Choristers of the Abbey Afterwards was chosen one of the Gentlemen of the late Kings Chapell and having spent much time and

money in travelling for the obteyning of his qualitie was made Master besides of the Choristers of the said Abbey, in which Employm:t hee took such assiduous care and paines That the Deane and Prebendaries often promised him a Singingmans place and a better reward for it But their dissolution immediately following yo:r Petiton:r not onely lost their intended additon: to his estate, but his place att the Chappell and all his meanes elsewhere hee and his children having ever since lived in great want and necessitie And are att psent in debt and in a wanting condition the small stocke hee had being exhausted for his and their preservaton:

In this sad case yo:r Petiton:r being 70:tie and odd yeeres of age his strength and faculties decayed, his wants dayly increased and his charitable freindes neere all deceased

Humbly beseecheth yor Hono:rs in tender pittie and comiseraton: of his deplorable condition to bee pleased to give him a Share in the Monuments w:th the rest of the Singingmen or some other way of reliefe By w:ch y:r noble Charitie hee and his Children will be relieved and the small remaynder of his dayes closed upp wth comfort

And hee shall ever pray &c
Walter Porter

The petitonr likewise intends (Being put into a Capacitie) to sett up a meeting for Musick once a fortnight and to traine up two or three boyes in the Art of Musick, such as may be thought fitt to be Chosen out of Westmr Schoole besides their other Learning.

Another undated petition makes equally sad reading:

May it please your Honor

The Lease of the Keeping of the Monuments was obteyned of the Deane and Chapter for three lives, It was not all purchased by the Singingmen but severall Gentl: charitably contributed the greatest parte of the mony

That Mr. Edward Hooper being both Organist and Mr of the Choristers put himself in as Organist and left himselfe out as Mr of the Choristers and the Choristers allso, who ought to have had a proportionable share of that charitable gift as well as any other for that they were members of that body

The Organist and Mr of the Choristers are distinct places, and had distinct ffees and allowances

The number of the Singingmen att first were 17:

Of those 17 there are but 4 left wch enjoy the benefitt of the Gift and one who was not of the Quire. wch is Mr Tingell.

That I was bredd a chorister and arrived after a long time and study to bee Mr of the Choristers And for my paines taken therein was promised a Singingmans place wth a great reward by the Deane and Prebendaries

That the Mr of the Choristers was of the Quire will appeare by the Records of the Colledge in the Raigne of Queen Elizabeth when shee settled a Deane Prebendaries a Chanter, a Mr of the Choristers an Organist and Singingmen

The reason of my not enstallment was because Ministers Deacons and Priests onely wch were to execute Ministeriall offices were enstalled, wch neither the organist or my selfe were capable of, but admitted onely as laymen to officiate as a teacher and organist by the Deane and Prebendaries wch was by the ArchBishopp of Canterbury and Yorke; and the Subdeane of Westminster.

The notwithstanding the Pattent was granted to continue to them and the longest liver of them yett humbly conceive (wth your honors favours) that it was not the Deane and Chapters, nor those charitable Gentlemens intent who trooly gave the greatest parte of the mony for the purchase (the Singingmen themselves paying onely 30:*l* or thereabouts) that surviving life wth three or fower Singingmen or without (there being before 17 who had proportionable shares out of the benefitt of the Monuments) should ingrosse the whole benefitt thereof and have power to excepte against mee who was one of the Quire as Mr of the Chorist:rs

That upon the exhibiting of a former Peticon they all concluded mee a great Sufferer and much impoverished yett would not by any meanes admitt of my coming in, pretending the Admittance of mee would bee an ill President and so consequently iniurious to them.

(Unsigned but obviously by Walter Porter. Probably a draft or copy.)

This third petition by Walter Porter is also undated but may have been the first in time:

To the right hoble Comittee of Lords and Comons for ye Colledge of Westmr

The humble Petiton of Walter Porter late Mr of ye choristers Sheweth that y:r Petr in respect of his said place had p ann ye severall paiem:ts and allowances following: viz 33*li* 6*s* 8*d* stipend, 10*li* for tutordige, 20*li* Augmentaton, 5*li* for dinners, 78 bushells of wheat, 26 bushells of malt and 20 yards of Cloth to make ye said Choristers gownes beeing then in number 10. Out of wch severall allowances, hee, his children and servants had their livelihood, whose imploym:t beeing taken of, it pleased this Comittee to take of the said allowances & to order him 50*li* for his arreares, wch hee hath thankfullie received, & 10*li* p ann' stipend.

So now it is, the Pet:r is growne old & not able to travaile & take paines for a living as formerlie hee hath done having spent much monie in his travaile & taken great paines to better himselfe in his qualitie, is now exposed to great necessitie & want having 4 children to keepe whereof 3 were Choristers wch he hath bin forced to keepe at his own charge, who together wth himselfe are all likelier to perish wthout yor ho:ble favr herewth extended

Maie it therefore please yo:r honors in regarde me yr allowance is verie small & his charge verie great, & for that he feareth everie daie to be cast into prison for debt) to take ye premisses into consideraton, & to Order that hee may either enioy his augmentaton of 20*li* p annum, settled vpon ye Mr of ye Choristers by Chapter Act, beeing pt of ye *Cli* p annum freelie given by ye late Duke of Buck' for the use of those belonging to ye choire; Or els that hee may haue ye benefitt of one of ye void singingmens places formerlie promised by ye Deane as ye rest of ye Choir can testifie, Or otherwise such an additionall allowance to his x*li* stipend out of his former allowances as in yr graces' wisdomes shall seeme most hereby hee may render himselfe equall therein to ye rest of his fellowes in ye Choir

And (as in dutie bound) hee and his familie shall daylie praie &c

Walter Porter

Porter was buried on the 30th of November 1659, only a few months before the Blessed and Happy Restoration of His Sacred Majesty King Charles II.

Chapter Ten

HIS MAJESTY'S HAPPY RESTAURATION

INHERENT IN THE Restoration of the Stuart Monarchy was the return of the Established Church, and that at the Abbey meant the reconstitution of the choral establishment. Christopher Gibbons, a son of Orlando, became organist and Henry Purcell Master of the Choristers. Until the critical research of Professor Westrup, it had been thought that he was the father of the great composer who was organist of the Abbey from 1679 to 1695, whereas it would now appear to be conclusive that he was the uncle and that the composer's father was Thomas Purcell, also a Gentleman of the Chapel Royal and brother of this Master of the Abbey Choristers.

Christopher Gibbons, perhaps owing to a cavalier disposition, was not at all suited to ecclesiastical surroundings, and in December 1660 the Chapter made a highly significant order:

18th Dec. 1660

It was ordered that the Backe doore of the Organ Loft bee shutt upp and that the organist come into the quire atte the beginning of Prayers in his Surplice and betake himselfe to his Stall till towards the end of the Psalms (except on festival dayes when the Answeres are to bee performed with the Organ) then to goe upp the stayers leading from the quire to the organ and performe his duty. And 'tis further ordered that neither the organist nor any other permit any pson to bee in the Organ Loft during the time of Divine service And that the Organist and the blower keepe themselves private and not expose themselves to the view of the people during their Stay in the Organ Loft.

There were as yet no choristers available as we learn from the Precentor's Book. This, one of the very few to have survived, has never been published and is so valuable in its uninhibited accounts that many entries are worth quoting verbatim. It is greatly to be regretted that the corresponding one for Purcell's period as organist disappeared long ago and nothing is known of its contents.

The appearance of the book suggests that the newly appointed Master of the Choristers who paid for it in lieu of a fee to Philip Tynchare alias Tinker must have been very little out of pocket. John Hill the cornet player who died in 1666 was paid to remedy the lack of treble voices, though the fact that he was still being paid £4 for doing so in 1664 need not necessarily mean that their quality was poor!

The Precentor's Book

1660-1 February 16 . . . and with them Henry Purcell, Edward Bradock, William Hutton, Richard Adamson and Thomas Hughes were installed singing men and the aforesaid Henry Purcell, Master of the Choristers also, by Philip Tynchare, Chaunter, for whose installation the Chaunter received 5/- each. Mr. Purcell, instead of Mony, this book.

. . .

Feb. 17 1661 (in another hand) The Febr 17, 1661, The Loady Elizabeth Queen of Bohemia was layd in a vault by her illustrious brother Princ Henry for or attendance at her funerall we received -0 -0 -0.

1660-1 March 22 Funeral of the honourable Lady, Anne Barlow by night at whose funerall were used 3 doz of torches and 9 pound of wax candles and for the attendance of the Quire was payd, to the Chaunter for his fee -0. 10s. 0d. and to the whole company of petticanons and singingmen with the organist — 6*li* 13*s* 4*d* which was thus divided. . . .

To Mr Purcell for the Choristers 10*s*. 0*d*. but this was paid ignorantly, no fee being received for them and none attending to perform any service

1661. March 30th. Funeral of the Princess Royal, Mary the King's eldest sister, mother of the Prince of Orange, was layd in a vault. At this time there were no Choristers and therefore no fee was demanded for them.

Funeral of Lady Elizabeth of Richmond and Lennox April 29 at midnight 1661, Nothing received for the Choristers, none attending for the funeral.

But they had already come into being in time for the coronation of Charles II on April 23rd.

John Evelyn.

23rd April was the Coronation of his Majesty Charles the Second in the Abbey Church of Westminster; at all which ceremony I was present. . . .

(The next day, being St George's) he went by water to Westminster Abbey. When his Majesty was entered, the Dean and Prebendaries brought all the regalia, and delivered them to several noblemen to bear before the King, who met them at the west door of the church, singing an anthem, to the choir. Then, came the peers, in their robes, and coronets in their hands, till his Majesty was placed on a throne, elevated before the altar. Afterwards, the Bishop of London (the Archbishop of Canterbury being sick) went to every side of the throne to present the King to the people, asking if they would have him for their King, and do him homage; at this, they shouted four times 'God save King Charles the Second!' Then, an anthem was sung. His Majesty, attended by three Bishops, went up to the altar, and he offered a pall and a pound of gold. Afterwards, he sate down in another chair during the sermon, which was preached by Dr Morley, Bishop of Worcester.

After sermon the king took his oath before the altar to

maintain the religion, Magna Charta, and laws of the land. The hymn V e n i S. Sp. followed and then the Litany by two Bishops. Then the Archbishop of Canterbury, present but much indisposed and weak, said 'Lift up your hearts'; at which the King rose up, and put off his robes and upper garments, and was in a waistcoat so opened in divers places, that the Archbishop might commodiously anoint him, first in the palms of his hands, when an anthem was sung, and a prayer read; then, his breast and betwixt the shoulders, bending of both arms; and, lastly, on the crown of his head, with apposite hymns and prayers at each anointing; this done, the Dean closed and buttoned up the waistcoat. After this, was a coif put on, and the cobbium, sindon or dalmatic, and over this a supertunica of the same, spurs, and the sword; a prayer being first said over it by the Archbishop on the altar, before it was girt on by the Lord Chamberlain. Then, the armill, mantle, etc. Then, the Archbishop placed the crown-imperial on the altar, prayed over it, and set it on his Majesty's head, at which all the Peers put on their coronets. Anthems, and rare music, with lutes, viols, trumpets, organs, and voices, were then heard, and the Archbishop put on a ring on his Majesty's finger. The King next offered his sword on the altar, which being redeemed, was drawn, and carried before him. Then, the Archbishop delivered him the sceptre with the dove in one hand, and, in the other, the sceptre with the globe. The King kneeling, the Archbishop pronounced the blessing. His Majesty then ascending again his royal throne, whilst T e D e u m was singing, all the Peers did their homage, by every one touching his crown. The Archbishop, and the rest of the Bishops, first kissing the King; who received the Holy Sacrament, and so disrobed, yet with the crown imperial on his head, and accompanied by all the nobility in their former order, he went on foot upon blue cloth, which was spread and reached from the west door of the Abbey to Westminster stairs, when he took water in a triumphal barge to White-hall, where was extraordinary feasting.

Samuel Pepys, who had a much closer view at the coronation of James II, returned to the Abbey on 29 December, Lord's Day 1661.

> And so I dined at home, and my brother Tom with me, and then a coach came and I carried my wife to Westminster, and there meeting with Mr Hooper, he took me in among the quire, and there I sang with them their service, and so that being done, I walked up and down till night for that Mr Coventry was not come to Whitehall since dinner again.

As has been pointed out this Hooper was probably the grandson of the Organist and Master of the Choristers of James I's reign. His death is reported in the Precentor's Book.

As was customary the choirmen had a share in the money for stands at the coronation.

April 1 1661. Spent at an agreement made between the Quiremen for the setting up of Scaffolds for the Churchyard for the seeing the King coming to his Coronation 0-2-9.

The Organist being a good gainer by his organ loft and scaffolds therein erected had no place with the rest of the Quire.

The high born prince Charles Duke of Cambridge sonne to his Highness prince James Duke of York was buried May 6, 1661. . . . Also for the Choristers and Deliver'd to Mr Purcell their master £1-0-0.

Dr Dolben installed Dean of Westminster Dec 3 1662. . . . To Mr Purcell for the Choristers 6/-.

Dec. 13, 1662. Mrs ffrancis Gorge the wife of Dr Gorge one of the prebendaryes of this Church was buried in the South Isle of this Church between the two doors. The Dr gave to the Quire for their attendance as a token of his love 20s to be spent in a collation which was doune at the Chaunter's house, the whole company of Quiremen and boys having their shares therein; but fees should have been payd.

In June-July 1663 the senior singingman, Mr Hooper, died because on June 30 appears Mrs Hooper, and in July 'To ye Widow Hooper'. She was paid until October.

On August the 13th (1664) 'Mr Henry Purcell one of the gentlemen of his Majesty's Chappell Royall and Master of the boyes of Westminster was buried in the great cloyster near Mr Lawes'. August 1664 'Widow Purcell' is paid a share in the Monument money. Immediately after, in the same month, Thomas Blagrave became Master of the Choristers. He continued in that office until 1670.

August 15, 1664. Mr Thomas Blagrave one of the Gentlemen of his Majesty's Chappell royall was admitted to be one of the Clerks of the Collegiate church of Westminster he first serving a year of approbation from the day above written and subscribing as followeth.

Then follows the customary oath.

June 26, 1665. Sir Edward Braughton who received his deadly wound in His Majesty's service at sea in fight against the Dutch and shortly after in returne home, dyed thereof, was buried in the north part of the crosse, neere the doore which openeth into the upper end of the Quire.

The Quire and officers of the Church were payd their full fees for the funeralle of the sd Sir Edward Braughton May 12, 1666 by his Lady, but not without some trouble to her Ladyship, her coach and horses being first attached for the payment thereof.

The fees for the Earle of Marlboroughs funerall were forgiven he dying poor and his friends not being able or willing to pay the money, they gaining nothing by his death.

The following entries when the Great Plague was at its height and a Pest House was on Tothill Fields need no embellishment.

July 1665. At the funeral of the Rt Hon Sir Wm Killigrew only the Chanter, Mr Tynchare junior, Mr Hazard, Mr Hughes, Ambler, Shorter & Corny were present, the rest of the Quire being absent by reason of plague.

Collected in July 1665 for the monuments the sum of £1-19-1 most of the Quire beeing out of toune, it was decided by those that were in toune that it might be divided amongst them, and if the rest did not think well of it, they were to pay back againe so much as would make every man's part alike, it was thus divided.

(Later) It was ordered yt in regard they had nothing for showing ye monnuments yt they should have 2s a peece.

Payment to the choristers appears again for the funeral of the celebrated Mr Thomas Chiffinch on April 14, 1666.

Precentor's Book has the entry:

In the year 1665 by reason of God's Visitation by the plague of pestilence, no wax Lights or Tallow candles were used in the Church, but the Service was dayly performed by day light by Mr John Tynchare, one of the Petticanons, and by him alone from the beginning of July to almost the end of December.

August 25, 1665. Thos Corny one of ye quire was buried of ye sickness.

Oct. 15, 1665. Richard Ambler one of ye quire was buried of ye sickness.

(It will be noticed that both Corny and Ambler were present at the funeral on July 17 of Sir William Killigrew.) 'Feb. 12, 1666. John Hill that played on the cornet in the Quire was buried.'

Although the Great Fire of 1666 was down the river from the Abbey, the Dean at the time was John Dolben who had distinguished himself at the Battle of Marston Moor. On September 2nd (according to Taswell, a contemporary Westminster boy)

126

On Sunday between one and eleven forenoon, as I was standing upon the steps that lead up to the pulpit in Westminster Abbey, I perceived some people below me running to and fro in a seeming disquietude and consternation. . . . Without any ceremony I took leave of the preacher, and ascended Parliament Steps near the Thames. The wind blowing strongly eastwards, the flakes at last reached Westminster.

On the following day,

the Dean, who in the Civil Wars had frequently stood sentinel, collected his scholars together, marching with them on foot to put a stop, if possible, to the conflagration. I was a kind of page to him, not being of the number of the King's Scholars. We were employed many hours fetching water from the backside of St Dunstan's in the East. The next day, just after sunset at night, I went to the King's Bridge. As I stood with many others, I watched the gradual approaches of the fire towards St Paul's. About eight o'clock the fire broke out in the top of the church . . . and before nine blazed so conspicuous as to enable me to read very clearly a 16mo edition of Terence which I carried in my pocket.

The Precentor's Book includes an example of the generosity of Richard Busby, Headmaster of Westminster.

Memorandum that Dr Busby delivered to the Chaunter for a dinner to be made for the petticanons, Singingmen and choristers the last Christmas the sums first of four pounds, which dinner was held at the Chaunter's house Jan. 5 . . . but the expense exceeding the sums received by—1s. 7d. the Dr gave orders that nothing requisite or convenient be wanting he payd also to the Chaunter freely and willingly the sayd sum of 1s. 7d. and ten shillings more for Mr Hazard who at that time lay sick and could not be at the feast.

Busby reigned so long and so completely at Westminster

that the story of Charles II's visit to the school is particularly fitting. He alone wore his hat in the King's presence explaining to Charles that he had kept it on, not out of disloyalty, but because it would not have done for the boys to think there existed a greater man than himself.

For each organist, Master of the Choristers and singing-man the Precentor's Book contains the customary oath of allegiance. On December 3, 1668, John Blow's name appears when he takes the customary oath on being admitted in the place of Mr Albertus Bryne (or Bryan or Brian—the name is spelt many ways), Organist of the Collegiate Church of Westminster. Albertus Bryne last appears in October 1668 under payments for the monuments. Blow was son-in-law to Edward Braddock who was Master of the Choristers 1670-1704.

There is one entry which provokes a smile, 'May 1670. Mensis mensium or the month of months, none like it before and none likely to be like it hereafter. Deo gratias agite. Collected for the sight of the monuments the sum of £138. 6s. 3d.'

The reason for this phenomenal sum was the funeral effigy of George Monck, Duke of Albemarle which lay in state in full magnificent armour. Each of them, chanter, organist, etc., received £6. 10s. 6d.

Information concerning the showing of the Monuments and the varying distribution of the emoluments therefrom could fill a book by itself. A contemporary broadsheet *The Tombs in Westminster Abbey . . . as chanted by Brother Popplewell* is now in the British Museum. There is possibly more than meets the eye in its title as it was printed for Obadiah Blagrave and a Thomas Blagrave had been Master of the Abbey Choristers from 1665-8 and a Gentleman of the Chapel Royal, and a William Blagrave was at Westminster School under Busby, went up to Peterhouse and received his M.A. in 1659 but was ejected from his living for Nonconformity.

It was included in

Wit and Drollery. Jovial Poems.

Printed for Obadiah Blagrave, at the Bear in St Paul's Church-Yard, 1682.

You must suppose it to be Easter Holy-Days: At what time Sisly and Dol, Kate and Peggy, Moll and Nan, are marching to Westminster, with a Leash of Prentices before 'em who going rowing themselves along with their right Arms to make more hast, and now an then with a greasie Muckender wipe away the dripping that bastes their Foreheads. At the Door they meet a crow'd of Wapping Seamen, Southwark Broom-men, the Inhabitants of the Bank-side, with a Bucher or two prick't in among them. There awhile they stand gaping for the Master of the Show, staring upon the Suburbs of their dearest delight, just as they stand gaping upon the painted Cloath before they go into the Poppet Play. By and by they hear the Bunch of Keys which rejoyces their Hearts like the sound of the Pancake-Bell. For now the Man of Comfort peeps over the Spikes and beholding such a learned Auditory, opens the Gate of Paradise, and by that time they are half got into the first Chapel, for time is very pretious, he lifts up his Voice among the Toombs, and begins his Lurrey in manner and form following.

Here lies William de Valence
  A right good Earl of Pembroke
And this is his Monument that you see,
  I'll swear upon a Book.

He was High Marshal of England,
  When Henry the 3d did Raign,
But this you may take upon my Word
  That he'll nere be so again.

This once was John of Edelston,
  He was no Costermonger,
But Cornwal's Earl; And here's one Dy'd
  Cause he could live no longer.

            .   .   .

Now think your Penny well spent good Folks;
  And that you are not beguil'd,
Within this Cup doth lie the Heart
  Of a French Embassadors Child.

But how the Devil it came to pass,
  On purpose, or by chance,
The Bowels they lie underneath,
  The Body is in France.

            .   .   .

This was Queen Mary, Queen of Scots,
  Whom Buchanan doth bespatter,
She lost her head at Totingham,
  What ever was the matter.

            .   . .   .

Now down the Stairs come we again,
  The Man goes first with a Staff,
Some two or three tumble down the Stairs,
  And then the Peeple laugh.

(Dol: How came she here then? Will: Why ye silly Oose could not she be brought here after she was dead?)

For now the Show is at an end,
  All things are done and said,
The Citizen pays for his Wife,
  The Prentice for the Maid.

            .   .   .

Curiously, shortly before the totally unexpected death of the King, which was to bring so much change, the Chapter Acts of 12 January 1685 issued a command for greater reverence in the Abbey:

Ordered that when any of ye Prebendaries shall come into the Quire the Schollers & the Singing boyes there shall stand upp to shew their Respect to them according to ye Old Custome & practice

And also That they doe pay all due respect to them in all other places

And that all Orders relating to the Schollers shalbe written in a table and hung upp in the Schollers Chamber

Ordered That the Quiremen as they passe in the Quire to doe their offices shall according to the Old Custome come into the Middle of the Quire and there mak due Reverence towards the Deanes and Prebendaries Stalls after they have first done it towards the Alter.

By a Chapter Act of 29 March 1686:

It is Ordered that the Quiremen and all the Officers and servants of this Church & Colledge doe receive the Holy Comunion in this Church 3 times in ye yeare att least (according to the Rubrick) (viz) att Easter Whitsontide and Christmas and particularly this next Easter day after the date of this Order And that a Copy of this Order be delivered to the Chanter who is to give notice thereof

Evelyn's note of February 14th reads:

The King was this night very obscurely buried in a vault under Henry the Seventh's Chapel at Westminster, without any manner of pomp, and soon forgotten after all this vanity, and the face of the Court was exceedingly changed into a more solemn and moral behaviour. the new King affecting neither profaneness nor buffoonery. All the great officers broke their staves over the grave according to form.

Clarke in his *Life of King James the Second*, published 1816, fills this out and may well close the references to funeral obsequies with which our documents during the reign have been so concerned.

One of the first things that required his Majesty's attention was the funeral obsequies of the late King, which could not be perform'd with so great sollemnity as some persons expected, because his late Majesty dying in, and his present Majesty professing a different religion from that of his people, it had been a difficult matter to reconcile the great ceremonys, which must have been performed according to the rites of the Church of England, with the obligation of not communicateing with it in spiritual things; to avoid therefore either disputes on the one hand or scandal on the other, it was thought more prudent to doe it in a more private manner, tho at the Same time there was no circumstance of State or pomp omitted, which possebly could be allow'd of: for (besides, that while the body lay in state the illuminations and mourning was very solemn) all the privy Council, all the household, and all the Lords about Town attended the funeral.

Chapter Eleven

THE LATER STUARTS

T HANKS TO SANDFORD'S account of the coronation of
James II, we know the names of the Abbey boys who
sang on that occasion and although little is known of them,
they are worth naming as they were under the great Henry
Purcell. Eight were chosen to sing, though there were ten
choristers by statute. Sandford, with the illustration which
shows four of them, describes them as follows:

Children of the Choir of Westminster in Surplices,
   Four a-Breast, the youngest first, viz
1. William Christian. 2. Thomas Price. 3. George Rogers.
4. William Morley. 5. John Bates. 6. John Walker. 7. John
Howell. 8. William Williams.

The Funeral Book says: Buried February 14, 1699 William
Christian one of the Choir, in the North Cloister.

Colonel Chester in his *Westminster Abbey Registers* said
that he considered Alice Christian who, an infant, was buried
in the South Cloister on August 6, 1697 was the daughter
of William Christian. There was also a Thomas Christian,
also called Christmas, a Child of the Chapel Royal, whose
voice broke in 1692.

A John Howell was admitted to the Chapel Royal, March
23, 1696-7, one of the private musick for the voice, in the
place of Mr Alphonso Marsh deceased. There is a slight
puzzle here as there is in another volume of the Lord
Chamberlain's Accounts a Warrant for £120, being arrears

133

due to each of several musicians of whom John Howell is one.

A Mr William Williams on November 6, 1697 was appointed musician in ordinary to His Majesty in the place of Mr Morgan deceased. In the following year he is mentioned third in the list of payments for liveries and he was still there amongst twenty-four instrumentalists in 1699, each receiving £40. The name of course was a common one, but he may be—for his age—either the son of Henry by Mary baptized St Margaret's, Westminster, August 1, 1675, or the son of Rowland by Mary baptized August 27, 1671, both children being called William Williams.

Henry Purcell was responsible for the setting up of an additional organ for the coronation in the Abbey in April. It appears from Sandford's celebrated reproduction (see page 64) that this stood on the south of the altar and the singers were accommodated in the gallery beside it. The instrumentalists were in a gallery on the opposite side of the chancel; and, because of the vast gulf between the performers, Purcell's job of making them harmonious must have been difficult indeed. The singers of Westminster went with the clergy to make obeisance to the King in Westminster Hall. When they had taken their place the procession to the Abbey began. Henry Purcell walked amongst the basses as he was a lay clerk; but he also played the organ, and his own anthem, *My Heart is inditing of a good matter*, was amongst the nine performed. It was noticed that the King showed little or no devotion and did not move his lips at the responses.

The choristers were also present on the sensational occasion when the Declaration of Indulgence was read. The Abbey was, according to Evelyn, almost the only church in London where it was read. Burnet writes

As soon as Bishop Sprat (who was Dean) gave orders for reading it, there was so great a murmur and noise in the

Church, that nobody could hear him; but before he had finished, there was none left but a few prebends in their stalls, the choristers, and the Westminster scholars. (Patrice states that Sprat sent it 'to one of the Petty Canons to read'.) The Bishop could hardly hold the proclamation in his hands for trembling, and everybody looked under a strange consternation.

When the Seven Bishops were acquitted the Abbey bells were rung in concert with the peals of many London churches. Sprat immediately ordered them to be stopped, which was done under protest.

Another story of Sprat's time at the Abbey concerns the organ loft. He had invited the great Barrow to preach. Barrow was a lengthy preacher and his second sermon was given on a holiday. Bradley quotes from Dr Pope's *Life of Seth Ward* to describe what happened.

It was a custom for the servants of the church on all Holidays, Sundays excepted, betwixt the sermon and evening prayers, to show the tombs and effigies of the Kings and Queens in wax, to the meaner sort of people who then flock thither from all the corners of the town, and pay their twopence to see The Play of the Dead Volks, as, I have heard, a Devonshire Clown most improperly called it. These perceiving Dr Barrow in the pulpit after the hour was past, and fearing to lose that time in hearing which they thought they could more profitably employ in viewing, these, I say, became impatient, and caused the organ to be struck up against him, and would not give over playing till they had blowed him down.

There is only one direct reference to the boys during Purcell's years. On the 23rd of January 1690 it was 'Ordered that the Choristers doe weare to Church their Gownes & Surplices'.

Thomas Brown in his *Works* deals with the men, though one hopes the satirist may have overdrawn a little.

135

I have no novelties to entertain you with relating to either the Abbey or St Paul's, for both the choirs continue just as wicked as they were when you left them; some of them daily come reeking hot out of the bawdy-house into the church, and others stagger out of a tavern to afternoon prayers, and hick-up over a little of the L i t a n y, and so back again. Old C l a r e t - f a c e beats time still upon his cushion stoutly, and sits growling under his purple canopy, a hearty old-fashion'd bass, that deafens all about him. Beau B u s h y - w i g preserves his voice to a miracle, charms all the ladies over against him with his handsome face, and all over head with his singing. Parson P u n c h makes a very good shift still, and lyrics over his part in an anthem very handsomely.

Reprehensible behaviour did not belong only to the singers if one may judge from the treatment meted out to Purcell himself. It is the only reference to him in the Chapter Acts, and concerns the famous quarrel from which the Chapter can scarcely escape criticism.

Chapter Acts: 25 Martii 1689

It is order'd that All such Money as shall be raised for Seates at the Coronaton within the Church Organ Loft or Churchyarde shall be paid into the hands of the Treasurer to be distributed as the Dean & Chapter shall think fitt; and that all vacant Places both in the Church and Churchyard wch are not taken up and imployed for the Kinges use be disposed of by the Dean & Chapter of Westm as they shall think fitt.

Act' in Capit' die Jovis 18 die Aprilis 1689
present'   Domino Decano
                        Subdecano

Dr Busby	Dr de l'Angle
Dr South	Mr Berkley
Dr Brevall	Mr Sartre

It was order'd that Mr Purcell the Organist to ye Deane &

Chapter of Westm doe pay to the hands of Mr John Needham Receiver of the Colledge All such Money as was received by him for places in the Organ Loft at the Coronacion of Kinge William & Queene Mary by or before Satturday next being the 20th day of this instant Aprill. And in default thereof his place is declared to be Null and void. And it is further Ordered that his stipend or sallary due at our Lady Day last past be deteyned in the hands of the Treasurer untill further order.

These are the only entries under these dates; and it would appear that the meeting of the 18th was for the sole purpose of bringing Henry Purcell to book.

An impression of the atmosphere in the Abbey very different from Thomas Brown's is given in Ned Ward's *The London Spy* (1698-1703).

By this time the bells began to chime for afternoon prayers and the choir was opened, into which we went, amongst many others, to pay with reverence that duty which becomes a Christian. There our souls were elevated by the divine harmony of the music, far above the common pitch of our devotions, whose heavenly accents have such an influence upon a contrite heart that it strengthens our zeal, fortifies the loose imagination against wandering thoughts and gives a man a taste of immortal blessings upon earth, before he is thoroughly prepared for the true relish of celestial comforts.

Chapter Twelve

PUDDING DAYS

THE EIGHTEENTH CENTURY in many ways is a detest-able century. In spite of Johnson and Horace Walpole—and anyone can name a pair of redeeming individuals to his own fancy to save Sodom—the veneer is thin. The wigs and the clothes are elegant, the punctilio engaging, but under-neath are Prinny and Chesterfield, Hervey and Louis Quinze.

In Ecclesiastical History the century does not bear think-ing about. It was an age of mildew, of getting a maximum of money for a moment of time, and this at the Abbey was interrupted by outbursts of ostentatious praise.

Those times however have gone from the Abbey when thirteenth century Gothic choir stalls were destroyed for 'improvements', and it is irrelevant to labour the point. As regards the singers it was not until Samuel Horsley's time (1793-1802) that anything serious was done for them and this was so much appreciated that although Horsley was translated to St Asaph and died four years later the choir, demonstrating an unanimity in this respect that had not been shown since the death of Purcell, went en bloc to his funeral at St Mary's, Newington, to testify their gratitude.

It seems that, although the choristers were by statute members of Westminster School, the attendance of some of them was a polite fiction, and they were little regarded.

As there are no names in the Treasurer's Accounts, as the

Precentor's Books, which might have given their names, have gone, and as the indefatigable compilers of *The Record of Old Westminsters* state that the choristers are little more than surnames, it is lucky that their records show the details of a few because from them it is possible to draw several conclusions.

There are twenty-three boys of whom nothing further is known beyond the date of their entry into the school, their age and, sometimes, that they were still in the school two years later. This does show however that they generally entered the school (and the choir) in their eighth year. The names of some twenty-four others prove that they were not ineligible for being, nor incapable of becoming, King's Scholars. One of the things which militated against the choirboys was the singingman. As a rule he was a pluralist hack scratching for a living, and the Westminster opinion of him is quite clear.

The present writer believes that the late J. S. Bumpus had access to information which is not now apparent. Bumpus stated that certain boys were in the Abbey Choir and he has proved to be right. He has here been taken as the authority for stating that Joseph Drury, later Headmaster of Harrow School, entered Westminster School as a chorister.

William Croft, who was organist at the Abbey from 1708 until his death in 1727, was thirty-one years of age at his appointment. He was at the same time composer at the Chapel Royal and is best remembered for his collection of words and anthems. He had been a chorister at the Chapel Royal under Blow whom he succeeded at the Abbey.

He cannot have had a very easy time with the Abbey boys to judge from a Chapter Act of 6th May 1710.

Whereas Several Butchers & other Persons have of late especially on Market days carried Meat & other Burdens thro' ye Church, & that in time of divine Service to ye great Scandall & Offence of all Sober Persons And whereas divers disorderly Beggars are dayly walking about & begging in ye Abbey & Cloysters & do fill ye same wth Nastiness whereof great Offence is given to all People going thro' ye Church and Cloisters & whereas many Idle Boys come into ye Cloisters dayly & there play at Cards & other plays for Money & are often heard to curse and Swear: For Remedy whereof It is this day order'd by the Dean and Chapter that Charles Caldwell ye College Beadle do dayly attend in ye Church and Cloisters and do hinder all persons whatsoever from carrying meat or other Burdens thro' ye Church And that if any Person or Persons shall be refractory & force their way thro' ye said Church wth any Burden, that ye said Beadle shall forthwth make a complaint of such Person or Persons to ye Deputy Steward of ye City & Libty of Westm or to some other of her Majties Justices of ye Peace for ye City & Libty to ye Intent that such Person or Persons may be dealt with according to Law. And it is further Order'd that ye sd Beadle shall keep out all Beggars Men and Women from ye said Church & Cloisters & doors thereto belonging & not suffer them to loiter there And that he do likewise keep out of ye sd Church and cloisters all Idle Boys & not suffer them to play there And it is further Order'd that if any Boys yt go to ye Gramar School or are Choristers of this Church do play there yt he do forthwith give in ye Names of such Boys to one of the Masters that they may be punished according to their fault. And it is likewise Ordered that the Bellringers Porters & other Inferior Officers shall be assisting to ye sd Beadle in remedying ye disorders abovementon'd

Order'd further that the sd Beadle have Ten pounds And Allowed for ye same from Lady day last.

In 1725 the Order of the Bath was inaugurated and there was the usual raising of scaffolding for the accommodation of spectators. The distribution of the money which resulted from such occasions occupied much of the time of the Chapter Meetings and considerable space in their books. The choir and those concerned in the Tombs Money had leave to build stands in one part for their joint advantage. The Chapel of King Henry VII was appointed for the Order and the banners of the Knights still make a brave show. The last time the late King George VI came to the Abbey was for an installation when, after meticulous preparation the evening before, he carried out his all-important part to perfection.

The choristers received the right to exact a fine from anyone who wore spurs in the Chapel. It is not known how the custom began but John Timbs in his *Curiosities of London* records:

The choristers had a right to levy a fine on any person who entered this Chapel with spurs. Bishop Finch had to pay eighteen pence for offending; and even the Royal Duke of Cumberland, excusing himself with this reply, 'It is only fair I should wear my spurs where they were first buckled on,' complied with the custom. It was made the Chapel of the Knights of the Bath, May 18, 1725, and the last installation until modern times occurred in 1811. On May 9, 1803, according to old custom, the King's cook met the knights at Poets' Corner with a chopping knife, and addressed them with these words, 'If you break your oath, by virtue of my office I will hack your spurs from off your heels.'

A clue to the diet of the boys at the school is to be found for an allowance to be made for those who did not go home (although in fact no one failed to go).

14 Dec. 1736

Ordered That so long as that Custome shall continue there be allowed Twenty pounds per annum for Roots Greens and other Kitchen herbs with their boiled meat five days in the week butter, and vinegar and pepper included.

Ordered That a Crown a Quarter be allowed the Bed-maker

141

of the Dormitory for Fire to air the Room and warm the Boys Beds at the end of each Breaking up.

In order to lessen the temptation of racing and its attendant betting, horseraces were to be allowed on Tothill Fields 'only on the three days at Bartholomewtide when the school is broken up'. That was in July 1737, a few months before the funeral of Queen Caroline, a manuscript account of which with underlinings has survived amongst the Muniments.

The Ceremonial at Her Majesty Queen Carolines Funeral Dec. 17th 1737.

The Choir met in the Organ-Room before 4 o'clock, and for their Admittance at the Cloyster-Gate had Each of them Tickets from the Earl Marshall.—From thence they proceded between 5 and 6 o'Clock to the North-Gate of the Abbey they King's Scholars walked first then the Children of the Choirs. Then the Gentlemen, then the Master and Undermaster of Westm School and then the Sub-Dean of the Chapels Royal (who was also Chanter of Westm): the Prebendaries in their Copes: and the Ld Bp of Rochester Dean of Westm immediately before the Royal Corps. They staid near the North-Door of the Abbey and fell in after the Abp of Canterbury before Norroy King of Arms. They Procession was made up the North-Isle as far as Sr Godphrey Kneller's Monument, and then crossed over to the South Isle from whence they proceded to H. the 7th Chapel.— Being come there it was ordered that Both the psalms in the Burial Service should be sung to the Organ: *which* (*by some accident*) *was omitted*. The Hymns in the Burial-Office was sung in the Organ Loft. The Organist of Westm performed in the Church of Westm and the Organist of the King's Chapel in H. the 7th Chapel. *The Lesson was omitted*. After the Anthem (compos'd for voices and Instruments) was performed. The Stiles being pronounced by the King of Arms the whole Ceremony ended.

Leave was given by the Rt Rev'd the Dean to the Chanter to place his friends in his Vestry in the North-Isle.

The organist on that occasion was John Robinson. On Croft's death at the age of 50, he had become organist on September 20, 1727 and had been his assistant for several years, having been like Croft a Chapel Royal boy under Blow. He remained at the Abbey until his death in 1762 at the age of 80. His assistant from 1746 onwards was Benjamin Cooke who succeeded him in 1762. His first wife was the celebrated singer Mrs Turner Robinson who was popular in Handel's oratorios.

Chapter Thirteen

EIGHTEENTH CENTURY WORTHIES

I

SEVERAL OF THE choristers prospered, became King's Scholars or singers or went into the Church. A few deserve more extended notice.

Caesar Danby Piguenit, probably the son of John Piguenit of Brentford, Middlesex, entered the choir in 1748 and became a bookseller, first of Berkeley Square, and afterwards of Aldgate. He was also an author and collaborated with Samuel Arnold in an Entertainment called *Don Quixote*, which was sung at Marybone Gardens in 1774 and at the Theatre Royal in Covent Garden in 1776.

In 1792 he printed a two volume edition of *The Arabian Nights Entertainment Freely Transcribed from the original Translation*. His Advertisement gives us several clues to himself:

These celebrated tales are too generally known and admired to receive new fame from the present editor's pen. It may perhaps, be thought necessary for him to account for the very unusual liberty he has taken with them.

Having devoted his attention, as a bookseller, for the greater part of the past twenty years to the service of schools, his first idea was to select a portion of these tales, as a miscellany which would not perhaps be unacceptable to those who superintend the education of youth. Mr Knox, speaking of *The Arabian Nights Entertainment* says 'They

The North Prospect of Westminster Abbey

From a print *circa* 1700

are well calculated to kindle a flame (of genius) in the bosoms of boys.'

But on looking over them for that purpose, the stile appeared to the editor to be dry, encumbered and tautological. He was tempted, therefore, to present them as tales twice told, and he hopes he shall not, by doing so, have vexed the patience of the reader.

The circumstances of the stories have generally been retained, perhaps a little too scrupulously. Wherever the editor hath ventured to deviate, he trusts it will be found to have been in favour of probability or of good morals. Aldgate April 10, 1792.

Samuel Arnold, of whom there will be reason to speak later, was organist at the Abbey from 1793-1802, but even before 1763, when only 23 years of age, he was engaged by Beard to refurbish other composers' works for him at Covent Garden. In 1769 he took the rent of Marylebone Gardens for burlettas and operas, but owing to the dishonesty of one of his underlings lost ten thousand pounds by speculation. In the seventies he produced religious spectacles during Lent at Covent Garden and the Haymarket.

Four choristers of this period deserve mention—Parsons, Crosdill, Drury and Knyvett. Sir William Parsons born 1746 (?) was a chorister under Robinson and Cooke. There is no record of his having been at Westminster School. Before the year 1768 he tried to join unsuccessfully the company at Covent Garden; and so went to Italy to improve his technique. Like so many, on his return he was successful as a teacher of singing. In 1786 he became Master of His Majesty's Band, and was composer and conductor of the Odes and Minuets which were performed at Court on the King's birthday; his salary was £300. In 1790 he became Bachelor and Doctor of Music of Oxford University. In 1795 he visited Ireland and attended the Lord Lieutenant, Lord

Camden, who knighted him for his services, and in the following year he was made instructor to the Royal princesses. It was the Princess Amelia and her sister Sophia who encouraged Samuel Arnold. Amongst his many interests Parsons had a predilection for the law, and attended Bow Street Police Court as a subsidiary magistrate, later becoming a stipendiary magistrate at Worship Street (perhaps at Marlborough Street). Apart from his professional membership of the Catch Club, he was a Fellow of the Society of Antiquaries, and an early patron of Michael Kelly. A portrait of him appeared in the *European Magazine* of August 1808 and he died in 1817.

John Crosdill, born probably in 1751, was educated musically under Robinson and Cooke in the Abbey Choir, (Robinson being organist and Cooke Master of the Choristers from 1757) and was admitted to Westminster School where he became friendly with Lord Fitzwilliam and remained so for life. In 1768 he was made a member of the Royal Society of Musicians. He studied the cello under John Pierre Dupont. In 1769 he played at the Gloucester Festival, and was principal cellist at the Concerts of Antient Music in 1776. On March 10, 1778 he was appointed violist at the Chapel Royal on the death of Nares and held the post until his own death, at the same time being a member of the King's private band. In 1782 he was appointed Chamber Musician to Queen Charlotte, and taught the cello to the Prince of Wales. In 1784 he was the principal cellist at the Handel Festival in the Abbey. He married a lady of fortune Elizabeth Colebrook, widow, on May 31, 1785, and retired from his profession, although he came out of his seclusion to play at the coronation of George IV in 1821, and lived happily in Titchfield where his old friend Fitzwilliam often stayed with him. Dance painted his portrait which, in profile, was engraved by Daniell. Crosdill died in 1825.

Joseph Drury, born 11 February, 1750, son of Thomas Drury, of London, a member of an old Norfolk family, by Elizabeth daughter of John Hilton, of the City of London, was admitted to Westminster School at a date unknown, became a King's Scholar in 1765, was elected to Trinity College, Cambridge in 1768, admitted pensioner June 1, 1768, and re-admitted as a ten-year man June 2, 1774. By the customary stages he became a Doctor of Divinity in 1789. As he was unable to continue at the University because of the lack of funds, he became an Assistant Master at Harrow School under Doctor Sumner in 1769. Six years later there was a serious split at the School on the appointment of Dr Heath, and Drury was almost persuaded to follow the celebrated Samuel Parr who left with a number of boys and founded a rival school at Stanmore. Instead he remained, and four years later married the Headmaster's youngest sister, Louisa. A very efficient teacher, when his brother-in-law resigned in 1785, Drury, who was then in his thirty-sixth year, was elected to succeed him. He was Head Master for twenty years and throughout that time exerted a fine influence over the boys who, after a preliminary drop in number after the secession of Parr, increased during his mastership from two hundred to three hundred and fifty. These boys included many subsequent celebrities and, considering the numbers, a very large proportion of the nobility. He seems to have been the first Head to exempt the Sixth Form from flogging, and encouraged as almost unheard-of co-operation between Headmaster and Prefects. The system of delegated caning by monitors grew up in his time. In 1805 he retired for two reasons—the indisposition of his wife and his wish for a country life. Paradoxically, it may seem, he had a love for the theatre which led to his acquaintance with Edmund Kean whom he helped to establish at Drury Lane. In his retirement he went to Lockwood, near Dawlish, Devon. For some time he was Vicar of Aldwinkle in Northamptonshire but did not live there. He was a Prebendary of Wells from April 1, 1812. He had three sons, all in Holy Orders, one at Eton, another at Harrow, and the third a Rector in Shropshire. He also had a daughter, and the family of the second and third generation were closely connected with Harrow School.

His name however will be perpetuated by one of his famous pupils, Lord Byron, who wrote of him in the note to Canto X, 75 of *Childe Harold*:

I was not a slow, though an idle boy; and I believe no one could, or can be, more attached to Harrow than I have always been, and with reason:— a part of the time passed there was the happiest of my life; and my preceptor, the Rev. Dr Joseph Drury was the best and worthiest friend I ever possessed, whose warnings I have remembered but too well, though too late, when I have erred,—and whose counsels I have but followed when I have done wisely or well. If ever this imperfect record of my feelings towards him should reach his eyes, let it remind him of one who never thinks of him but with gratitude and veneration,—of one who would more gladly boast of having been his pupil, if by more closely following his injunctions he could reflect any honour upon his instructor.

Presumably all these three sang at the coronation of George III though Parsons may have been too old. The fourth of this distinguished quartette did not enter until afterwards, though he took part in many later occasions.

Charles Knyvett, only son of Charles Knyvett of Westminster, born February 11, 1751-2, was admitted to Westminster School, 1762 and was still there in 1764. He became a Member of the Society of Musicians in January, 1778, and was one of the principal alto singers at the Handel Festival of 1784. He was a Gentleman of the Chapel Royal from

1786 until 1808. In 1789 he directed a series of oratorios at Covent Garden. Two years later, in 1791, he established the Vocal Concerts at Willis's Rooms, with former colleagues and contemporaries at the Abbey. On July 25, 1796 he was appointed Organist to the Chapel Royal. For many years he was Secretary to the Noblemen's and Gentlemen's Catch Club, and was considered 'one of the best singers of glees' and 'perhaps the best catch singer in England', according to Parke's *Musical Memoirs*. On June 16, 1772, he married Rose, daughter of William Alleway of Sonning, Berks, and died on January 19, 1822.

II

Benjamin Cooke, born in 1734 and Master of the Choristers since 1757, succeeded Robinson as organist in 1762 and ever since then the two offices have been held by the same person, except for a while at the beginning of the nineteenth century. His father had kept a music shop in Covent Garden and the boy was placed under the celebrated Dr Pepusch whom he succeeded at the age of eighteen as conductor of the concerts at the Academy of Antient Music. So brilliant was he that when only twelve years of age he deputized for Robinson. He was an enthusiastic member of the Catch Club and of the Madrigal Society. Cambridge made him a Doctor of Music in 1775, and Oxford followed suit in 1782. For the Installation of the Duke of York as a Knight of the Bath in Henry VII's Chapel in 1772 he wrote an anthem. In 1782 he became organist of St Martin-in-the-Fields and two years later was an Assistant Director of the Handel Festival. He and Samuel Arnold (his successor at the Abbey in 1793) were at loggerheads in the Society of Antient Music and he refused to meet Arnold in 1789. He suffered from gout and spent his summers at various Spas, dying shortly after a return to his house in Dorset Court, Westminster.

It would seem that whatever his personal responsibility, there were, as in 1603, many disorders amongst the choristers.

The toughness of school life at this period needs as little repetition as the Ecclesiastical decay, but Westminster after two hundred years of greatness was passing through a bad period and little control was exercised over the boys. Bullying, flogging, sadism and fights on a Corinthian scale were the order of the day. Boys scratched names all over the tombs, slept in the coronation chair and carved their names on it.

One of the favourite delights was 'Water'—sailing, rowing, swimming in the Thames. So reckless were they that an astonishing number were drowned, and, as was to be expected, these included some choristers, the earliest of whom was William Marshall, who was buried in the Dark Cloister on July 19, 1765. According to the Funeral Book he died 16th July, aged 8 years. 'He was a Practiceing Boy in the Choir, and had the misfortune to be drowned'. In *The Record of Old Westminsters* he appears as Marshall ——; b.——; in school lists 1765.

Three years after Marshall, another chorister, John Taylor, was drowned, in 1768. He is presumably the Taylor who appears as in school lists 1764, and left 1767. He was in the Under Third in October, a little low in the School for a boy of 14. The Abbey Registers give a different ending: 'Mr John Taylor buried August 12, in the Dark Cloister.' The Funeral Books says that he died on 10th August aged 14 years 9 months and adds 'was one of the choristers and had the misfortune to be drowned'. It was left to *The London Chronicle* of August 11th to fill out the picture with its own odd punctuation: 'Last night, as Master Taylor, one of the Singing Boys belonging to the Choir at Westminster, was washing, off the wooden bridge at Westminster, in the Thames, he was drowned.'

Another short-lived chorister was George Newton who was admitted to Westminster School on February 26, 1770. The Abbey Registers contain the entry 'Master George Newton, aged 12 years, in the Cloister leading to the School'. The Funeral Book says 'he was one of the choristers' and that he died on the 1st of May, 1772.

More fortunate was John Hindle, son of Bartholomew Hindle of Westminster, born 1761, who entered Westminster School on February 26, 1770; and left at Whitsuntide, 1774. In 1785 he became a Lay Vicar of the Abbey, and sang there until his early death in 1796, when only thirty-five. At the age of thirty he matriculated on November 16, 1791 at Magdalen College, Oxford, and took the degree of Bachelor of Music. He was a celebrated countertenor and sang before members of the Royal Family at the Worcester Musical Festival of 1788, and often at the London Vocal Concerts in 1791-2, singing with another Abbey chorister, Charles Knyvett. He was the composer of many glees and songs, of which the most well known and popular was *Queen of the Silver Bow*.

Five new boys joined the choir on June 12, 1770.

Robert Crucifix was the first. His family were Huguenots. Robert Crucifix the grandfather was a watchmaker, of St Margaret's Parish, was born about 1690 and had two sons Robert and John. The latter in 1792 was a reduced Ensign in the 108th Foot.

The second, Robert Greville, son of Caleb Greville, the parish clerk of St James's, Westminster, left December, 1773; matriculated, Christ Church, Oxford, July 13, 1779, aged 19; became a B.A. 1783, and eleven years later a B.C.L. from Pembroke College, Oxford. Amongst other compositions, he wrote the hymn, *See the bright morning star*.

Another boy, Albany Charles Wallis, seemed destined by

fate for a distinguished career. The only son of Albany Wallis of Norfolk Street, Strand, an eminent solicitor, by Elizabeth Vaughan, he too was drowned in the Thames, on March 29, 1776, aged 13. The Burial Registers of the Abbey state: 'Master Albany-Charles Wallis, a Westminster scholar, in his 14th year; in the East Cloister.' The boy's mother had already been buried in the Temple Churchyard, 3rd March, 1773. At the death of his son the father was inconsolable, became bitter, and seems never to have recovered (although he lived to the age of 86) and was buried in the same East Cloister on September 10, 1800.

The boy had previously been painted by Sir Joshua Reynolds, and the picture was sold in 1916, on June 7th at Christie's and was bought for 500 guineas for Messrs. Knoedler's, who have given permission for its reproduction here. The portrait almost immediately went to America where it is in a private collection.

The painting measures $29\frac{1}{2}$ inches by $24\frac{1}{2}$, and shows him 'in mauve slashed dress with vandyck collar and cuffs, in a landscape, sketching'. (See page 160.)

The boy's father, also painted by Reynolds, was a close friend of David Garrick, the actor, who composed the inscription to the boy. As apparently this was done and the memorial erected as a surprise and without the father's knowledge, there is a discrepancy in date according to Chester, as The Funeral Book, presumably quoting the coffin lid, says 'in his 14th year', whereas Garrick's inscription gives the boy's age as 13. The discrepancy is more simply attributable to the common practice of referring to someone aged 13 as being in his fourteenth year.

Garrick's epitaph translated runs:

Below has been buried amid the genuine tears of his fellow pupils Albany Charles Wallis—the only hope of his most loving father—who alas! too much taken by the forbidden delights of the River Thames was torn away by its untamed force and perished on the 29th of March 1776 aged 13. Stop O youth; consider the end of this boy.

When Garrick died, Albany Wallis, the boy's father, erected at his own expense the memorial to the great actor which stands in the Abbey today, while the tablet to the boy is equally clear in the cloisters. In the 1928 edition of *The Record of Old Westminsters*, the late Russell Barker did not state his authority for saying Wallis was a chorister.

The fifth of the boys to enter the choir on June 12, 1770 was John Wheler, the son of John Wheler of Evesham in Worcestershire. He did well at the school and in 1772 at the age of 13 became a King's Scholar, was elected to Christ Church, Oxford in 1776 and matriculated on June 25, but a service career appealed to him and he became a 2nd Lieutenant in the Royal Marines on December 17, 1777, and a 1st Lieutenant on August 18, 1779; he married and was placed on half pay on September 1, 1783.

Comic relief is never far from the Abbey and *The Public Advertiser* of Wednesday, December 18, 1776, provides it:

The crowd of people was so great in Westminster Abbey, to see the funeral of her Grace the late Duchess of Northumberland, that the Lord Bishop of Rochester and the gentlemen and boys of the choir could not perform the service. Although the corpse entered the Abbey a little before eleven o'clock, it was not interred till between one and two o'clock. The old Gothic screen or fence belonging to St Edmund's Chapel, supposed to have been built between four and five hundred years, by the number of people climbing upon it, fell down. The Lord Bishop of Rochester, narrowly escaped being dangerously hurt; one man had his leg broke, as had a woman her arm, and three other persons were carried out of the Cathedral very much bruised, to be taken care of by their friends, and considerable damage was done to the monuments.

Five years later the funeral of another of the Percies, Lady Charlotte, was the last non-Royal occasion performed by torchlight.

James Bartleman, born September 19, 1769 presumably had left. He was a chorister at the Abbey but does not appear to have been at the school. He was a distinguished singer even as a boy, and Sir John Hawkins took a great interest in him, so that he is mentioned in the *Anecdotes* of Hawkins' daughter. His first appearance as a bass was in 1788 at the Concerts of Antient Music, which had more than a sprinkling of ex-Abbey choristers, and there he continued to appear until ill-health compelled him to retire. Contemporary critics speak of his voice as being more agreeable than a bass, and it is possible that he would now be called a baritone. He had an unusual compass from E below the bass stave to G above it. Both Crotch and Callcott, whose artist brother was in the Abbey choir, wrote songs specially for him. He was also a beautiful copyist of music and an example of his work is a set of madrigals by Marenzio, now in the British Museum. He died unmarried at the Middlesex Hospital in Berners Street, on April 15, 1821, aged 53, and was buried from his house at 45 Berners Street. He was interred in the west cloister of the Abbey on April 21, his memorial setting out his virtues.

There were threats from many nuisances, and one in particular reminds us how close the Abbey and College were to rusticity:

14 Jan. 1745-6. Whereas great application has been of late made for putting up Monuments in our Church, which is almost full of them; and our Fabrick (now the Aid of Parliament is at an end) will stand in more need than ever of Monument money to be laid out on our Repairs: and whereas our Church Yard, which formerly lay in a manner open and exposed to dogs and swine and other nuisances is

now enclosing with Iron-rails upon a Stone plinth, and will be a very decent Burial place.

The Dean and Chapter decreed that the two cloisters and covered ways were in future to be considered as a part of the church.

The composition of the congregations in the Abbey must obviously be a concern of the choir as well as of the authorities who pay their stipends, so that a Chapter Minute of March 4, 1748 is worth quoting. It deals with the making of more room in the pew for the families of the Dean and of the prebendaries which the Chapter favoured, as it would take

but little from the adjoyning Pews, in wh the Tenants and other Inhabitants within or near our Precinct, have satt time out of mind; and what they give has been a perquisite to one of the Bellringers; whose Places are extreamly small; and are of this further Use, that in the Summer Months, when the Ladies Pew is commonly in a manner empty, they help to make the thinness of the Congregation less Observable.

As to the Accommodation of Servants, the Answer is a satisfactory and clear one; viz That neither here nor in any of the Cathedrals in England, or in the Kings Chapels, it is expected or supposed, that servants are to attend on Choir Service, but on the contrary, in all those Places provision is made for early Prayers daily throughout the year and the Statutes of Cathedral expressly, take Notice that the Provision is designed for the Accommodation and Convenience of their servants; Accordingly our Minor Canons take it by turns either themselves or by Deputies, to perform the daily Service in our church for the Purposes before mentioned; and for their greater Encouragement and Diligence have an additional Allowance granted them by the Dean and Chapter.

That the boys were difficult to control is exemplified in Horace Walpole's letter concerning his mother's tomb, which he had erected in the South Aisle of Henry VII's Chapel:

Will you believe that I have not yet seen the tomb? None of my acquaintance were in town, and I literally had not courage to venture alone among the Westminster boys; they are as formidable to me as the ship-carpenters at Portsmouth.

November 17, 1750 also must have been an extra special gala day because Westminster Bridge was opened for traffic at midnight. It had been started as long ago as 1738 and was the centre of much admiring wonder though its apogee was to come with Wordsworth's sonnet, 'Earth hath not anything to show more fair'.

The Abbey surroundings were still those of the Civil War days. The Minutes note the amelioration of Tyburn Lane into Park Lane; but the population of the Horseferry Road and the poverty-ridden districts surrounding it was increasing and making comparison with Engels' later descriptions of Manchester.

The country was vanishing under almshouses, slums and ragged schools. A completely new district was springing up; although as yet Tothill Fields were still common land and a centre of vice, and Vincent's enclosing of the square which bears his name was done only just in time. It was formerly the site of the Pest House of Westminster, the place so vividly described by Defoe.

It is quite clear from the Minutes that the houses on the site of the Great Almery still provided money for the singingmen, and leases 'of the Singingmen's Rents' were sealed 'for the benefit of the Singingmen'. In particular, in May 1756 it was

Ordered that two or more Prebendaries take a View of the Houses and Ground belonging to the College, within the plan and Design of the Rev. Dr Markham and Thomas Salter Esq., and endeavour to obtain an Account of the true yearly Rents paid by the Occupiers to the Dean and Chapter's Lessees, and also some Account of the yearly Value of Houses &c now in hand, or Such as belong to the Minor Canons, Singingmen or Almsmen, as particularly, and as soon as may be.

Three weeks later Dr Markham attended in order to come to an agreement with the Dean and Chapter and the following was concluded, although in the margin is written 'I dissent from this. Tho. Wilson'; concerning the intended new square and other buildings in or near Dean's Yard, subject to an Act of Parliament. Clause three reads 'That the Dean's Stables &c The Minor Canons Houses: the Singingmen's Rents: the Almsmens Houses, and those They live in, are not to be comprized herein; but are to be considered separate Estates To which Proposals the Dean and Chapter agreed.'

Chapter Fourteen

STATE AFFAIRS AND MONSTER CONCERTS

A GREAT DAY IN the history of Westminsters and choristers was the bicentenary of Queen Elizabeth's foundation and the Dean and Chapter rose to the occasion. On April 30, 1760 they ordered

That on Monday the 2nd day of June next be kept a solemn Jubilee in Comemoration of our Royal Foundress Queen Elizabeth, upon the Completion (as on ye day before Sunday) of a second Century since Her Foundation of this College: and that the Dean, the Prebendaries, Masters, Scholars, Officers, Ministers, and all others belonging to the Choir or Foundation; be invited to attend on that day, in the College Hall, & to go from thence in Procession to the Morning and Evening Prayers in the Choir, and to dine altogether in the Colledge Hall: The whole to be conducted according to the Directions, which the Dean shall think proper to give on this Occasion.

The Gentlemen of the Choir, with one eye to a fitting tribute to Elizabeth but the other, a weather eye, to the money that was likely to come to them for its exhibition, decided that it was high time a new effigy was made of the great Queen. Accordingly the Chapter Minutes of June 3rd record:

The Gentlemen of the Choir having requested Leave that they may set up a waxen Effigy of Q. Elizabeth within the Tombs at their own Expence, the said request was agreed to, and it was Ordered that the College Carpenter do make a wainscot-case for the same, at the College Expence, as hath formerly been done on like Occasions.

This effigy and case today forms one of the exhibits in the waxworks now housed in the Norman Undercroft of the Abbey.

The Chapter Minutes proceed directly to an account of the day's events:

Ordered that an Entry be made in the Chapter Book of the proceedings of the Jubilee kept this day in such manner as his Lordship shall direct, which Entry his Lordship directed to be as followeth:

All the Members of the Collegiate Foundation having been sumoned to be present this day in the College Hall at ten of the Clock in the morning; they set out from thence and proceeded to the Choir, two or three absent, and the Juniors preceding the Seniors.

In the Choir Purcell's Te Deum was performed, and one of his Anthems was sung; and when the morning Service was ended, a Sermon was preached by the Dean on the solemn Occasion. After this all the Members proceeded in the same Order as before, from the Choir to the College Hall, where an English Oration and several Copies of English Verses were spoken by the King's Scholars from the Gallery in the Hall.

About a quarter after 2 of the Clock the whole Company sat down to a Dinner in the Hall, the Dean, Prebendaries and upper Officers of the Church being at the upper end of the Hall; the Minor Canons, Gentlemen of the Choir, Singing Boys & inferior Servants of the Church on the Eastern side of it, the King's Scholars on the Western side, and the Almsmen at a Table placed in the middle.

At half an hour after four of the Clock they all rose from Table, and proceeded to Evening Prayers in the Choir, where another of Mr Purcell's Anthems was sung, and when the Evening Service was ended, the whole Company was dismissed, and the Dean and Prebendaries repaired to the Jerusalem Chamber, where a Chapter was then held and the Business before mentioned was despatched.

When in that same year George II died, the Dean and Chapter erected scaffolding everywhere (and benches in the organ loft) to accommodate the spectators, amongst whom was Horace Walpole who wrote to George Montagu:

Nov. 13, 1760.—Do you know, I had the curiosity to go to the burying t'other night; I had never seen a royal funeral. . . . But the charm was the entrance to the Abbey, where we were received by the Dean and Chapter in rich robes, the choir and almsmen all bearing torches; the whole Abbey so illuminated, that one saw it to greater advantage than by day; the tombs, long aisles, and fretted roof, all appearing distinctly, and with the happiest chiaroscuro. There wanted nothing but incense, and little chapels here and there, with priests saying mass for the repose of the defunct—yet one could not complain of its not being catholic enough. I had been in dread of being coupled with some boy of ten years old—but the heralds were not very accurate, and I walked with George Greville, taller and older enough to keep me in countenance. When we came to the chapel of Henry the Seventh, all solemnity and decorum ceased—no order was observed, people set or stood where they could or would, the yeomen of the guard were crying for help, oppressed by the immense weight of the coffin, the Bishop read sadly, and blundered in the prayers, the fine chapter, Man that is born of a woman, was chanted, not read, and the anthem, besides being unmeasurably tedious, would have served as well for a nuptial. The real serious part was the figure of the Duke of Cumberland, heightened by a thousand melancholy circumstances. He had a dark brown adonis, and cloak of black cloth, with a train of five yards. Attending the funeral of a father, however little reason he had so to love him, could not be pleasant. His leg extremely bad, yet

Albany Charles Wallis: a portrait by Sir Joshua Reynolds

forced to stand upon it near two hours, his face bloated and distorted with his late paralytic stroke, which has affected, too, one of his eyes, and placed over the mouth of the vault, into which, in all probability, he must so soon himself descend—think how unpleasant a situation! He bore it all with a firm and unaffected countenance. This grave scene was fully contrasted by the burlesque Duke of Newcastle. He fell into a fit of crying the moment he came into the Chapel, and flung himself back in a stall, the Archbishop hovering over him with a smelling-bottle—but in two minutes his curiosity got the better of his hypocrisy, and he ran about the chapel with his glass to spy who was or was not there, spying with one hand, and mopping his eyes with t'other. Then returned the fear of catching cold, and the Duke of Cumberland, who was sinking with heat, felt himself weighed down, and turning round, found it was the Duke of Newcastle standing upon his train to avoid the chill of the marble. It was very theatric to look down into the vault, where the coffin lay, attended by mourners with lights. Clavering, the Groom of the Bedchamber, refused to sit up with the body, and was dismissed by the King's order.

Preparation for the coronation of George III began. The carpenter had a most suitable name. On August 12, 1761 'Mr Bacchus the Carpenter acquainted the Chapter that the Church Wardens of St Margaret insist on taking a piece of Ground before part of the 259 feet of Ground (for which he hath Agreed) to make a Scaffold for a Fountain of Wine & a Band of Mewsick.'

One Chapter Minute ten days before the Coronation presents a hilarious picture.

12 Sept. 1761. It being reported that a Chain & Padlock had been put on the West Door of the Choir, which made the Church Key of no use; It was Ordered that the College Smith be sent to take off the said Chain and Padlock, which was done accordingly in the presence of the Chapter.

On the 21st William Hickey set off to the crowning:

The Coronation of His present Majesty being fixed for the month of September, my father determined that all his family should be present at the ceremony. He therefore engaged one of the Nunnery's, as they were called, in Westminster Abbey, for which he paid fifty guineas. They are situated at the head of the great columns that support the roof, and command an admirable view of the whole interior of the building. Upon this occasion they were divided off by wooden partitions, each having a separate entrance with lock and key to the door, with ease holding a dozen persons. Provisions, consisting of cold fowls, ham, tongues, different meat pies, wines, and liquors of various sorts were sent into the apartment the day before, and two servants were allowed to attend. Our party consisted of my father, mother, brother Joseph, sister Mary, myself, Mr and Miss Isaacs, Miss Thomas, her brother (all Irish), my uncle and aunt Bolton, and their eldest daughter. We all supped together in St Albans Street on the 21st of September, and at midnight set off in my father's coach and my uncle's, and Miss Thomas's chariot. At the end of Pall Mall the different lines of carriages, nearly filling our street, our progress was consequently tedious, yet the time was beguiled by the grandeur of the scene, such a multitude of carriages, with servants behind carrying flambeaux, made a blaze of light equal to day, and had a fine effect.

Opposite the Horse Guards we were stopped exactly an hour without moving onward a single inch. As we approached the Abbey, the difficulties increased, from the mistakes of the coachmen, some of whom were going to the Hall, others to the Abbey, and getting into the wrong ranks. This created much confusion and running against each other, whereby glasses and panels were demolished without number, the noise of which, accompanied by the screeches of the terrified ladies, was at times truly terrific.

It was past seven o'clock before we reached the Abbey,

which having once entered, we proceeded to our box without further impediment, Dr Markham having given us tickets which allowed our passing by a private staircase, and avoiding the immense crowd that was within. We found a hot and comfortable breakfast ready, which I enjoyed, and which proved highly refreshing to us all; after which some of the party determined to take a nap in their chairs, whilst I, who was well acquainted with every creek and corner of the Abbey, amused myself running about the long gallery until noon, when notice being given that the procession had begun to move, I resumed my seat. Exactly at one they entered the Abbey, and we had a capital view of the whole ceremony. Their Majesties (the King having previously married), being crowned, the Archbishop of Canterbury mounted the pulpit to deliver the sermon, and as many thousands were out of the possibility of hearing a single syllable, they took that opportunity to eat their meal when the general clattering of knives, forks, plates, and glasses that ensued, produced a most ridiculous effect, and a universal burst of laughter followed.

The sermon being ended, the anthem was sung by a numerous band of the first performers in the Kingdom, and certainly was the finest thing I ever heard. The procession then began to move towards Westminster Hall, at which moment my father received a paper from Lord Egmont, enclosing four hall tickets, two of which he gave to Mr Thomas and me, desiring us to make the best of our way.

On April 30, 1767 an echo of the coronation returns to the Minute book:

Whereas several of the Iron Bars which extended from Pillar to Pillar in the Abbey have been at former Coronations taken away and carried off by Stealth to the great hazard of damage to the Pillars It is agreed and Ordered that as many new ones as are wanting be placed in the room of those taken away.

The choir was again altered in 1773 when a Chapter Minute requested whether

it is the Sense of the present Chapter that the Screen at the Entrance of the present Choir with the Monuments against the same be removed, and that the Entrance into the Choir be advanced one Intercolumniation nearer the Altar, Eastward and the Organ be placed at the East End of the Choir, or not.

A lease ten years later shows that the tenements in the Great Almery were still considered as belonging to the singingmen. A pencilled note in the margin is to that effect.

There is an echo of the War of American Independence when, a couple of months before the Declaration, on May 17, 1776, were voted 'ffifty Pounds being the Dean and Chapter's Subscription towards the Relief of the Clergy of the Church of England in North America'.

And so one comes to the great Handel Festival of 1784, the forerunner of so many mammoth performances and the natural father of the Albert Hall and of the Royal Festival Hall. Many ex-choristers took part as singers and instrumentalists, and the names of some of the boys are known.

Arthur Thomas Corfe, third son of Joseph Corfe, organist of Salisbury Cathedral, born April 9, 1773, came into the School March 3, 1783, and sang at the Festival. He studied music in the choir under Cooke, and was a pupil of Clementi. In 1796 he married Frances Davies, daughter of the Vicar of Padworth, and they had fourteen children. On the resignation of his father in 1804, he became organist of Salisbury, and in 1813 it was said that the choir was 'in a very fine state of perfection'. In 1828 he organized a Festival at Salisbury with outstanding success; and on that occasion he conducted while his son John Davies Corfe, who was organist for more than fifty years at Bristol Cathedral, was at the organ. He composed a service, some pianoforte pieces, anthems and a treatise *The Principles of Harmony and Thoroughbass*.

On January 28, 1863, he was found dead in the early morning kneeling at his bed as if in prayer.

Charles Burney provides us with the information about the Festival of 1784:

3 Master Ashleys, Master Bellamy, Ten Chapel Boys, Master Dorion, Two Master Knyvetts, Master Latter, Master Loader, Master Lowther, Master Matthews, Ten St Paul's Boys, Master Piper, Master Taylor, Eight Westminster Boys, Six Windsor Boys. There were also ten ladies named and Signor Bartolini.

The basses included Mr Greatorex of Burton on Trent, and Mr Greatorex junior of Newcastle. The Principal Violoncellist was Mr Crosdill. Money received Westminster

Abbey Weds. May 26, 1784	£2966	5	0
Second Performance in the Pantheon Thurs. May 27	£1690	10	0
Third Performance in the Abbey Sat. May 29	£2626	1	0
Fourth Performance in the Abbey Thurs. June 3	£1603	7	0
Fifth Performance in the Abbey Sat. June 5	£2117	7	0
At three separate rehearsals, in Westminster Abbey & the Pantheon,	£944	17	0
His Majesty's most gracious donation	£525	0	0
By sale of printed books of the words	£262	15	0
	£12736	12	10

Doors open at 9 o'clock, and the performance will begin precisely at Twelve. Tickets One Guinea each. The Festival had been originally planned for the 20, 22, 23rd, but a sudden dissolution of Parliament having taken place, it was

thought more proper to defer the festival to the 26, 27, &
29 May, which seems to have been to its advantage: as so
many persons of tender constitutions, who ventured to go
to Westminster Abbey in warm weather, would not have
had the courage to go thither in cold.

More than 500 managed to get into the general rehearsal
in the Abbey in spite of every endeavour to shut out all but
the performers. . . .

and so the organizers fixed a price of half a guinea as the
price of admission for any such occasion.

Charles Burney continues:

Early in the morning, the weather being very favourable,
persons of all ranks quitted their carriages with impatience
and apprehension, lest they should not obtain seats, and
presented themselves at the several doors of Westminster
Abbey which was advertised to be open at Nine o'clock, but
the doorkeepers not having taken up their posts, and the
Orchestra not being wholly finished, and, perhaps, the rest
of the Abbey quite ready for the reception of the audience,
till near Ten o'clock; such a crowd of ladies and gentlemen
were assembled together—as became very formidable and
terrific to each other, particularly the female part of the
expectants; for some of these being in full dress, and every
instant more and more incommoded and alarmed, by the
violence of those who pressed forward, in order to get near
the door, screamed; others fainted; and all were dismayed
and apprehensive of fatal consequences: as many of the
most violent, among the gentlemen, threatened to break
open the doors; a measure which if adopted, would, probably, have cost many of the most feeble and helpless their
lives; as they must, infallibly, have been thrown down,
and trampled on, by the robust and impatient part of the
crowd.

It was a considerable time after a small door at the west
end was opened, before the press abated: as tickets could not
be examined, and cheques given in return, fast enough, to

diminish the candidates for admission or their impatience.

However, except dishevelled hair, and torn garments, no real mischief seems to have happened. In less than an hour after the doors were opened the whole area and galleries of the Abbey seemed too full for the admission of more company; and a considerable time before the performance began, the doors were all shut to every one but their Majesties, and their suite, who arrived soon after Twelve; and on entering the box, prepared for their reception, pleasure and astonishment, at the sight of the company and disposition of the Orchestra and Performers, were painted so strongly in their countenances, as to be visible to all their delighted subjects present. Eagerness and expectation for the premier coup d'archet were now wound up to the highest pitch of impatience: when a silence, the most profound and solemn, was gently interrupted by the processional symphony of the Coronation Anthem composed in 1727, Zadock the priest and Nathan the prophet anointed Solomon King.

Now as the orchestra in Westminster Abbey seemed to ascend into the clouds and unite with the saints and martyrs represented on the painted glass in the west window, which all added to the appearance of a continuation of the orchestra; I could hardly refrain, during the performance of the Alleluia, to imagine that this orchestra, so admirably constructed, filled and employed, was a point or segment of one of the celestial circles. And perhaps, no band of musicians ever exhibited a more respectable appearance to the eye, or afforded a more extatic and affecting sound to the ear, than this,

> 'So sung they, and the empyrean rang
> With Allelujahs.'

Chapter Fifteen

LATER WORTHIES

ONE OF THE most distinguished of the ex-choristers missed the Festival, nor is there any record of his having been at Westminster School.

Sir Augustus Wall Callcott, born Kensington, February 20, 1779, was brother of Dr John Wall Callcott, composer of music, who was not at the Abbey. Augustus had a great taste for music as well as for painting and was a chorister for six years, earning, as he said, '£7 a year and 3½ yards of coarse black baize'. He became a student at the Royal Academy and came under the influence of Hoppner. He scored a success at the Royal Academy Exhibition of 1799; and after 1804 exhibited only landscapes for many years. In 1806 he became A.R.A.; and R.A. in 1812. On the accession of Queen Victoria in 1837 he was knighted, and made conservator of the Royal pictures in 1844. Both Turner and Stothard admired his work, and nine of his paintings were left to the nation by Vernon. Two of his figure paintings, Anne Page and Slender, and Falstaff and Simple, as well as several of his landscapes in oil and sketches in water colour, are in the Sheepshanks Collection at the Victoria and Albert Museum. *The Wooden Bridge* reproduced here is at the Tate Gallery. As a man he was well known for his open-handedness, and for his generosity and kindness towards young artists. His wife, an invalid for many years, was the well known authoress of *Little Arthur's History of Britain*.

The Art Union Monthly Journal of the Fine Arts in its October number of 1844 recorded:

Sir Augustus Wall Callcott. We regret to learn that the health of this accomplished artist is such as to leave but little hope of his ultimate recovery. His loss will be severe to the profession he has so long honoured, not only by his admirable works, but by his high and irreproachable character; in private life no gentleman is more universally respected; and few have ever been so esteemed and regarded by an extensive circle of loving friends.

In 1845, the *Art Union* added:

'In accordance with a codicil in his will, his works in oil were not sold in public but disposed of amongst his personal friends. They were all bought at once—six were purchased by His Royal Highness Prince Albert.'

These are still amongst Her Majesty the Queen's collections of pictures.

William Henry Champnes who was Callcott's contemporary in the choir, entering on June 30, 1788, was one of the group of Champnes found amongst the Old Westminsters and Lay Vicars.

The last choristers of the eighteenth century whose names are known include a bevy of Walmisleys, but not the composer. Most of them were connected with the Houses of Parliament and several held important posts.

George Parry Marriott, a native of Bedfordshire, entered the school on April 24, 1786; admitted pensioner, St John's College, Cambridge, March 5, 1795 and became a Foundress Scholar, November 3, 1795. He took his B.A. in 1800; M.A. in 1808 and assumed the name of Marriott in lieu of Wakefieldon, on December 6, 1799. He took Orders and was ordained September 19, 1802; became Rector of Hazeleigh, Essex, from 1804; Vicar of Eynsford, Kent, November 13, 1807; sometime Minor Canon of Canterbury, Prebendary of

York from December 30, 1829. Married October 2, 1809, Jane Bonham, second daughter of John Bax, of Great Baddow, Essex. His voice and vigour were so remarkable that at the age of seventy-one, he sang Tallis's Litany with the Reverend Joshua Stratton, the Precentor, at the enthronement of Archbishop Sumner in Canterbury Cathedral in April, 1848. Four years later, on March 6, 1852, he died.

William Beale, born at Landrake, January 1, 1784, was a chorister under Arnold but was not at Westminster School apparently. When his voice broke he joined the navy and served as midshipman on board the *Révolutionnaire*, a 44 gun frigate captured from the French. He was nearly drowned through falling overboard in Cork Harbour. When his voice settled to a pure baritone, he left the sea for music. On December 1, 1811, he was made a Member of the Royal Society of Musicians; on January 12, 1813, he won the prize cup of the Madrigal Society for *Awake, sweet Muse*. On January 30, 1816, appointed a Gentleman of the Chapel Royal, he remained there until 1820, when he was on November 1st appointed organist of Trinity College, Cambridge. On December 20, 1821, he returned to London where, thanks to Attwood, he became organist of Wandsworth Parish Church and St John's, Clapham Rise. He sang in public until late in life, and in 1840 won the prize at the Adelphi Glee Club for his glee for four voices entitled *Harmony*.

The cycle of festivals which would probably have revolved was broken by the Napoleonic Wars and it was not until 1834 that, rather contrary to the wishes of the Dean and Chapter, William IV, anxious to emulate his father, determined to hold a glorious festival.

To George III on April 2, 1789 the Chapter drafted an address 'On Your Majesty's Recovery from a severe Visitation of the Almighty'.

Chapter Minutes

Beer appears as a subject for discussion in the 1780's. On May 3, 1788 it was ordered

that the Butler do always take care to supply the Scholars with as much Beer as they shall desire without any limitation but that he likewise take care as a part of the proper duty of his Office as Butler that no more be charged on account of the Scholars than they shall really have consumed.

'23rd May 1794. Ordered that an alteration be made in the Choir for the better disposition of the King's Scholars and the Choristers there.'

24 Feb. 1796. Application having been made by the Organist and Singingmen or Lay Clerks of this Church for an Augmentation of their Stipends It is agreed and Ordered

That an addition of twelve Pounds be made to the annual income of the Organist who is considered as one of the Lay Clerks

That an addition of twelve Pounds be made to the annual income of each of the ten Lay Clerks on condition that no Lay Clerk who shall not personally attend his duty in the Choir fifty times in his month of waiting shall be entitled to any part of the said augmentation for that month unless in case of illness he shall be dispensed with by the Dean or in his absence by the Subdean or Prebendary in residence

That an attendance of a Lay Clerk at morning and evening Service on any Sunday in his month of waiting shall be deemed equivalent to an attendance of any two other days in the week

That no Lay Clerk shall incur a forfeiture by his absence on those days when Choir Service is not performed and the whole Choir have of ancient custom been allowed to be absent

That the order of personal attendance shall be understood that every Lay Clerk shall be allowed to procure the attendance of any other Lay Clerk of this Choir in his stead who is not in waiting for himself in the same month.

That if it shall happen at any time that three Lay Clerks shall not be attending a fine of five shillings shall be imposed upon each of the absent Lay Clerks who may be in waiting

That these Orders do take effect on the first day of March next and the augmentation to be paid quarterly by the Treasurer

That copies of these Orders be sent by the Chapter Clerk to the Organist and every one of the Lay Clerks.

Samuel Arnold, whose reign in the organ loft coincided with Samuel Horsley's in the Deanery, edited at the King's request the works of Handel. This he began in 1786 soon after the first Handel Festival. He was noted for his open-handedness and cheerful good fellowship and wrote Tory Squibs in the papers, some of which he doubtless tried out on his boys, as Bridge did his rhyme about 'Labby'. He was very popular and it was a cause of genuine sorrow when he fell from his library steps in Duke Street and broke a tendon in his leg. Unfortunately he also received internal injuries which proved fatal.

He was succeeded by Robert Cooke (son of Benjamin) who had become organist of St Martin-in-the-Fields on his father's retirement. Amongst his compositions was an *Ode to Friendship* in the style of Purcell which he wrote for the singer and ex-Abbey chorister James Bartleman. After twelve years at the Abbey, in 1814 he went mad through being crossed in love and drowned himself in the Thames.

The education and payment of choristers in general during the first fifty years of the nineteenth century was scandalous and a Miss Maria Hackett set about altering the situation. Her main interest was St Paul's Cathedral, of whose choristers she collected material and wrote a history: but she made it her aim to examine every choir school in the country at least once every three years. She became known as 'The Choristers' Friend' and was their Florence Nightingale, causing as many heartburnings as that redoubtable lady. She published in 1824 *A Brief Account of Cathedral and Collegiate Schools* and in writing of the Abbey left a blank under the heading of the boys' education. She continues:

The School, the more immediate subject of this inquiry, seems to have been coeval with the monastic establishment, and to have shared in all its vicissitudes. It was in existence prior to the re-building of the Abbey by Edward the Confessor, for Ingulphus, in his *History of Croyland*, informs us, that he received his education there; and the same regulations which were universally observed in the other great Benedictine Abbeys, would no doubt be adopted.

Westminster was one of the new Bishopricks designed by Henry VIII. It was finally established as a Collegiate Church by Queen Elizabeth who is commemorated as the foundress. The constitutions and statutes agree in substance with those of the Cathedrals on the new foundation, and they have in general been more faithfully observed. The Choristers, however, here, as in other Choirs, have been too much neglected. They are sometimes admitted to the benefit of a classical education in the Royal Grammar School; but their maintenance '*De bonis ecclesiae*', has been commuted into a very inadequate money payment.

The whole period before 1848 smacks of neglect and incompetence, but it would be futile to consider it without its background, the aftermath of the long-drawn-out wars against Napoleon, which were to lead to the Year of Revolution in 1848, the Chartist Riots and the Communist Manifesto of Marx.

A few of the choristers went to Westminster School, but only a handful in fifty years. An anonymous ex-chorister writing in 1911 looked back to the year 1841 when, he said, he and Macfarren went to the school but no one else.

Even so Walter Macfarren's name is not in the *Record of Old Westminsters*. Macfarren, who died in 1905, after leaving the Abbey studied at the Royal Academy of Music and became Professor of Pianoforte there in 1846. He was a prolific composer, some of his overtures to Shakespeare's plays being very popular. He wrote a considerable body of orchestral works including a symphony, a pianoforte concerto, church music and solo works for various instruments.

Samuel Matthews was admitted as a chorister to Westminster School in 1809. He became a Lay Clerk of Winchester Cathedral and a Mus. Bac. of Cambridge in 1828, after being appointed organist of Trinity and St John's in 1821. He also was a composer of glees and church music but his career was cut short by his death in his early thirties on December 9, 1832.

An instructive and salutary comment on the purpose of the Abbey choir is given by Simon Andrew Forster, who was born on May 13, 1801, admitted to the school as a chorister at Midsummer 1811 and left in 1817. He was the fourth in descent in a line of instrument makers, the first being born in 1713. The family played the instruments they made, especially the cello and Forster says of himself that his progress in early years was not very rapid. 'However at that period, perhaps the work room may have been neglected, as music was studied as a profession in the Choir of Westminster Abbey, which gave the right of education in Westminster School.'

Forster made instruments for many of the musical, including the Prince Regent, and by a happy coincidence made cellos for the former chorister John Crosdill. When Crosdill died seven of his finest cellos were sold on May 7, 1826. One in particular was wanted by Robert Lindley but the former Regent, now King, had sent someone to buy it. Happily for Lindley, the man was in the other room at the moment of the sale and he was able to buy it for 50 guineas.

Forster collaborated with another Old Westminster, William Sandys, F.S.A. in *The History of the Vision and other instruments*, published in 1864 by John Russell Smith and with a chorister's flourish 'Dedicated (with Permission) to Lord Gerald Fitzgerald, and the Nobility and Gentry of the Society of Wandering Minstrels'.

During these early years of the nineteenth century there was a temporary reversion to the practice of having the offices of Organist and Master of the Choristers separate. It had begun in 1794 on the appointment of Samuel Arnold as organist. Richard Guise became Master of the choristers, receiving £10 and £33. 6s. 8d. for the choristers, being £3. 6s. 8d. for each of them. There were of course augmentations as the value of money decreased; and this change was summed up in a Chapter Minute of 1815 which follows in a moment. Richard Guise remained Master of the Choristers throughout Arnold's rule, from 1794 until 1802 and continued in his office on Robert Cooke's appointment as organist, until 1805 when in the Treasurer's Accounts his name is crossed through and Robert Cooke's name is opposite the entries. Since then there has been no division.

Robert Cooke was succeeded by George Ebenezer Williams who was at the Abbey only from 1814 until 1819.

The whole position with regard to the financial position was made clear in the Chapter Minutes of February 27, 1815.

Ordered that the Organist and Master of the Choristers he required to make a further allowance to the choristers making the whole payment to the four Senior Boys ninepence per day and to the four Junior Boys sixpence per day and that the Organist shall be paid an increase of Stipend of thirty five pounds per Annum in consideration of the additional allowance to the Choristers and that he shall be subject to the regulations drawn up by the Dean approved this day in Chapter and entered in the Receiver's Books. . . .

Ordered that twenty pounds be given to the Choristers Fund out of the Mulcts and that the sum of ten pounds be given to Mrs Vine out of the Mulcts.

Regulations respecting the Organist and Master of the Choristers referred to in the Order previously entered this Chapter.

	£	s.	d.
Organist: Stipend	10	0	0
House	8	0	0
Augmentation 1796	12	0	0
Dinner Money 1759	5	3	0
Tombs (supposed)	45	0	0
	80	3	0

	£	s.	d.
Master of the Choristers:			
Stipend	10	0	0
Choristers' Diet	33	6	8
Augmentation	20	0	0
House	10	0	0
Wheat and Malt	64	0	0
	137	6	8

In lieu of Boarding the Choristers the Master has hitherto paid the eight Boys Seven Pounds each

	£	s.	d.
	56	0	0
	81	6	8

But he is now required to pay the four senior Boys nine pence a day each that is a Guinea per month of 28 days each Boy amounting together per Annum to   54 12 0
likewise to pay the four junior Boys sixpence a day each

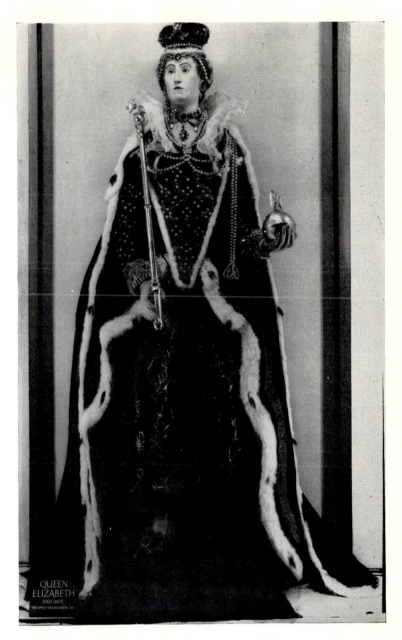

Effigy of Queen Elizabeth I, made for the Bi-centenary in 1760

or 14s. per Month of 28 days amounting together per
annum to

	£	s.	d.
	36	8	0
	91	0	0
	56	0	0
difference between £56 and £91	35	0	0

To make good this difference to the Master It is proposed
to allow him £12 to be added to the Augmentation 1796 in
consideration of his attendance as Organist twelve months
instead of Six.

It is proposed moreover to make an addition to his Stipend
of £23

£12 making together

£35

which is the difference between the £56 he formerly paid
and the £91, he is now to pay the Boys.

The Stipend due to the Boys now, is to be paid monthly
into the hands of their Parents, and the Master is to certify
annually in the Receiver's Book, that he has paid such
Stipends—before he receives the augmentation.

The Master may stop the allowance in case of irregular
attendance, bad behaviour in Church or out, neglect of
cleanliness in person, Surplice &c, But if the stoppage has
been continued for one week without effect, he is to report
the offender to the Dean, Subdean or Prebendary in
residence.

Choristers of good conduct, morals and proficiency in
music, will receive £10 upon quitting the Choir by certifi-
cate of the Precentor and Master:—who are desired not to
certify, unless the merits of the Boys may justify their
testimony.

Choristers leaving the Choir before due age are not
entitled to £10.

Ordered that upon the admission of a Boy as Chorister, the Master deliver to the Parents in writing, the Emoluments he is entitled to, with the Service required of him, and the rules for the conduct, behaviour and cleanliness.

As will be seen from this order, only eight boys are accounted for, yet the Treasurer's Accounts allow for the statutory ten. By a Chapter Order of April 6, 1831, a further entry allows for two probationary choristers and they in July 1844 are raised to four.

Robert Cooke the suicide was followed by George Ebenezer Williams who seems to have been ineffective and equally unfortunate.

Two Chapter Acts, the only references there are to him, seem to sum him up:

Chapter Acts Tuesday 9 March 1819

An application by the Organist for an increased Stipend. Ordered that an addition be made to his Stipend as Organist and Master of the Boys of thirty eight pounds 10s 3d. provided a report be made to the Chapter by the Dean of his Satisfaction of the Management of the Organ and the Boys. The addition to begin from Michaelmas 1818 but the whole of the payments to the Organist are not to exceed two hundred pounds yearly.

March 30 1819 Mr Williams the late Organist having died very much distressed Ordered that forty pounds be given his Family out of the Mulcts.

Deputy to both Robert Cooke and Williams was an ex-chorister, John Jolly, who was organist of St Philip's, Regent Street.

James Howe was born in 1820-1, entered the school at the age of 7 in 1827 and his treble voice did not break until he was 21 years of age. He was one of the principal soloists at the Royal Musical Festival in 1834 and was a composer of glees.

The coronation of George IV in 1821 was another pageant—perhaps the most lavish coronation that ever took place—with a magnificent banquet, though the proceedings were somewhat marred by the attempt of the Queen to gain admittance to the coronation of her husband.

On July 14, 1821, it was ordered that the Subdean Dr Edwards and Mr Webber being on the spot and any other Prebendaries who may be desirous of attending be a committee for making arrangements with the Committee of the Westminster Hospital on the Subject of the music to be performed in the Abbey after the Coronation for the benefit of the Westminster Hospital which has been permitted by the Dean and Chapter.

On the very same day a request from the Headmaster was heard by the Chapter:

An application having been made by the Head Master of the School to place the Town Boys in the Western part of the Choir for the purpose of their more effectually hearing Divine Service.

Ordered that the bringing the Town boys into the Western part of the Choir be acceded to as an experiment and that preparation be made to effect it, on the restoring of the Choir when the scaffolding of the Coronation is removed. The Dean and Chapter at the same time will have the firmest expectation that the Head Master, and Under Master, will regularly attend the Church; together with a sufficient number of the Ushers; to maintain an effectual inspection, and control, of the conduct of the Boys, while attending service.

John Larkin Hopkins, who was born on November 25, 1819, was educated musically under Turle and continued with a musical career on leaving, turning especially to the organ. At the age of 22 he became Organist of

Rochester Cathedral. In 1842 he received a Mus. Bac. Cantab. and in 1856 resigned from Rochester to become Organist of Trinity. In the following year he became a Mus. Doc. He wrote glees and a madrigal, Cathedral services and a book on singing, *A New Vocal Tutor*, published London 1855. He died on April 25, 1873, at Ventnor

Another boy who sang at the 1834 Festival was James Coward, who was born in 1824 and died in 1880. While in the choir he sang many solos and duets with Madame Malibran. He and his brother were celebrated for their duets in the Abbey, especially of Boyce's *Turn Thee unto me*. His first appointment as an organist was at Lambeth Parish Church which he left to become organist of the Crystal Palace on its removal to Sydenham, and remained there until his death. He was an enthusiastic conductor of glees and madrigals, being conductor of the Abbey and City Glee Clubs and in October 1864 succeeded Turle as conductor of the Western Madrigal Society. He combined these offices with the organ of St George's, Bloomsbury 1866-9, the Sacred Harmonic Society and the Grand Lodge of Freemasons. His last appointment—held like all the rest concurrently with the Crystal Palace—was at St Magnus the Martyr, London Bridge. He wrote glees, part songs and organ pieces and some anthems.

Neither he nor any of the other five Abbey boys named in the 1834 Festival lists was at Westminster, although in the Muniment Room there is a pencilled note on the back of No. 60,056 amongst the Precentor's MSS concerning an unusual boy: 'Feb. 8 1828 Was removed his voice having suddenly broken and received the salary for half the current Quarter and his Father not wanting him to go thr Westm School he was removed entirely from the foundation.'

An indication of the kind of schooling the choristers received in these years is found on the other side of 60,056.

A Report of the conduct of the Scholars attending the Choristers School Westminster Abbey. For the latter portion of the month of November 1847

	Good Marks	Bad Marks
John Rhodes	12	0
Henry Lissant	6	0
John Davis	13	0
Alfred Howe	11	0
Edmund Davis	10	0
Francis J. Bavin	7	0
James R. Murray	12	0
Charles Quarterly	11	0

December 1st 1847
W. Sanders

At last in 1834 William IV, anxious to emulate the mammoth performances of his father's reign, came in state to listen to the Royal Musical Festival in Westminster Abbey.

Amongst the 45 Principal Singers is Master Howe, Westminster Abbey, who was born in 1821 and kept his treble voice until the age of twenty-one.

'Amongst the Chorus:

Masters Coward   Westr Abbey.
      Cunningham

At the 3rd Performance, Gloria in excelsis, by Mozart, The Solos by Master Howe, Master Smith, Mr Bennett and Mr J. B. Sale.'

'Dotted Crotchet' writing in the *Musical Times* in 1907 quotes J. S. Bumpus to state that Thomas Greatorex, Organist and Master of the Choristers for the Coronations of George VI and William IV, and who was succeeded by Turle in 1831-2, was in the Abbey under Benjamin Cooke. There are two Greatorex in *The Record of Old Westminsters*, who would have been contemporaries of Thomas, but his name does not appear. He was a favourite of George IV whose humour led him to say that he might be George Rex but Thomas was Greater Rex. William Hutt, according to the same authority, became organist of Winchester College, and J. B. Allen took his Mus. Bac. and became a well known Vicar Choral of Armagh Cathedral. John Leman Brownsmith was organist of St Gabriel's, Pimlico and first organist of the church built to commemorate Waterloo, St John's Waterloo Road which in 1951 became known to many thousands as the Festival Church.

Yet one more boy there is to mention—Charles Herring, who performed the feat of singing at the coronation of Queen Victoria and that of Edward VII sixty four years later. He was a nephew of John Herring senior, the animal painter, was born August 19, 1825, was admitted to Westminster School in October 16, 1838, as a chorister, was for many years a Deputy Vicar Choral of St Paul's Cathedral and surpassed his coronation span with sixty seven years in the sign writer's office of Messrs. Barclay, Perkins & Co., the brewers, to whose beer he may have been indebted for his long life. He died on October 26, 1908.

PART TWO

HEARSAY

Chapter Sixteen

DARK ENTRY

A T LAST, WHEN it was long overdue, a separate school for the choristers was established in 1848 and the direct connection with Westminster School was finally broken.

The whole organization of the Abbey needed reconditioning. Almost completely surrounded by an appalling neighbourhood, its hygiene was in a chaotic state. Mr G. M. Young in his *Early Victorian England* reminds his readers that

An outbreak of fever in the cloisters of Westminster Abbey led to the discovery that there lay beneath a network of old cesspools, barren drains and brick sewers, crammed with 500 cartloads of stagnant filth. The fact was that the whole subsoil of London was sodden with seventeen million cubic feet of decaying residuum. . . . Belgrave and Eaton Square as well as the whole splendid neighbourhood of Hyde Park Gardens stood over sewers abounding in the foulest deposits.

At the Abbey reconstruction was begun. A Chapter Minute for December 22, 1847 states: 'Ordered that a privy be made at the Porter's Lodge to clear itself without a cesspool, the present privy and cesspool being in a very offensive and unwholesome state as reported by the Clerk of the Works.'

Three months earlier William Sanders had been appointed

185

as Schoolmaster. The Chapter Minutes of September 7, 1847 record the conditions:

the Dean having informed the Chapter that he had appointed Mr W. Sanders to the vacant office of Sacrist on condition that so long as he held the Place he shall perform the duties of School Master to the Choristers such hours of the day as the Dean may appoint. Ordered that the sum of £21 16 8 be be added to the stipend heretofore paid to the Sacrist for the performance of such duties as above required and until the Dean and Chapter provide him a house should they have it in their power and think fit to do so.

In January 1848 a bill for a chimney pot to the choristers school room was paid, and charged to the Fabrick Fund; and in the following month a Chapter Minute of 9th February 1848 Ordered 'that the whole Expense of the building and, fitting up of the Choristers new School Room be taken out of the Fund set apart by the Dean and Chapter and called by them the Choristers Fund, and that the Annual Expenses attaching to that Room and the Augmentation of the Sacrist's Salary to whom the instruction of the Choristers is committed by Order of Chapter of the 7th September, 1847 shall be paid out of the interest arising from the said Fund.'

A new Precentor's Book was begun, and opens with the announcement that

The Chorister's School for Daily Instruction, was opened by the Reverend Dr Wordsworth, Canon in Residence, on Monday January 17th 1848—the Choristers having, since November 16th 1847, been assembled for that purpose in a Room at *The King's Arms*, Bowling Street, Westminster.
Mr William Sanders—Schoolmaster & Sacrist.
The Pay of the Choristers is as follows.

The 4 seniors	3	8	3 per Quarter.
The 4 next	2	5	6 per Quarter.
The 4 Juniors	2	0	0

This pay was later increased, as an undated entry follows:

The 4 seniors	per Quarter	£5	0	0
The 4 next		£3	15	0
The 4 Juniors		£2	10	0

The present writer was fortunate in receiving a verbal description of this school from an ex-chorister aged 91, William Kay Waterson, who took him round to what remains to be seen and explained that it was a single room. It had been specially built and was, for its time, 'modern'. It stood in the north-east corner of Ashburnham House and access to it had been made by cutting through the ancient wall in Little Cloister at an angle with the South Cloister and at the beginning of the Dark Entry. A few steps led up into the room.

On the east side there were four tall cupboards, each of which held surplices, four in each as there were at that time sixteen choristers. Above it was a bookcase for the school stock text-books, and above that a fanlight. On the south side was the desk of the Master. There was a fireplace and, outside the west corner, a tiny cubicle with a single w.c. and one tap which supplied cold water into an angle fitted hand basin. On the west were two four-seater desks with another fanlight above them. On the north were two more four-seaters, while on the north-eastern corner was a coal cupboard. Lighting was by gas.

When the schoolroom was not occupied, the key had to be kept at the Porter's Lodge, although the senior boy usually retained it during divine service.

Thanks to the energy of the Rev. W. B. Dams, who was Headmaster from 1908-15, some school magazines were published containing at times reminiscences of earlier days. One of these articles was contributed by A. F. Clement, who was in the choir from 1856-63. He was 'a practising boy' for about fifteen months, and was then raised to the status of a chorister. Practising boys had to go to the schoolroom in the cloisters on Tuesday and Friday mornings from 9 until 9.45, then into the Abbey for morning service. Charles Jekyll, who later became organist of the Chapel Royal, was senior boy and used to instruct them in the music, but left just as Clement joined. For the first two or three years of his Abbey life Clement used to walk from Clapham and back each day. When his two brothers Horace and Arthur were also admitted as choristers, their father presented them with a pony and village cart in which they drove over Westminster Bridge. There was a stable in Dean's Yard at the south-western corner at the foot of a terrace, and here lived the Abbey organ blower and cleaner, named Cooper.

Edward Lloyd was a contemporary, but left in 1860. The boys had no cassocks, so that long surplices were worn to hide the variations in leg wear. Some of the boys sang at the first Handel Festival in the Crystal Palace in 1859 and received bronze medals in commemoration.

An article of considerable interest was contributed by Charles E. Tinney, writing of the years around 1859.

Entered at the age of eight. No boarding house, at school by nine o'clock. Provided own surplices and had to keep them clean. There were not two alike, and from the appearance of some of them they must have been made at home. Once a fortnight on Sunday mornings and before morning service the boys could be seen carrying brown-paper parcels containing these surplices through the cloisters on their way to the schoolroom. Two or three friends of the boys, including the Minor Canon the Rev. Lupton tried to get this state of things altered, but it was several years before the change was effected. The rehearsals were held in the Practice Room in the Little Cloisters or at times in Mr Turle's house where he had a small organ.

There was considerable jealousy (mainly owing to the financial considerations), over promotion and a precociously successful boy sometimes had a rough time from the others. At least one case is known of a mother intending to remove her son.

Turle, like many of his contemporaries and predecessors in schools everywhere, had a strong partiality for the cane.

On one occasion Queen Victoria was present at a service held in the nave. Charles Tinney sang a duet with a boy named Clarke, and a solo by himself in the anthem. *The Times* next day mentioned that the solo had been beautifully sung by a lad named Tinney but did not mention the duet.

As luck would have it, Tinney happened to be in Clarke's house on the morning of the appearance of the report, and the boy's father said it was most unfair that his son should not also have been mentioned. Tinney agreed. Clarke's father said he ought to write to *The Times* about it, and Tinney agreed to do so if the father would word the letter. On the following day the letter duly appeared in *The Times* with the result that an infuriated reporter arrived, complained to Turle, and poor Tinney received the cane.

Tinney was thrice unlucky. On another occasion an Abbey habituée declared that he had travestied the Lord's Prayer, changing the word 'Heaven' into 'Hell'. The boy next to him was the culprit; but Tinney afterwards declared it was more than his life was worth to give away the real offender. He preferred the caning he received.

The third occasion concerned pay. Turle had on one occasion, perhaps owing to strained finances, kept everyone waiting a week over quarter day. He always wore a brown Inverness coat, and the boy who made the substitution in the prayer, shouted after him 'I say, Old Brown Coat, when are you going to pay us?' Turle was more than inclined to be deaf; but in this case he heard, and Tinney suffered.

At the funeral service in memory of one of the Dukes of Northumberland an anthem by Handel was sung. The quartet, *When the ear heard Him*, was sung by Charles Tinney, and Messrs. Foster, Montem Smith and Lawler. It is a beautiful quartet but very trying for the treble. On all the high notes the boy's voice broke and the quartet was ruined. He naturally wished a trap door would open and swallow him up. After the service one of the Vergers told him that Turle wished to see him in the Practice Room, in the Little Cloisters. He went in fear and trembling, sure that he would be caned. Turle had the weapon ready in his hand. 'You will now tell me the meaning of this terrible fiasco,' he demanded. The boy wept. Turle then asked how old he was and when the reply was 'Sixteen', thought the matter over, sat down at the piano and tried his voice. Finding that the boy could reach no higher than C in the third space, Turle said that the voice had gone. The boy went also.

It must be said in fairness that although Turle was harsh after bad work in the choir, in other ways and in other places he was kind and anxious to help the boys. On one occasion when the boys were playing football in Dean's Yard, Tinney was keeping goal. In the haste to get started, the boy had thrown his coat on to the railings. When he came to look for it at the end of the game, it had disappeared. He did not know what to do and went home very scared to meet the punishment he expected. Next day Turle met him in the cloisters on his way to school. It was a very cold day, and Turle asked him where his greatcoat was. Tinney told him it had been stolen while he had been playing football. 'After service you come to me,' said Turle. When the boy arrived, Turle gave him a note to take to a tailor in Bond Street, who made him a very fine coat of which he was intensely proud. Whenever there was a big solo to sing, the boy responsible used to go to his house for a sherry and egg. The order was to go straight up to his dining room, and on the sideboard would be a glass containing the mixture. It was a wise prescription, for there were occasions when a boy, faced with his first solo, broke down in the middle and burst out crying.

They had no playground except the cloisters. It was a common practice in those days. Occasionally they had the use of Dean's Yard, and the Racquets Court of Westminster School, but this was only when the School was on holiday.

As the new Choristers' School was beginning, a great occasion took place in the Abbey. This was the commemoration of Purcell in June 1848: and was shortly after the new stall work had been finished and the organ had been rebuilt and re-arranged. The music critic of *The Atlas* wrote:

On Thursday the choral Cathedral Service was revived in its splendour at Westminster Abbey in honour of Henry Purcell, on which occasion an entire morning service of his composition was performed, including three anthems. The Te Deum in B flat, the Jubilate belonging to the orchestral Te Deum in D; the anthems *Out of the Deep, O give thanks*, and another for eight voices, the title of which has escaped me, composed the music. The eight voice anthem was, perhaps, the only thing which did not thoroughly satisfy in the performance; the rest of the music was full of beauties. The style of the responses, the chanting, accompanied with an exquisite variety of effects by Mr Turle; the solos sung by Machin, Hobbs, Lockey, and others; the full and fine combinations of the choir with the judicious contrasts of the organ, which answers its object as an accompanying instrument most perfectly, altogether raised the cathedral service to a dignity and beauty which it never yet reached in our experience. The alterations in the Abbey— the removal of the wooden partitions between the choir and the transepts, are all greatly in favour of music, and make the most minute sounds tell. Then the organ. It is almost impossible to make a noise with so beautiful an instrument. When the whole of the stops are drawn, the effect is only what Shakespeare calls 'sweet thunder'. Now that this organ is thoroughly tuned and rendered smooth, it surpasses in volume anything that we have ever heard. No foreign organ can vie with it in weight and richness of quality—though that in the Royal Catholic Church at Dresden certainly speaks a more clearly defined C of 32 feet. In the accompanying of voices, however, this instrument is admirably designed—from the most minute and most delicate tones of the diapasons in the swell, to its grandest combination, it forms one immense engine of perpetual variety. Mr Turle employed it with the greatest taste and address; without overdoing his part—interfering with or covering the choir, he found an opportunity to let all the finest effects of his instruments be heard, and a noble illustration of Purcell it afforded. Such magnificent and extraordinary tones might almost have drawn the mighty master from his tomb. We seemed to realize his presence as the soft sounds of the Abbey clock mingled with the anthem, and the sunlight fell on the columns of the choir. Sounds and sights like these must have been the familiar things of the life of Purcell, and by the aid of sympathy and the strong vitality of his music, the composer may again be conjured into existence.

But what we remark with the greatest pleasure is the strong and growing passion of the public for his works. The immense crowd of hearers which filled all the open avenues of the Abbey, exhibiting the deepest interest in the music, afforded testimony to the progress of a composer who has not yet resumed his true position. The latest in this respect is always the greatest. Every year's experience tends to show that Handel must ultimately make way for Purcell, and that the German history of vocal music, sacred and secular, needs certain corrections in favour of England. Meanwhile we may thank the Purcell Society for their efforts on behalf of early English art, in declamation, in melody and counterpoint. Nor must Mr Vincent Novello, who arranged the

Interior of Westminster Abbey, showing the west (performing) end of the nave during the Commemoration—from a painting by Edward Edwards, A.R.A., exhibited at the Royal Academy, 1793

whole of Purcell's church music, be overlooked in the list of those to whose enthusiasm English art is indebted. Great things have been done in the present century for Purcell, in the preservation of works that would have been lost beyond recovery. The next thing is to preserve the tradition of his style by stated performances.

A friend of the choral establishment was Sir George Grove, a frequent visitor to the Abbey, and examiner of the choisters, who in his recollections wrote:

'Many an entrancing hour I spent in the Abbey at the afternoon services, in the winter months, with the dim candles below and the impenetrable gloom above, when I thought my heart must have come out of me with emotion and longing.'

But the soft sounds of the Abbey clock which delighted the critic of *The Atlas* produced a very different effect on the Rev. John Jebb. In his writing in the 1850's his account of *The Choral Service of the United Church of England and Ireland*, he damns the ordinary Abbey Service,

The service opened in a most careless manner; no decent procession was made and the striking of a wretched clock was a signal for beginning to race through the office: there was a squalid neglect in all the accessories of divine worship: the books were torn and soiled, and the custom of the place apparently enjoined on the choir boys the use of surplices more black than white. The whole of the Church plainly indicated the mechanical performance of a burdensome duty.

It must be admitted that this was too often the state of affairs everywhere in England, and not least at the Abbey. One has only to read Maria Hackett's correspondence to learn how disgraceful was the neglect in the highest places. It is a relief therefore to turn to the tribute of Dr A. Cleveland Coxe, Bishop of Western New York, who wrote

At the end, the clock strikes. The Protestant Fabulist tells a Policeman that he has heard Westminster Abbey talking. 'Bless me,' said he, 'where do you live? Let me see you safe home.'

One can almost imagine the figure of Mr Punch rising over the wall under a gibbous moon.

whole of Purcell's church music, be overlooked in the list of those to whose enthusiasm English art is indebted. Great things have been done in the present century for Purcell, in the preservation of works that would have been lost beyond recovery. The next thing is to preserve the tradition of his style by stated performances.

A friend of the choral establishment was Sir George Grove, a frequent visitor to the Abbey, and examiner of the choisters, who in his recollections wrote:

'Many an entrancing hour I spent in the Abbey at the afternoon services, in the winter months, with the dim candles below and the impenetrable gloom above, when I thought my heart must have come out of me with emotion and longing.'

But the soft sounds of the Abbey clock which delighted the critic of *The Atlas* produced a very different effect on the Rev. John Jebb. In his writing in the 1850's his account of *The Choral Service of the United Church of England and Ireland*, he damns the ordinary Abbey Service,

The service opened in a most careless manner; no decent procession was made and the striking of a wretched clock was a signal for beginning to race through the office: there was a squalid neglect in all the accessories of divine worship: the books were torn and soiled, and the custom of the place apparently enjoined on the choir boys the use of surplices more black than white. The whole of the Church plainly indicated the mechanical performance of a burdensome duty.

It must be admitted that this was too often the state of affairs everywhere in England, and not least at the Abbey. One has only to read Maria Hackett's correspondence to learn how disgraceful was the neglect in the highest places. It is a relief therefore to turn to the tribute of Dr A. Cleveland Coxe, Bishop of Western New York, who wrote his impressions of England after his visit during the Great Exhibition of 1851:

And now, having a whole day before me, I began by attending divine service in Westminster Abbey, and entered the door in Poets' Corner. Service was going on, and of course I gave myself as much as possible to the sacred impressions, but was unable to repress some wandering thoughts, as my eyes caught the long lines and intersections of nave and aisles, or turned towards the clerestory, where the smoky sunlight of a London morning was lingering along the old rich tracery and fret-work, to which every cadence of the chaunt seemed to aspire, and where just so, just such sunbeams have come and gone quietly over the the most speaking and eventful pageants of the British Empire. . . .

What thoughts of human splendour and of human no-thingness! The anthem was *Awake, my glory!* and it rose and fell and tremulously died away, distributing its effects among innumerable objects of decayed antiquity. I seemed to catch a new meaning in the strain of the psalmist.

Published in the same Great Exhibition year of 1851 is an anonymous pamphlet redolent of its period:

The Midnight Conference
between
Westminster Abbey & St George's Catholic Church
Overheard
by a
Protestant Fabulist.

In this the two churches are personified and, as the clock strikes, the Protestant Fabulist hears the Abbey speaking.

Westminster: . . . Talk not to me of pictures, statuary and relics, when I know what use was made of them to dishonour God, and to delude men; nor of tapers, music, frankincense and gorgeous robes, when I saw all these used by the priests as baits to attract the multitudes from the Bible and the care of their own souls. . . .

I can never forget that within my walls the immortal Caxton with a genius far beyond his time, first produced an English specimen of the great revolutionary art of printing. I think I see him now presenting his first sheet to our then Abbot, John Esteney, who received it as though he feared some Satanic magic in that which was a noble gift of Divine Providence. . . .

Yet, as I daily hear the lessons of Holy Writ read and chanted, by the half-sleepy canons and choir to a wretched congregation, I sicken for the want of earnestness and faith which seems to have taken their departure from a pampered Church. But to go back to the old leaven—to undo the work of Protestants—to restore the idolatries, the blasphemies, the falsehoods, the spiritual slavery of former ages, such as your priests and Cardinal would re-impose,—again, I say, I would rather perish.

St George's: . . . One cannot wonder that you should be tired of their dull and respectable mediocrity—the luxurious Dean and Chapter, with plenty of riches and no ecclesiastical power—the lazy Prebendaries doing duty to get a living—the humdrum Choir singing to your bare walls their professional praises, with now and then a gleam of extraordinary splendour, as on a coronation and other great days, to make the general poverty more sensible.

Westminster: . . . There are humble Missionaries, not sent by the Dean and Chapter of my Abbey, nor clergymen of our English Church, but connected with the despised sectaries, who daily go to and fro from one miserable abode to the other, gathering the ragged children into schools, and their elders, who live mostly upon theft and crime, into cottage rooms, for worship and instruction. . . .

At the end, the clock strikes. The Protestant Fabulist tells a Policeman that he has heard Westminster Abbey talking. 'Bless me,' said he, 'where do you live? Let me see you safe home.'

One can almost imagine the figure of Mr Punch rising over the wall under a gibbous moon.

Chapter Seventeen

DEAR OLD TURLE

A TOUCHING ACCOUNT OF the Rev. William Sanders was written by William Thomas Styles in one of the school magazines during the First World War. His reminiscences cover the years 1866 to 1872, just before the great changes—and it is easy to see how necessary they were. But the removal of inefficient kindliness from the path of essential reform is none the less tragic.

He finished his time with us now some 50 years ago, but I have a soft spot in my heart for his memory. Mr Saunders to me was always elderly, with a tall, cleanly, wholesome appearance. He was an old Victorian to the finger tips, and, as was the custom in those days, he moved in a groove. 'Let nothing disturb me', was his motto! No doubt it was grateful and comforting to all parties. He did his best for us in the circumstances, and was a man who acted well his part before innovations were the order of the day. Our Schoolmaster held various posts as well, Sacristan and Librarian at the Abbey, and away from all this was one of the Honorary Stewards of the *Sacred Harmonic Society*, whose concerts were held at the old Exeter Hall in the Strand. The Stewards wore evening dress, and our Schoolmaster was fond of telling the story that a dear old lady whom he was showing to her seat in the audience tipped him a shilling. He kept the shilling to save explanations, and as a souvenir. Mr Saunders had to retire to make room for a younger man in my time. We might have been at periods very troublesome;

197

I am afraid we took advantage of his age, but his leaving us was quite tragic. One morning after coming into the school-room he intimated he had something important to impart to us. It was very brief when he did speak. He simply said: 'Boys, I am going to leave you.' He could not proceed, but broke down and wept bitterly; and that was his going out from us as it were into the night. We had no previous intimation from any other source, and we were all very sorry and upset. The old man in a few days recovered his composure, and on the following Sunday seemed quite happy, taking up his duties as Sacristan.

The School in those days stood just at the corner end of the South Walk of the Cloisters, a sort of Hole-in-the-Wall. You went up a few steps to the door, a very dark entrance, and when you entered you went up a few more steps until you reached the floor of the building.

This building was about 20 feet long by 13 feet and fairly lofty. At the end of the School near the entrance were the four surplice cupboards. Above these cupboards was fixed a bookcase containing the School library. The books were old and musty, and the boys generally had no literary appetite for them. Over the mentelpiece was an old portrait of Henry Purcell. There were three form desks in the School, and with a blackboard you have the whole of the furniture of the defunct Choristers' School. Our school hours, unfortunately, were very limited, as our Organist, Mr James Turle, took us for choir practice every morning from 9 o'clock until about 9.45. We then went along to the School to be robed for service, entering the Abbey near on 10 o'clock to form up in procession. It was after morning service that school actually commenced. The first session was from 11 o'clock to 1 o'clock, and then an hour for dinner or lunch. This meal we provided for ourselves—more's the pity. We had a very little school from 2 o'clock until time for afternoon service. There might be a very casual assembly after this service, but not very often. Our preparation work was not very serious; so far as school was concerned it was a very happy-go-lucky life in one respect. I ought to mention Mr Turle had the first call upon us, and often he would knock at school door in the middle of lessons and say he wanted us for more music practice, and so school was disbanded for the time being. We were stirred to excitement occasionally when Dean Stanley would quietly knock at the school door to visit us and take us through any lesson that happened to be in hand. The Dean was so good and painstaking that he always went away wreathed in smiles. One can never forget the Dean Stanley of that time.

So far, I have not mentioned any space for recreation or exercise for the Choristers. This was intermittent, a few games of football in the field in Dean's Yard and an occasional game of cricket in Vincent Square sufficing. As the boys did not board at the school, we found time to indulge any further sport to our liking, swimming, running, jumping, etc. We did not do so badly, and in our annual cricket match with the Chapel Royal boys I recollect some very good cricket on both sides. This match, played on Vincent Square, was quite an event, and caused a fair amount of interest among the Abbey folk. One of our alto singers, Mr Robert Barnby, always provided a good lunch for both teams, also presenting us with a brand new cricket ball to be used in the match. We did the thing in style—our umpire was Ted Berrington, a Middlesex professional and son of the old Abbey Verger (West Door). We found the fee of half-a-guinea for umpire perhaps with some difficulty and self-sacrifice. We had a fair sprinkling of visitors and had much enjoyment. The match had to be played between the morning and afternoon services, and again resumed after the latter service.

During these years Charles Dickens was buried in the Abbey. A lucky chance has preserved the reactions of a chorister which reminds us of the warning, 'a chiel's takin' notes!'

We boys saw the cortège pass through the precincts of the Abbey before noon, but only those closely connected with the great novelist were allowed to witness the ceremony inside the Abbey, but directly the service was over we were allowed to view the grave. On the Sunday following the funeral, there was the usual funeral service given at the Abbey for the Great. Dean Stanley preached the sermon, and took as his text the story of Dives and Lazarus. There was an immense and varied congregation, and at times the feelings of many of those present were carried away with enthusiasm and spasmodic grief as the Dean discoursed on the character and goodness of Dickens towards his fellow men.

Unfortunately the sermon was marred somewhat because of the extreme hoarseness of the Dean, who frequently had to be relieved by taking a mixture he had in the pulpit.

Charles Dickens perhaps appeals most to cathedral men and cathedral boys in his *Mystery of Edwin Drood*. There is plenty of evidence that he took many of his characters from life; and in 'Drood' we get the Dean, Lay Vicar, and Verger—all types to the cathedral boy. As an ordinary man criticising, I do not think the character of the Lay Vicar, 'Jasper', could possibly exist; I have met and known many lay vicars in my time, but none had the vagaries or vulgar vices of a Jasper.

On Maundy Thursday, 1871, took place the first permance in England of Bach's *St Matthew Passion* (*Musical Times*, July 1, 1907).

Another account is worth quoting concerning the years 1870-4, as it takes a different view on certain important matters.

The Choir consisted of sixteen boys, eight a side, and subdivided into eight seniors and eight juniors. A number of practising boys were held in reserve to fill vacancies, usually drilled on Fridays, when the service was unaccompanied. On joining the choir, each boy had to supply his own surplice. This necessitated two at least, because a clean one was required for Sunday mornings.

All lived at home, most of them not far away, and they had to attend a daily practice at nine a.m. every day except Sundays. School began after the 10 a.m. service, lasted until 1, when an hour was allowed for lunch. School 2-2.45, then service at 3, a fair amount of home lessons to be brought to school next day.

Boys were provided with mortar boards during these years, as previously there had been considerable variations in headgear. This happened shortly after the change of schoolmasters when, on the retirement of Mr Sanders, Mr Shiel was appointed; a very welcome change all round, as many of the Abbey boys on leaving had to go to school again.

This change was undoubtedly brought about by the Rev. Troutbeck who, like Mr Shiel, came from Manchester, and took a great interest in the boys.

The Dean and his wife Lady Augusta Stanley also took a deep interest in the boys.

During this time occurred the Thanksgiving Service at St Paul's Cathedral for the recovery of the Prince of Wales (afterwards King Edward VII) from a very serious illness. The funeral of David Livingstone, the visits of the Tsar of Russia, who was later assassinated, and the Shah of Persia, caused welcome diversions, and especially interesting were the visits of the German Imperial Family who came regularly about once a year, usually to the Sunday afternoon service.

In the months of June and July the Sunday evening services were held in the Nave. On these occasions the choir consisted of ten of the Abbey boys and ten from the Temple Church, while there was a voluntary choir of gentlemen consisting of about fifteen on each side.

In or about 1873 there was a special invitation to visit Windsor, and the boys were shown the Castle, the Dairy, and the Aviary under the guardianship of Mr Shiel. At the same time, a gentleman unconnected with the Abbey obtained permission for the boys to use the boats which could be rowed on St James's Park lake. He also paid for them to use the swimming baths in Great Smith Street. These were greatly enjoyed in the summer time, and the latter privilege is still appreciated almost a hundred years later.

The last first-hand account of these years comes from the great tenor Edward Lloyd and is taken from an article contributed by him to the newspapers:

I was only seven years of age when I joined the choir of Westminster Abbey, under James Turle, the Abbey organist, who took me under his special care and had a great deal to do with my ultimate success. They were very happy days at the Abbey. I served as a probationer for twelve months, and was then entered as a full chorister. After a few years I became one of the first four, until at last I was promoted to head boy. The Dean was very kind to us, and in the evening would frequently invite us to the Abbey to play at 'bob-apple'. You know the game! An apple is suspended on a string and is set in motion, your hands are tied behind your back, and you try to bite the apple. The Dean was as merry as any of us, and revelled in securing as big an apple as possible.

I met many choir boys who have since become famous. In those early days Sir John Stainer was a senior boy at St Paul's, and we frequently met at the rooms of the old Madrigal Society in Lyle Street, where for our singing we were rewarded with a glass of port, a buttered biscuit, and two shillings. The two shillings were invariably spent before I got home.

I also met Sir Arthur Sullivan and Cellier playing at cricket. The boys of the Chapel Royal, St Paul's, and Westminster frequently opposed each other with bat and ball. Sullivan was my elder. Cellier was always the life and soul of us all at cricket, a thorough good fellow, though he did bowl me out once.

Although my voice may be said never to have really broken, I left the Abbey when fifteen years of age, and went to a school in Southwark.

Edward Lloyd was often one of those who came under the critical view of Cornetto di Basso, otherwise known as Bernard Shaw, who wrote of him:

11 March 1890. The large audience of the Crystal Palace on Saturday may be claimed for Mr Hamish MacCunn or for Wagner, according to bias. My own opinion is that the attraction was Mr Edward Lloyd.

Chapter Eighteen

THE SPAN OF 'WESTMINSTER' BRIDGE

I

FOR THE REMINISCENCES concerned with the years 1890 to 1895 no one has been so helpful as Mr Harold Bristol, who with a remarkable memory has corroborated, and supplied, much valuable information. He joined the choir in 1890 at the age of ten. The years of his presence there were typical and yet saw important changes.

The Choir House at the beginning was on the north side of Little Smith Street. In the basement kitchen was chiselled the name of one of William Pitt's friends. The house was about three hundred years old according to tradition and had certainly seen better days. There was one painted iron bath with an old coffee tin for the purpose of scooping off the blackbeetles which came when the earliest bathers turned on the hot water. Fortunately the water was so hot that the visitors did not long survive. Even so an occasional one might come popping up. A washing basin was set on the street side of the house, which was a dingy barn of a place.

The boys watched with great interest the new school which was being built for them across the road on the south side, and there were no regrets when the move took place.

Before that, however, there was a dramatic incident. Mr Harold Grant, now organist of Frome Parish Church, remembers the Headmaster, one evening, coming in hastily during a gale, saying, 'Now then, pack up your machinery and away with you.' Within an hour, they had all been dispersed to relations and friends, who fortunately did not live far away. The gale had become so threatening that he was afraid the house would collapse.

It did not fall; but when it was pulled down, a man was killed, as the house had been propped up and all that was required to bring it down was a rope round the wall end.

Until the new building was completed the boys attended only for services and practices, but they were re-housed in time to see the exciting demolition across the road.

The new establishment was of the solid plain type which was popular with the contemporary London School Board, but was a decided step towards the present superior buildings.

The juniors went to bed at 9 p.m. and the seniors at 9.30 p.m. On Saturdays they were allowed at times to go home: and zero hour for their return was the last stroke of Big Ben at nine o'clock. The same practice obtains today, though the hour is now seven. In the eighteen-nineties they might have to run the gauntlet of tipsy revellers.

The school possessed a well-stocked library in which the works of Kingsley and Henty were prominent, with those of Fenimore Cooper. Chess, draughts, and bagatelle were the main indoor recreations. Outdoor games around the school were confined to the small asphalt playground where the favourites were rough: Hop Barging and Jump-Jimmy-Knacker.

On Sunday mornings between the end of the morning services and dinner at 1 p.m., the boys were allowed to wander on their own, the favourite rendezvous being the trains at Charing Cross, Victoria or even Waterloo. Occasionally their popularity would wane temporarily and then the boys would induce spine-chilling thrills upon themselves by creeping into the Adelphi Arches, which even now can arouse morbid interest.

When the weather was unfit for football or cricket, they would be taken on walks, sometimes even as far afield as Kensington Gardens. Often it was the stroll in St James's Park, where once they met the Prime Minister, W. E. Gladstone.

School work, as regards languages (apart from Latin) consisted of French and German. At the prize-giving, plays in those languages were performed. The Headmaster, who was said to speak six languages, was also adept at mental arithmetic, at which he was unconquerable. There was one unforgotten occasion when he was defeated. Before the day was out however another lesson was devoted (and it was the only time it ever occurred) to a second spell of mental arithmetic, from which Mr Shiel emerged triumphant and smiling.

His method of teaching drawing consisted in choosing an etching of a building (it was usually that), placing it on an easel and moving the blackboard on to another easel beside it. He would then map out the principal sections on the blackboard and the boys had to copy it on to the large sheets of paper he had distributed. When the main details were in place he would complete the rest with almost mathematical exactitude.

His wife, a large woman, was matron. There was a maid named Jane, who was summoned to smear the boys' hair with a vile yellow pomade which was universally hated. In order to avoid it they would wet the hair with water, but it always dried too soon, whereupon Jane would be summoned and, furious at having to use the pomade, would plaster it thickly on the hair to the great detriment of the school cap.

The school servant, named Gates, was a big, stolid man, dark, with mutton chop whiskers, always wearing a green baize apron. He used to hand round the plates at breakfast time and would collect the empties. He made no sign of impatience at any time, even when the boys twisted their dinner plates as he took them, so that his fingers might land in the mustard. He never gave them away, and used to clean their boots.

The matron, Mrs Shiel, had an excellent appetite, and was especially partial to vegetables so that it was calculated that those on her plate rose to a height of two inches above the line of plates ready for the second course. When she began, the watchers would say, 'Top off!'; 'Half gone!'; finally, as she scraped the plate, 'All gone!'

Whenever possible they played cricket between afternoon service and tea time. The quickest way to Vincent Square lay through an appalling area, but time was urgent. They would run through the worst part, but even so the stench was dreadful. They always walked fast or trotted, except when the Master would check his stride and demonstrate special strokes with his walking stick. Newspapers would be bought for the cricket scores. On Wednesday, when the men alone sang the service, Vincent Square was in use by Westminster School, so that the choristers would form up into a crocodile and walk to Battersea Park. In the long summer days they would take the penny steamer down the river, and play for hours. Matches were held amongst themselves, often cantoris against decani. The only exception was a match with the Chapel Royal, St James's, who were the visitors. Then one day, a wealthy friend of the choir (Mr Jackson by name) suggested for the greater collaboration of the school with the boys of St Paul's Cathedral, that an annual match be played between the two choir schools.

The first game was played on the Crystal Palace Ground and it was a tremendous thrill to walk down bat in hand from a pavilion before an admiring throng. It was all done in great style with real white-coated umpires.

This first game led to the annual meetings between the

schools which are keenly contested, and the Jackson Cup has been followed by other cups for cricket, football and athletics. The separate and extra-splendid Jackson Cup is held by the school winning the majority of sports in any given year.

But an outstanding match of those years, and one of the most interesting of any year, began in the organ loft.

One day in June 1894 there appeared in one of the daily papers the following notice:

It would be interesting to know the real author of the playful notice posted a day or two since at the side of the organ upon which the Gresham Professor of Music presides at Westminster Abbey. It ran as follows:

'The Great or Swell occupants of the Organ Loft invite the Choir (if they can descend Solo) to a friendly Manual and Pedal exercise called Cricket. Every player is requested to bring a Full Score, and it is hoped many runs will be executed, although no "Great Shakes" are expected. P.S. A surgeon will attend.'

Its author is clearly lost in the Organ Loft. He would be a valuable acquisition to some of the Comic Papers.

It is to be assumed that Dr (later Sir Frederick) Bridge was the composer of the note. He certainly entered into the spirit of the occasion with great enthusiasm. There must have been an usually large number of deputies in the choir that day as so many of the gentlemen were away. It had been intended originally that the opponents' team should consist solely of Vicars Choral, but portliness prevailed so widely that two of the boys were borrowed to help with the fielding and bowling.

Sir Frederick's deputy at the organ was Dr, later Sir Walter, Alcock. He had a feeling that exception might be taken to the notice. He therefore got up very early and, reaching the Abbey at 7 a.m., he removed it. When (as

THE ABBEY CHOIR, 1888-9

Back Row: Jarman, Egerton, Stanley Roper, Clinton, Mansbridge, Murray, ———, Burnett, E. Bristol

Third Row; Wilson, ———, ———, Thompson, Mills, Pye, ———, Court, Finlay Dunn

Second Row; Harper Kearton, William Shiel (Headmaster), Carter, Scharteau, Dan Price, Robert Hilton

Front Row: Brown, Dalziel, Rev. Flood Jones, Dr Bridge, Sexton, Winter

Alcock was correct in his premonition), one of the clergy, accompanied by a verger, arrived to find the offending notice, it had already disappeared, and the whole thing was dismissed as 'another of those Press stories'. This sequel was told only many years after the death of the principal persons concerned.

The day of the match was gloriously fine without a spot of rain, with white fleecy clouds occasionally lessening the heat. The party went by train to Wendover in Buckinghamshire where elaborate preparations had been made at the famous Red Lion Hotel. It was in those days run by Mr Joseph Holland who had a large and very capable family. They successfully staffed it.

Behind was a lovely meadow in which the wicket had been trimly set. Not even Dingley Dell could exceed such a sight, was the opinion of the boys, nor could even Mr Pickwick be more benign than good Doctor Bridge.

The whole day was an immense success; but, as is often the case, there were two minor tragedies. The first was when the good-looking tenor, Edward Branscombe, acquitting himself nobly as a wicket-keeper was hit in the eye with a bumping ball, and bore for some days after, in spite of the usual remedy, a splendid black eye which caused much amusement when he fulfilled his more professional engagements.

The other was even more deplorable. Dr Bridge had come in to bat and had received, as was his due, much applause on his way to the wicket. Everyone, even the bowlers, genuinely wished him to make a good score. Harold Bristol was fielding near the wicket, and could not help seeing

that the very first ball sent down was a no-ball. The umpire however failed to spot it. Dr B. got it well in the middle of his bat and, with a resounding smack that must have given him a thrill, lifted it well into the long field—surely for four—but by the worst possible luck it went straight into

the hands of a surprised fielder and stuck there! Universal
regret as the Doctor went out and I keeping a discreet
silence as to the no-ball for how was I, a mere boy, to
challenge the umpire, a man in a proper white coat? I
never told Dr Bridge about his bad luck and sometimes
regret I didn't. I think he would have enjoyed it.

Good as the game was, luncheon and tea fully equalled it
and I can still remember the good things we had and the
convivial happy spirit that prevailed. There was a sirloin of
beef worthy of its knighthood, Yorkshire pudding, horse-
radish sauce, roast chickens with the usual trimmings and
apple tart with lashings of cream, trifle, custard, etc. etc.
For tea there must have been other good things but all has
faded except the enormous bowls of strawberries and cream
in great jugs.

The lunch was wisely preceded by the singing of 'Non
nobis, Domine'. Within the last few months one of the late
Mr Holland's daughters has written to suggest that it was
Raspberry and Currant Pie, not apples in June, and that
there were 'Aylesbury Ducks, such as we do not get in these
days of poor feeding for the birds'.

The Queen's Westminsters' Volunteers used to hold their
annual Church Parade in the Abbey. Harold Bristol had a
cousin in the Regiment and after the service it was his
proud privilege to meet him at the canteen and enjoy a
'real' lemonade all fizzy and sparkling. Then after a walk in
the park with the cousin-in-uniform, he would return to
the Choir House feeling more self-important even than the
boy who had collected the largest list of engine numbers.

Several of the boys of that period remember the Thames
as an indispensable part of life at the Abbey. The penny
steamers on the way back from cricket in Battersea Park
were a delight. In the winter time, with the fog signals
sounding every few minutes at times, it was a depressant.

It could be forbidding too, as on the occasion when they were walking along Millbank and saw the body of a drowned man lying on a barge.

There was also the winter when the river was almost frozen over and—shades of Evelyn and Pepys!—large blocks of ice came floating down and remained blocked and unable to get down on the tidal waters. Then there was much sliding and skating on St James's Park and the Serpentine. But the choristers were never allowed to join in.

Dr Bridge had been working for some time on a system of musical gestures for the easier understanding of music. Thus, two fingers placed across two fingers indicated a sharp: a thumb and forefinger turned into an oval and placed at the base of the left forefingers, stood for a flat.

At the lectures the boys would be primed to laugh at the right time. A favourite part of the lecture was when the eight boys chosen were lined up, each representing a note, and this he would sing as the Doctor pointed at him—doh, ray, me. They would then 'walk the scale', making a full step forward for a tone and a half step from a semi-tone. Once Bridge challenged Harold Bristol to sing less than a semi-tone, having first told the audience that it could not be done. The boy tried his best and still vows that he succeeded. The only comment was 'That's flat!' The 'notes' would then be formed into line and he would play tunes on them by pointing his baton.

The lectures were much enjoyed, although jokes made at their expense in front of girls' school audiences sometimes made them blush; but there is no doubt that it helped those boys who, later in life, had to appear on the concert platform.

Dr Bridge was expatiating once on his 'gestures' to his friends at the Royal College of Music, with demonstrations. The group was suddenly and quietly joined by Sir

Charles Villiers Stanford, whose centenary was celebrated in 1952. 'Why, Bridge,' he said, 'you've left out consecutive fifths.' And he extended his ten fingers from the end of the tip of his nose.

On the evening of the 20th May 1890 they went to the Holborn Restaurant to take part in the singing of Tallis's 40-part motet at the hundred and fiftieth anniversary of the Madrigal Society. Bridge conducted and the motet was encored. The undertaking had required most careful organization and rehearsal, and each boy was delighted to receive, besides refreshments, a beautifully bound copy signed by the President, Lord Beauchamp, and by the Secretary, Edward Street.

Occasionally they went as far afield as Rochester where, after singing, they were entertained at the famous Bull Inn.

They used to be lent to St Mark's, North Audley Street, where the Vicar was their own Canon Duckworth. Afterwards their surplices were crowded into fewer cases than they had brought, so that the remainder might carry the fruit, which the wealthy congregation had given them to eat, back to the Choir House.

On one occasion they went to the Chapel of Lambeth Palace, beside the battered ruins of which their successors now play cricket and enjoy scouting and cubbing, thanks to the kindness of His Grace the Lord Archbishop of Canterbury. On that occasion there was a great Convocation of Bishops, and the boys could not help noticing the unusual accompaniment of many gruff-sounding elderly voices who made up the bulk of the small congregation.

At the Convocation of Bishops Harold Bristol, then head chorister, had the privilege of carrying the train of the Primate of All England. The magnificent procession formed up in the Jerusalem Chamber of the Abbey and proceeded to Henry VII's Chapel, where the service was held. The

boy waited outside until it was time to return to the
Jerusalem Chamber, and afterwards received half a crown
by way of reward. Two or three years previously the Archbishop's chaplain had accidentally given the boy train-
bearer a penny by mistake. His disappointment did not last
long, however, as a day or two later the chaplain came back
and handed him an envelope which contained not only a
half-crown but a toothpick as well. The boy, believing he
had been given the Archbishop's very own toothpick, trea-
sured it as a semi-sacred relic.

It was in these years that the now most impressive
Maundy Service was first held in the Abbey. At their first
appearance amongst the Abbey boys the dainty little coins
were the objects of jealous admiration and justifiable pride.

Amongst episcopal preachers in the Abbey was Bishop
Philips Brooks of Massachussets, whose rapid delivery at
sermon time was the despair of reporters. Another Bishop
had a whistling S; while yet another was so well rounded
that when going to preach in the Nave pulpit he was unable
to get up the stairs and had to resort to the Lectern, from
which he delivered a forthright and pungent sermon.

Another visitor who caused even more interest and, un-
wittingly, much trouble was the then Prime Minister, W. E.
Gladstone. The boys were so impressed at seeing him that
they could not help at times looking in his direction. After
the service Dr Bridge caned the lot. Apparently he would
have done the same if Lord Salisbury had been present
'though with less pleasure, the Doctor being a good Tory'.

In connection with Bridge's political leanings, it is worth
recalling a rhyme of his at one Old Boys' Meeting. As
many will remember, Henry Labouchère was member of
Parliament for the Abbey Division. The Organist and
Master of the Choristers profoundly disagreed with his
political views. Accordingly, for one Old Boys' Meeting he

composed a parody of 'Sally in our Alley' the last lines of which were,

> *But when his seven long years are out*
> *Why then we'll bury Labbey,*
> *And then how eas-i-labbey'll lie,*
> *But not in our Abbey.*

Earlier that evening the boys had been subjected to a most ingenious device. They were given free time, lasting about three quarters of an hour, in the library and prep room. There they were allowed to 'let off steam'. At the end of the time, they were sent out, the windows opened for a few minutes, then closed again, and lo! the room was pleasantly warm for the Old Boys' Meeting. The twenty choirboys very much enjoyed these evenings, at which no one could have been more congenial than Dr Bridge. The meeting revolved in all its hubbub around him, and he would sit at the piano and sing humorous songs, often of his own composition especially for the occasion.

One of these, called *The Goslings*, was particularly popular and brought forth laughter and applause as he brought it to an end to the strains of the Dead March in *Saul*.

Afterwards he would persuade them to sing a part song such as *It was a lover and his lass*, or some Elizabethan favourite. Those were probably his happiest days at the Abbey, when he was at his peak musically, and so much had been achieved.

At times boys might be allowed with him in the organ loft during some of his evening recitals, if they were not themselves taking part. Then the full mystery of the Abbey would envelope them, and the loft was illuminated by one small light. The columns would soar into the darkness of the roof. Then Handel's Largo might be played as a violin solo; or a quartet would sing an item from Handel's *Ode to St Cecilia's Day*.

Even about Bridge's appointment there was a story. It seems that the final choice for the Abbey lay between Bridge and Dr Hiles. In the trial anthem, Dr Hiles set the words *The Lord will comfort Zion*. Bridge preferred *The Lord hath chosen Zion*. As it was, and often is, customary to abbreviate titles, the anthem was printed on the service paper as *The Lord hath chosen . . . Bridge*.

When a boy was admitted to the Choir School and went along to his first rehearsal, Bridge would look at him sternly and ask, 'Where is your shaving brush? You can't be a member of this choir unless you have a shaving brush. Kindly see that your father rectifies the matter when you go home on Saturday.' The dismayed child would often do as he was bid, and the irritated Headmaster would buy the brush from any boy who believed and obeyed the command.

Bridge had a cane which he called 'Tickletoby'. 'King Arthur had a sword called Excalibur. I have mine and I call it "Tickletoby".' In those days he used the cane very sparingly; but it was necessary to replace it, as it occasionally made a very useful poker for the fire in the practice room.

Above this room was Bridge's house, into the study of which protruded a speaking tube connecting it with the practice room. On one occasion the boys were awaiting the person who was to take the practice when the whistle from the tube sounded. Court, a boy who was standing next to it, had never used it before. Unnerved, he did not know what to do and said, 'What shall I do?' All the rest shouted, 'Blow, man, blow.' And he blew as hard as he could. As soon as the turmoil had subsided, contact was made with Bridge who angrily demanded that the offender should be sent up to his study with a cane. The unfortunate Court went, but Bridge did not cane him, nor did he afterwards ever refer to the incident.

The clergy included Dean Farrer who, they understood,

was the author of a series of brilliant boys' books. It is of interest here to remember that the author of *Eric—or Little by Little*, was the father of the lady who married Bishop Montgomery and became the mother of Viscount Montgomery of Alamein. Canon Farrer, as he was then, would have a most fatherly manner when he encountered the boys, and would walk along talking to them with a hand on a boy's shoulder. He and Canon Gore would invite them to tea, and would give them books on their leaving the choir. Another of the clergy had a glass eye, a fact which remained fixed in the boys' memory.

Two corporate visits were paid to Canon Farrer's house. On the first they recorded on Edison's phonograph—which was then the object of intense curiosity—a setting of Farrer's carol, *Christmas Bells*, to music by Bridge. A boy then sang a solo, and the record was completed by Farrer's reading of a poem. The second occasion was when he invited them to hear the prodigy, Mark Hambourg, then aged nine, play the piano.

The parties at the Deanery at Christmas were truly splendid. The Dean (Bradley) and his whole family would welcome the boys, and were kindness itself. The tea was huge and always there was some special attraction, such as a dwarf represented by a man cleverly disguised, or a Father Christmas, and always there was a great bran pie within whose sawdust lay a large number of presents which were distributed with sweetness and grace. Behaviour was excellent and it became the custom, whenever afterwards manners were slipping, to say, 'You wouldn't do that at the Deanery!'

The Rev. John Thynne, a son of the Lord John Thynne who had been Sub-Dean at Queen Victoria's coronation, was a Canon; and his family used to sit in the row of stalls which stretched in front of the choir. One of the daughters,

Agatha, was an outstandingly beautiful young lady and was
the object of much unspoken boyish devotion. One of her
silent admirers was greatly gratified when he chanced to
overhear his Schoolmaster, Mr Shiel, and his cricket coach,
Leonard Box, saying what a remarkably beautiful girl she
was.

This same boy was considerably hurt when Bridge one
day took him aside and accused him of not working as hard
as he might. The hurt lay in the fact that the beautiful
Agatha was sitting directly in front, and it was for her that
he was singing his heart out.

Accordingly he sang up; but so loudly it seems, that her
mother remarked to Bridge that the boy behind them had a
voice of rather devastating power; whereupon he was moved
over to the other side. This did not matter; as he could then
see all the family and sing for them at the same time.

Once, when using manuscript copies of an unaccompanied
trio, the only guide was a note of approximately forty bars'
rest. The boy member of the trio counted a bar short, and it
so happened that the note was in the favourite part of his
voice in the upper register. The result was that he came in
with such force that he was unaware he was singing alone
until the others joined him.

Esmond Bristol was the elder of the Bristol brothers and
joined the choir in 1888. When he was sixteen he won the
open sight reading competition for the pianoforte at the
Welsh Eisteddfod at Brecon, and studied at the Guildhall
School of Music.

He had a phenomenal memory for sea shanties and could
sing more than a hundred without music. Some of these he
sang at the Inaugural Dinner of the Master Mariners'
Association at the Guildhall, when the Prince of Wales, now
H.R.H. the Duke of Windsor, was in the chair.

The Westminster Glee Singers were then in their prime;

and, as some of the gentlemen of the choir were of their number, often used to practise in the boys' music room. Some of the boys would wait outside the door until the glee singers were in a particularly melodious part, and would then throw open the door and join in with the most appalling yells.

Amongst the generous friends of the early nineties, was the Mr Jackson (who presented the Cup), who used to give a fine silver fruit knife to each of the boys when their time came to leave. Another was a Mr Cunningham, who used yearly to provide a magic lantern show at which, through the dimness, he would talk and comment. During the splendid tea which he provided he would go round, a tall stooping figure with smiling face. One year a boy deliberately missed having any dinner so that he might do greater justice to the spread: but for some reason, which was never explained, on that one occasion, tea was not provided.

Equally a character was a rough old diamond of a Cockney who was engineer-in-charge of the donkey engine, and whom Bridge delighted to honour as his partner in the production of music in the Abbey.

One of the most poignant sights was the wedding of Sir H. M. Stanley to Dorothy Tennant, contrasted in her tall gracious figure and his stooping feebleness (the result of hardship in Africa), with the pair of them passing the grave of David Livingstone, which lies in the middle of the Nave aisle.

For the funeral of Alfred Lord Tennyson, each boy received the sum of 13s. 4d. which was wealth indeed in the year 1892. This was on October 12th. Everything had to be committed to memory; and Bridge, having specially composed the music for *Crossing the Bar*, was naturally anxious that it should be well sung. The other anthem was

The Silent Voices by Tennyson set to music by Lady Tennyson and arranged for four voices by Bridge. For the processional parts of the service the music of Croft and Purcell was used, the only hymn being Heber's *Holy, Holy, Holy*.

Another impressive occasion was the International Service held for the Y.M.C.A. The order of service was printed in nine languages. One of the hymns was *Onward Christian Soldiers*. Bridge, knowing only too well the tendency of congregations to drag out this particular hymn, had specially impressed on the boys and men that they must not let it happen. Up in the organ loft were six specially engaged trumpeters, who were similarly enjoined to keep the pace going. He with the organ would see that with the aid of the trumpeters, it did not slacken. All was in vain. The vast congregation wanted thoroughly to enjoy itself (and they would have gone on singing it indefinitely), and in the end the congregation won.

Madame Albani and Helen Quest were the soloists in a most memorable performance of Mendelssohn's *Hymn of Praise*. Albani sang 'Prahse' quite unblushingly on the top B flat.

As the result of a letter in *The Daily Telegraph*, the present writer received some notes written in 1920 and 1921 by the late Fritz Hart who was born in 1874, entered the choir on March 14, 1885 and left on April 4, 1889. He died in 1949 but fortunately his widow had preserved his notes and sent them from Honolulu, Hawaii. Fritz Hart was a Fellow of the Royal College of Music and lived in Australia for almost a quarter of a century, as conductor of the Melbourne Symphony Orchestra, as well as being the Director of the Albert Street Conservatorium where he worked with Dame Nellie Melba. In 1931 he came as guest conductor, during Australia's summer, to Hawaii. He returned yearly until 1937, when he became permanent conductor, and died there on July 9, 1949.

When he first came to the Abbey, Hart remembered how very impressed he was by the sight of Henry V's saddle, helmet and shield, and how they helped to pass even the long and tedious sermons.

He remembered best a certain afternoon service when the choir was augmented by a surpliced man with iron-grey curly hair, short and of swarthy complexion, who was waiting under the organ screen and joined the procession as it went by. From his place on the decani side, Hart noticed that the stranger was immediately behind him. The anthem was Mendelssohn's *Be thou faithful unto death*, and the solo was sung by the object of the boys' very natural curiosity. He never afterwards forgot the tones of that superb voice. Both in its soft and loud notes it had the quality of a true trumpet tone. Such was its resonance that the boy could imagine the Abbey walls rattled at the last note.

Only a few weeks later, a month or two at the most, the Abbey choir sang at the singer's funeral. On that occasion Spohr's quartet, *Blest are the departed*, was sung by Albani and Patey, Edward Lloyd and Charles Santley. In the days of his prime that great singer had died and his name was Joseph Maas.

During Hart's years in the choir there was often a shortage of copies, as many of the older anthems were only in manuscript, so that he would sometimes make out as many as six extra copies under cover of his surplice during the long lessons. Occasionally he had to slip across to the other side with these, hoping that Bridge was not watching. If he were, he never made any comment.

It was the custom when making a transcription of any music for a boy to sign his name at the bottom, and Hart recalled the thrill he received when he saw the name of the great Edward Lloyd at the bottom of the copy from which he himself was to sing that day.

He remembered Charles Santley singing, on another occasion, *Why do the nations* so fervently that his hands and copy book shook with the passionate intensity of his concentration.

Sir Arthur Sullivan stood beside them one day as they sang an unaccompanied anthem which he had arranged from some Russian music. He stood very quietly and conducted with his hand.

Once a year the Abbey boys used to journey to St Paul's Cathedral for a performance of Bach's *St Matthew Passion* during Holy Week. Every year to the end of his life he would be impelled by memory every Good Friday to play the chorus 'In tears of grief we here recline'.

Wesley's *Wilderness* was the great favourite; and there was one afternoon service at which Mendelssohn's two daughters were present, two modest little figures in black for whom the choir sang *Hear My Prayer*, with its ever popular solo, 'O for the wings of a dove'. Afterwards Bridge introduced them to the boys.

Sterndale Bennett was popular, but it was Wesley's *Wilderness* which was the prize, with its superlative last section, 'And sorrow and sighing shall flee, shall flee away'. This would bring tears to the eyes of many a soloist; nor has this been unknown even in the twentieth century.

II

Not always was there perfect behaviour. At the end of the nineteenth century there existed on each side of the aisle a pew, set in front of the choir stalls. In these pews were members of the congregation. Schoolgirls used at times to occupy them, and once, during a long sermon, one of the boys noticed two pigtails dangling tantalizingly in front of him, and quietly drew the two plaits of hair around the iron candle stand and fastened them together. The beating he received afterwards stung but the pleasures of memory stayed.

Sometimes the congregation provided the amusement. One man rose to his feet on the opening words of the First Lesson and began to read instead of the Canon in Residence. He was a huge fellow with a big voice, and there was a rough and tumble before the vergers were able to remove him.

Another oddity was the man who sat in a sweeping cloak of black until a certain point in the service when he arose, flung back the cloak and revealed himself clothed in scarlet tights. He stood in the middle of the aisle capering and yelling 'Hell! Hell! And the Wrath to Come!' until he too was removed from the delighted sight of the choristers.

Far more serious was the time towards the end of the nineteenth century when a mass of unemployed men forced their way into the Abbey. Great beams had been lashed across the entrance from the transepts to the altar steps, but even these seemed to be in danger of being burst by the great press of men. The master in charge of the boys trembled for their safety. The men shouted and cat-called all through the service, although the organ was loud enough temporarily to drown them. The only time there was quiet came when during the anthem a boy sang a solo. Utterly unforgettable was the stillness broken only by the clear untrembling voice. Immediately afterwards the shouting broke out again, but the safety of the boys was never again in doubt.

A recurrent source of disorder and amusement was the militant movement for Women's Suffrage. The Suffragettes' main target in the Abbey was Canon Wilberforce. Knowing he was opposed to them, the women would pop up from their seats in different parts of the Abbey whenever he was reading the Lesson or was due to preach. 'Votes for Women! Votes for Women!' would echo through the church as the demonstrators were removed. Finding themselves too easily expelled, they would chain themselves to the seats, whereupon the vergers lifted chair and woman and dumped them outside.

Serious damage might have been done to the Coronation Chair on one corner of which a small bag was surreptitiously hung. The explosion did little material damage except to the corner, though it brought down a great quantity of dust, but an aged verger who happened to be standing nearby was so shaken that he had to retire and died not long afterwards.

In the last quarter of the nineteenth century, and coincident with the appointment of Frederick Bridge, there was a change in the processional procedure.

Deanery, Westminster   Dec. 13, 1875

The Choristers and the gentlemen of the Choir are to precede the clergy and the Dean in leaving the Choir: the Schoolmaster to precede the Choristers, and the Choristers, on leaving the Choir, to proceed to the West End of the Nave and then to return by the North aisle, and pass out of the West Cloister door, and go to the North Cloister to their schoolroom.

A. P. Stanley, Dean.

An indication of contemporary prices is given by another entry in the same book.

Fees in lieu of Fittings at Westminster Abbey 1874, April 18th Dr Livingstone's Funeral,

	£	s.	d.
Precentor	1	1	0
Organist Mr Turle	1	1	0
18 men of Choir at 21/-	18	18	0
22 boys at 10/6 each	11	11	0

An old chorister who was present at that funeral remembered Livingstone's 'black boy' standing before the grave, and felt sure that he saw him cast something into the grave. This ex-chorister was that William Kay Waterson who, born on December 22, 1860, came to lunch at the school in February 1951, and afterwards pointed out the earlier sites of the school.

He also remarked, as have many others, what an astonishing likeness there was in the figure of Dean Stanley on his tomb to its original; and that the boys often said they expected him to get up and join on the end of the procession.

When the choristers' schoolroom was not occupied, the key had to be kept at the Porter's Lodge, although the senior boy retained it during the hours of divine service.

Before 1873 the boys slept at home. They brought their midday meal, and sometimes cooked it over the fire of the schoolroom. In or about the year 1873 a charge was made and a full hot meal was provided at a cookshop in Marsham Street. Tea was given in the schoolroom, if the boys were kept back for an evening service on special occasions such as the Sons of the Clergy Festival, or if they took part in madrigals or glee singing at a banquet or similar gathering. The practice of using the choristers for secular entertainment was of course a common one and in one form or another went back to the Reformation. Through the glee clubs and societies of the nineteenth and eighteenth centuries by way of Mr Handel and Signor Buononcini, it is easy to trace the descent from the 'little eyases' and 'squeaking Cleopatras' who might boy the Elizabethan players and oust them from the boards.

We are reminded of what lies below the surface not only of the Abbey but around it, by the fact that Vincent Square is the site of Westminster Pest House set up by the City of

Choristers in 1890: from WESTMINSTER ABBEY by Loftie
and Railton

Westminster at the time of the Great Plague of 1665. Amongst the bones and skulls dug up there are clay pipes, perhaps smoked by those engaged in the ghastly work of mass burial, in an attempt to keep off infection. This reminds one of the occasion when the Record Office was moved from the Chapter House. The bottom of the floor underneath the great mass of papers stank with rot and with the bodies of putrescent rats, and this was cleared by three workmen so heavily sodden in whisky that they were just able to use the necessary spades in clearing the place.

Regular members of the congregation were generous, sending sweets, taking favoured boys on visits to the tuck-shops, and paying bills for a party to the Marsham Street swimming baths, a bare fifty feet from the school at that time. Others took them on the boats in St James's Park.

The school, newly made into a boarding establishment in 1869, consisted of twelve choristers, fully fledged and on the establishment; four probationers who sang in the choir every day, and four junior probationers who attended all rehearsals and who were anxious for their seniors to fall ill so that they could take their places. Sickness was rare, although there was one boy who was removed from the school for ill health and died in the following year of what was then called 'stoppage of the bowels', and may have been appendicitis, virtually unknown until the time of Edward VII.

According to the testimony of some contemporary choristers, they were well taught. They found that by doing $1\frac{1}{2}$ hours' 'prep', they were not handicapped in their later education. They were taught French and German, and it is interesting that they were set to act scenes from plays, for example, Molière's *L'Avare*, and *Le Médecin malgré lui*. Latin was not taught.

The old Choir House had two cones outside the door

where link boys used to thrust up their incandescent torches to extinguish them after conducting any visitors there in foggy weather. These torches were of tarred ropes and gave out more smoke and smell than light. The inside of the house was comfortable according to the standards of the day, but the playground was small, approximately ninety feet by thirty.

Passing on down the Dark Cloister, the boys came to the beautiful, and happily still mainly intact, cloister with the fountain in the centre and a miraculous air of stillness. The music room used to be there and the prospect from it must indeed have been beautiful. A *memento mori* was encountered in the tablet erected by the Dean and Chapter to the chorister, Henry Quittendon Roper, (brother of the present organist of the Chapel Royal) who died soon after leaving the choir.

There was a library in the Choir House, including some books which had been presented by Princess Louise. There were two pianos and the practices required were twenty minutes to half an hour once or twice a week, less demanding than nowadays. Apparently no tuition was given, so that it was frequently a question of trial and error. If a boy liked an anthem, he picked out the treble part, and went on from there.

They could on the other hand sing anything on sight. On one occasion in 1875-6 they were asked to go round to sing part of *Judas Maccabaeus* to James Turle, then an old man. He used a very old score with a figured bass and explained to the boys that he preferred it as it left him more or less free with the accompaniment. Turle could, according to Bridge, stretch an octave and four notes.

Practice for the daily services was from 9 a.m. until 9.45 a.m. If there were any spare time, it was spent on learning parts of *Elijah, Creation, Lobgesang, Christmas*

Oratorio, and *A Woman of Samaria*, and these were all performed at various times in the Nave of the Abbey.

The practice room in 'Little Cloisters' was between forty and fifty feet long and fifteen to twenty feet wide. It contained a small two manual pipe organ and a piano. There was only one fireplace and the room was intensely cold in the winter with a smoking fire only just lit, and at times the boys, who had been snowballing, had frozen fingers. Practices were intensely serious, but it is possible to realize now, better than the boys did at the time, what Bridge had to combat and how finely he achieved his aim. The boys in general hated Bach, and disliked, after a hard practice, to have to learn the fugal choruses of the *Christmas Oratorio*. When this was sung in the Nave, one of the boys for dramatic effect was placed in the triforium to sing the echo part in the solo 'Ah! my Saviour', and we may be sure that the Victorian audience greatly admired the result.

The boys were taken on one occasion to hear Jenny Lind sing in the oratorio *A Woman of Samaria*. The boys had sung it in the Abbey, and her husband, Otto Goldschmidt, gave it in St James's Hall. The boys were lent to a rehearsal to give a stiffening to the choir. Jenny Lind sang the solo part only at the rehearsal, as she had not sung in public for many years, but the boys were told to pay particular attention to her, as they would remember it in after years. With the typical prejudice of the young, they found the timbre of her voice very different from their own and did not altogether appreciate her naturally foreign pronunciation as in 'Komm zee a mon', for 'Come see a man'.

That they were prejudiced is well shown in the way they sang Gibbons or Tallis, whom they regarded as 'dreary old codgers', if ever left to themselves. These composers were sung on Fridays, unaccompanied; and the boys considered that this must have some connection with the fact that

227

Friday was a fast day, when one had to do without something good. One day Dr Bridge put on a surplice and, by using a secret trap door from a side aisle (operated by lifting a seat in the stalls), suddenly appeared in the middle of the men. The boys did not discover his presence for some time; but when they did, the singing greatly improved. The repentance came too late however, and each boy received a caning which was well administered.

Toward the end of the nineteenth century the educational development of the boys seems to have been fortuitous, or at least erratic. Work, according to a senior master of the 'eighties, depended very considerably upon the whim of the organist. If he wished to keep the boys for two hours instead of one, time stood still and work began if possible afterwards: but it is only fair to Sir Frederick Bridge to remember that he came to the Abbey in 1875 after a period of truly appalling neglect, when the music of the Church of England was in dire straits. Complete rehearsals were unknown, as the gentlemen of the choir did not consider that their duties required a 'run through'. Again it is necessary for one to remember that this state of affairs was universal. The boys however were trained thoroughly.

Games were never organized from above. The boys at the Abbey seventy years ago were there to sing and their games had to be self-organized. These, as is usual with English boys, were of the jostling, vigorous kind. The nearness of Vincent Square perhaps was even more of a boon than it is now. Cricket had been played there for two hundred years, but the idea of a series of matches against other schools was not entertained.

To offset this there was the generosity of private patrons; wealthy, sometimes titled, persons who frequented the Abbey as a place of worship. It was they who took the boys to 'The Diving Bell', to the Crystal Palace (where an ex-

Abbey chorister was organist after its removal to Sydenham), to Hyde Park, and to the country, then so much nearer than it is now.

At the end of the century the school buildings were a hundred yards or so south-east of their present site, where the southern cliff of Church House now rises. A wide underground garage has its exit exactly where the school entrance used to be. It was a dingy place by all accounts although it had once been the house of William Pitt. To the north was the Abbey beyond Dean's Yard; but to the south there was squalor that accorded with the pages of Dickens. He indeed knew the district well and compared St John's, Smith Square, to a prehistoric monster lying on its back with its four legs sticking up into the air. It is indeed a helpless monster in its present bombed state.

Where Faith House now stands, and sideways to the school, was a filthy public house where in the evenings a squalid woman sang hymns by Moody and Sankey to the accompaniment of an untuned guitar. Fights were frequent and the police never went alone. It is not difficult even now as one walks at night between the bombed houses, raising their ruined emptiness, to see destitute human beings carrying the sores of poverty.

The boys were however inured to a Spartan existence and even flourished. Bullying usually was rare and a lively intelligence provided its own interests. Occasionally there would be cross-country runs, and one of the boys broke a blood vessel which ended his career as a singer. This same boy, a youthful eighty-four in 1952, remembers a contemporary of his who sang a duet with Madame Albani—he singing top A to her top C. This was in an Abbey closed to the public in which Queen Victoria and her family moved in the semi-darkness. When the boy's voice broke, he rested it carefully so that he might sing again as a tenor; but the power never returned and he fell into a decline and died of a broken heart.

Sir Frederick was an exacting, but inspiring, Master of the Choristers. He was known as 'Westminster Bridge' in contradistinction to his brother who was organist at Chester. Many testify that he was often unpredictable. On one occasion while the choir was rehearsing *God is a Spirit*, his voice came quietly from the organ loft, 'All right, gentlemen, all right. You are just half a tone down exactly.'

Once one of his choristers, a boy named Collard, saved the situation. Bridge was about to begin *God Save the Queen* when the boy, recognizing that it was not the Queen, signalled to Sir Frederick who had the presence of mind to change the intended chord in mid-air into the opening of the voluntary which lasted until Her Majesty's arrival.

On the day on which Dr Bridge's knighthood was announced, he entered the Song School, to be greeted with the customary 'Good morning, Dr Bridge'. The Master stood as if thunderstruck, drew back and declared, 'Good morning Dr Bridge? What a greeting! Is that the right and proper way to greet someone whom the Queen delights to honour? Really, boys, really! I shall now leave the room and when I return I hope you will have decided how such a person should be received.' Some wit among the boys thought quickly; and when Bridge came back, he found them lying prostrate on the ground with their faces to the floor.

Boys who came for voice-trials in those days have said how overwhelming was the first view of the Abbey, especially if the candidate approached from the bottom of Parliament Square. Inside there grew up an intimacy in time which made the shadows lean more nearly, and even the figures of Gladstone and Disraeli whom they saw in the flesh faded among the innumerable great.

A favoured boy would be taken by the porter on the

rounds with his hurricane lamp. Then the shadows in cloister and Abbey were less friendly, and the monumental dead would seem to be grinning and grimacing.

The men in the mid-nineteenth century sat on the back row of the centre stalls under the canopies, the boys in the middle row and members of the congregation in front. Candlelight added to the mystique of the Abbey, and anyone who has seen the colours when the candles alone are burning, knows what has been lost in the dulling light of electricity.

The Precentor was the Rev. Flood-Jones, who had a long beard and a habit of closing his eyes while intoning the service. On cantoris side of the choir, the basses were Hilton and Lawler; Hilton a big man with a splendid sandy beard, who gave great point, as he sang lustily, to the words, 'Say to them of a fearful heart', from Wesley's *The Wilderness*; Lawler was an older man, past his hey-day, with a fine reputation behind him. He was black-bearded.

The tenors were Montem Smith who was splendid in declamation and whose voice had a husky quality; and Carter who founded 'Carter's Choir', but whose voice seemed to the boys to be somewhat strident. The altos were a wine merchant named Birch who came up from Brighton every day; and Foster who as a small boy had stood on William IV's dining-table to sing to the guests and whose photograph as one of the singers at Edward VII's coronation appears in *A Westminster Pilgrim*. He was particularly fond of Tallis and Gibbons, and used to say to the boys that Farrant's *If ye love Me* was one of the finest pieces of church music; he must have been a man after Bridge's own heart.

On the Decani side, the basses were Whitehouse, a corpulent figure with a white beard; and Bell, who although small and bandy-legged, had a fine, resonant voice. The tenors were Harper Kearton who was, to one of the boys at least, the only tenor he had ever thoroughly enjoyed hearing. The boy thought that 'a tenor was not a voice but a disease'. The second tenor was Dalzell, but Kearton was the boys' favourite. When the choir were lined up in the nave and waiting to move up into the service, he used to play *God Save the Queen* by squeaking out the notes by pressing the palms of his hands together. The boys naturally tried to copy him, so that it was just as well that the clergy were at their assembly point some distance away. The altos were Sexton and Schartau, both possessing good voices but not liked by the boys, who objected to their singing the solos which they regarded as their due. Sexton possessed black 'mutton-chop' whiskers and a heavy black moustache, and used to sing out of the side of his mouth. The boys considered he 'looked like a tom-cat and sounded like one'; but it is doubtful whether they were very good judges.

The boys used to come into contact with one of the Minor Canons, the Rev. Troutbeck, who was very friendly towards them and used to give 'Penny Readings' and concerts at his church, St John's, Smith Square.

These concerts and readings, at which the boys helped with three and four part glees and part-songs, included such contemporary favourites as Roberti's *The Nights* and Smart's *Coralled Caves of Ocean* and *King Rene's Daughter*. One speciality was Reinechi's *Little Snowdrop*, which Troutbeck had translated from the German and read during the items. The boys liked the music and enjoyed singing it. Mr Troutbeck did many French and German translations for Novello's.

Another of the Minor Canons used always to drop a semitone or more while intoning the Creed or the Confession.

Of the clergy the boys saw little except for special occasions. They saw two Miss Troutbecks and their mother, and the two Misses Flood-Jones. The two latter were large young ladies; but little was seen of their faces as, after the custom of the time, they were heavily veiled when out of doors. Their features were glimpsed only when they lifted their veils to blow their noses or apply a little smelling salts, both of which performances involved much jangling of wrist ornaments and attracted the attention of the boys.

School uniform consisted of the popular Eton suits, superbly designed for chastisement. The 'college caps' or mortar boards were provided by the Dean and Chapter. One wrote 'Golgotha' in the space provided for his name, and was whacked for it. Football, surprisingly it seems nowadays, was played in one of the railed-in fields in St James's Park: and after the boys had seen some bargees swimming quite naked under Westminster Bridge, they wanted to emulate them in the Great Smith Street Baths.

One winter was so severe that they saw great blocks of ice floating down the river, and Dean's Yard, where the Westminster schoolboys were allowed to play football, was turned into a skating rink and was artificially lit. The choristers made slides in their little yard at the Choir House, although they had no skates such as their modern successors have.

They were allowed to go to the Westminster Play of which they understood not a word. They sat in the gallery with the junior school. In front of them sat two of the Queen's Scholars with copies of the script, so that whenever there were amusing lines or topical allusions they could wave canes to and fro. Thereupon the school laughed or applauded.

Victoria Station was a popular port of call where they used to make friends with the drivers of the yellow engines of the London—Brighton Railway. The technical terms concerned with the coupling of wheels, turntables, and the social status of trains were as familiar to them as the scores of oratorios and creeds.

Chapter Nineteen

THE TWENTIETH CENTURY AND
THE WARS

M<small>R AND</small> M<small>RS</small> Shiel retired at Michaelmas 1896, and a Mr Hove, with his wife as matron, took the places of the Shiels. Two years later they were followed by the Rev. R. Carveth Blackmore and his wife, who remained at the School until 1908, though at the end of 1904 he suffered a painful facial paralysis.

Mr Herbert Dawson, a serving officer of two world wars, who has been Organist of St Margaret's, Westminster for the past thirty-three years, came to the Abbey School in 1895. He was in the choir for eight and a half years, and on joining was so tiny that he used to stand on a soap box in the Song School.

His Headmaster was the Rev. Carveth Blackmore whose wife was a most unusual woman; a graduate of Oxford University. The Undermaster was Harold Lake who under the pen-name of Harford wrote the words for *I hear you calling me*.

The Blackmores were progressives, she being in the advance guard of feminists and he a Fabian. Mrs Blackmore used to help boys out of school hours.

On Wednesdays the men of the choir sang Evensong, so that the boys were free after Mattins. In those days the Litany was sung on Wednesdays as well as on Fridays which seemed to the boys to be a rather unnecessary penance, and it was a matter of importance who was Canon in Residence as the length of the Litany might vary considerably.

234

In those years the Precentor was very much the head of the Choir School and had a good deal to do with the time table. Latin had been restored and was taught with mathematics, English, history, geography and French, though there was no time to indulge in scholarship. Plays of necessity were in abeyance, but the introduction of regular exercise was long overdue and most welcome.

On the way to Vincent Square the boys repeatedly saw the owners of vegetable carts take their ponies or donkeys into their ramshackle tenements leaving the carts outside, though this was certainly more humanitarian than the reverse would have been.

The School buildings of those days still stand practically unaltered. They were in good condition, but Tufton Street was a grim thoroughfare, and the boys could still see appalling things on Saturday nights. The din was frightening and drunkenness and fights were the rule. The Westminster boys were still forbidden to use the short cut to Vincent Square and it was only because time was so short for the choristers that they were allowed to go that way—though things were better than in 1863, when cholera was so rife that a black flag was stretched across Marsham Street which lay on the route to the playing fields.

A considerable change was noticeable in the attitude of the clergy, who were friendly again towards the boys, and took a great interest in their welfare, inviting them to tea four at a time.

Still the only connection with Westminster School was the Latin Play, to which they went uncomprehendingly to laugh and applaud in the appropriate places.

During the summer the evening services were held in the Nave; the hymns being displayed on huge posters attached to the columns.

The gentlemen of the choir took monthly turns. They

were twelve in number and could have deputies, provided they were regular and had been approved by authority. On Sundays full attendance was required. The services were simple; broad churchmanship which would offend no one, and it was not until after the World War that the stately-simple ceremonial which is a cathedral's right was introduced.

At the coronation of Edward VII the two daughters of Sir Frederick Bridge sang in the choir. Rehearsal for the coronation was actually in progress when the news came that the King was to have an emergency operation—whereupon the Litany was said and everyone dispersed.

When the postponed ceremony took place it was magnificent; but there was one hitch. Some person in authority mistook an arrival for the King and the great procession was set in motion. It proceeded up the Abbey until the moment when the cry of *Vivat! Vivat!* should come from the King's Scholars of Westminster. It was then discovered what had happened and everyone had to go back and begin again.

Mr Herbert Dawson is one of those who owed his matriculation to Mrs Blackmore after his voice had broken. Bridge would sometimes say to him, 'You can play a hymn. Go and play it.' It was as well that this had happened, because one day Bridge was taken ill, Alcock was away and Stanley Roper was playing at the Chapel Royal. Dawson had to play all the morning services including a Choral Communion to music by Basil Harwood. Halfway through it he received a note from the Precentor, the Rev. Daniell-Bainbridge: 'Bravo! It's going splendidly.'

The Diamond Jubilee of 1897, for another boy, was chiefly remembered for the long and most wearisome march back from St Paul's. Once he sang *O Rest in the Lord* at Evensong and was presented afterwards to Princess Christian who presented him with five shillings. At the Diamond Jubilee of course all the boys' eyes were on 'Bobs' (Lord Roberts) as he marshalled everyone from his white charger.

The Rev. W. B. Dams came to the school from St Paul's Cathedral Choir School to be Headmaster in 1908. He, a member of a family much connected with the Abbey and including his nephew, the present Precentor, stands very much in his own person for the years he was at the school. His departure coincided with the opening of the new Choir House. The practices were still in the dark room in the Little Cloister, connected by the speaking tube with Sir Frederick Bridge. An immense number of anthems and services lined the walls of that now ruined room. Mr G. C. Tarbutt, Treasurer of the Westminster Abbey Old Choristers' Association, founded in 1892, remembers what a strenuous job it was to take the music for the following week round to the Abbey on a trolley, as it was the duty of the senior boys to help the choirmen and much of the music was in huge bound volumes. Most of it is now up in the desolate spaces of the triforium.

On Tuesdays the boys rehearsed with the men, preparing music both for the Abbey and for Gresham College. Gradually the madrigals, ballets and canzonets were returning to the repertoire, though by 1910 the boys were no longer allowed to sing at City Company dinners.

The boys were going then to good schools. One had gone on to Pembroke College, Oxford, and the ex-choristers provided three organ scholars in a row at Exeter College. Seeing the improved standard of the education the Governors of Westminster School empowered their Headmaster to offer an annual exhibition remitting all tuition fees (30 guineas a year) to any boy under 15 from the Choir House who had reached a sufficiently high standard.

The year 1911 closed the Abbey for six months when the choristers 'became ordinary boys again'. It was a bad year for epidemics in many schools and institutions but the Choir House was immune—but only just, as one of the boys, named Haddock, developed measles only forty-eight hours after the actual coronation. The probationers were allowed in somewhere, and the choir were much fascinated afterwards to see themselves on the cinematograph, someone suggesting that in future the division of the choir should not be between Cantoris and Decani but between round mouths and square mouths. A Dr Gow sent between fifty and sixty tickets for everyone to see the Royal Procession.

One very great gain to the school was a gift of £1,000 from Canon Hensley Henson, then Rector of St Margaret's, Westminster. This sum he set aside from profits on the stands erected in his churchyard and it was used to set up a scholarship of some £35 a year.

One of the boys who was helped by the School in these years was Harry Sebree Price, who came from Handsworth, Staffordshire. Born in 1891, he was admitted to Westminster School from the Choir School in 1908 and went to Exeter in 1911 as an organ scholar following Laurance (sic) Collingwood. When the war came, he was twice mentioned in despatches in 1917 and was awarded the Military Cross on New Year's Day 1918. His years in the Choir School affected his life in an unusual way, as he married the sister of his contemporary, Herbert Dawson.

Amongst the special treats of 1911 were visits to *A Midsummer Night's Dream* and—a forerunner of many more—to Lord's Cricket Ground. The Abbey reopened early in September.

Two of the best known of the men went from the choir about this time. Hilton retired immediately after the coronation and died in 1915. He had come to the Abbey in 1870 at the age of thirty, had sung a solo at the 1887 Jubilee and had been to Osborne to sing *Nazareth* to the Queen. He had given great pleasure to Gladstone by his singing of W. E's Latin setting of *Rock of Ages* with music by Bridge. He had sung in oratorios and operas in 1875 with Sir Charles Santley, had been a great singer of glees and was, according to *The Daily Telegraph* in a heartwarming obituary, 'a man with the appearance of a Viking and the heart of a boy'.

Boys were admitted as choristers by the Dean himself, in St Faith's Chapel as a rule and once, as the coronation scaffolding was still standing, in the Jerusalem Chamber.

To increase the amenities of the boys, Bridge presented them with a gramophone which was voted 'a very entertaining machine'. From Canon Duckworth's will came the case of statues of Christ and His Apostles which had been carved by the Danish sculptor Thorwaldsen and given to Duckworth by the Princess of Wales (later Queen Alexandra), and her sister the Queen of Denmark in 1874. The gift survived the blitz and stands today at the end of the school dining room. His crowning legacy was disclosed a few months later in the £1,000 left for the good of the boys. He loved children as much as his friend Lewis Carroll had done, in the days when Alice Liddell lived in Dean's Yard, and both went with the three little girls on the river on the day that *Alice in Wonderland* was born.

The Dean and Mrs Ryle took the boys to Maskelyne's to see the conjurors and had them to tea at the Deanery in groups. At Christmas a huge 'fish pie' or 'luxury dip' brought everyone presents; and another very popular event, now lapsed, was an annual dance at Fulham Palace. The boys declared for another comparative newcomer: 'The motor bus was a great success, and whisked us home in grand fashion.'

The choristers had the use of the tennis court in the Abbey Garden and worked hard to keep it in good condition; and they enjoyed going to the Westminster Baths to swim.

These were the days of Welsh Disestablishment and F. E. Smith, and the subject was as hotly debated in the school as in the nearby Parliament House.

The start on the new Choir House, as it was called, was made in 1913 with the intention that it should be finished before the end of 1915, and this schedule was maintained, though the skies were to fall during its building.

Nothing in the magazines shows more vividly the gap between 1914 and our own day than the facetious articles and stories which appeared in the school magazine for the first year of the war. The October number speaks of the prophets being confounded because the war has already lasted ten weeks: it says the encouragement given to the khaki-clad old boys was so great that 'they simply can't help getting the V.C. and pretty soon'. It is all very gay and exciting and the wet Flanders plain is dry of bones.

Amongst those praised in the Examiner's Report of the school in the summer of 1913 was the late Alan Howland, who went on to Dulwich, served with distinction during the War and afterwards went to Worcester College, Oxford, where he became Captain of the XV, and President of the O.U.D.S. in 1922. After acting at the St Martin's Theatre for several years, he joined the B.B.C. in the days of 2LO where he was 'Uncle Peter' and became Director of the Children's Department. About 1935 he left to become a free-lance journalist and commentator, but re-joined in 1939 as an announcer, and there will be few who listened then who do not remember his reading of the News during the war years. He died in 1947 in his forty-eighth year.

Similar to him, in that his career was interrupted by war, is David Valentine Willcocks, Fellow of King's College, Cambridge. During the 1939 war he served with distinction and was awarded the Military Cross. In 1947 he was appointed organist of Salisbury Cathedral and has since moved to Worcester.

The school remained in the buildings in Little Smith Street until the new Choir House was opened in October 1915 in Dean's Yard. Here at long last the choristers had come back within sight of the Abbey and faced the ancient buildings, taking their rightful place.

The new buildings were a very great improvement and were in keeping with the progressive trends in education. External progress was matched inside: and it became the custom, rather than the exception, to go to some famous school after leaving the Abbey. It is good to read of those who later went on to the Universities.

The Headmaster, the Rev. W. B. Dams, obviously had the affection and respect of his pupils and numbers wrote to him in after life from all over the world. Unfortunately he had to resign, owing to a breakdown in health, in September 1915, a month before the new buildings, to whose erection he had given so much of his enthusiasm, were ready.

The Rev. H. O. Cavalier succeeded him and stayed until January 1918. The School had its baptism of fire when the Rev. V. Dams, brother of the former Headmaster, was in charge as Senior Master. The December 1918 Magazine announced:

It may be of some interest to some of our readers to hear, perhaps for the first time, that one German bomb of quite unusually large size, fell in the back premises of the School. In its flight it caught on a window ledge and tore off the thin container where the explosive material was kept: on reaching the ground the forepart of the bomb made a considerable hole and buried itself 8 feet in concrete, but did no serious damage. Had the container not been torn, the probabilities are that a large part of the School would have been destroyed.

An inscription was put up, which the Rev. V. Dams came to see in 1952: but it had gone, having been destroyed by another German bomb, which fell in the same place in 1940.

After the resignation of the Rev. H. O. Cavalier in December 1917, the Rev. E. H. Muncey came to be Headmaster but suffered from asthma and stayed only a few months. He was followed by the Rev. W. E. Morgan who had been a Chaplain in France, and was the first married man since the Blackmores. He stayed only until 1922.

The great spectacle of 1919 was the Peace Day of July 19th, when the boys went with the choristers of St Paul's and of the Temple Church to sing in the ceremony at the Cenotaph. Walford Davies, later Sir Walford, conducted the boys and the London Symphony Orchestra. The position at the Cenotaph was ideal for the boys as they were at the procession's most impressive point, at which the Commanders saluted the symbol of their dead companions. In the evening the older boys were taken out into St James's Park to see the fireworks and bonfires.

Immediately after the Prizegiving everyone went to the Abbey where a service was held to commemorate fallen ex-choristers. The Dean gave an address and the choir was composed entirely of present and past choristers. Today the Memorial has been revised to include the dead choristers of 1939-45.

At Christmas 1919 the whole Royal Family came to the Abbey.

In 1918-19 the school was formally classed as a *bona fide* preparatory school and the Headmaster became a member of the Association. Another development which was to be of great benefit was the foundation, led by the Headmasters of St Paul's, King's College, Cambridge and the Abbey, of a Choir Schools Association. The first meeting took place at the Abbey, and a resolution was passed to the effect that 'In view of the urgent educational requirements of the present time a Choir Schools' Association be formed at once'. The meetings began soon afterwards.

Another big break was the departure of Dr Alcock, who went to Salisbury and was knighted for his services to music. E. Stanley Roper C.V.O., a distinguished and greatly loved ex-Abbey boy, had been assistant at the organ during the war and it was an occasion of great rejoicing when in 1919 he was appointed Organist of the Chapel Royal. After sixty-four years' connection with the Abbey, he was one of the musical committee of the coronation of Elizabeth II.

Edward Lloyd, who must have seemed semi-immortal, sang at the age of 70 at the Lady Mayoress's concert for Belgian refugees on February 3, 1917, and Laurance Collingwood C.B.E., who had been born in 1887 and left the Abbey in 1902 had gone from his Organ Scholarship at Exeter College Oxford to study at the St Petersburg Conservatorium. He lived in Russia, married Anna Koenig, a Russian lady, and worked with Albert Coates. In the year 1918 he escaped to England after the October Revolution and was principal conductor at Sadler's Wells from 1931 until 1946.

During all those years a great visitor and willing lecturer at the school was the Rev. Dr Jocelyn Perkins, who still entertains Old Boys' Meetings and is President of the Old Choristers' Association, and who in 1919 gave a talk on Fiume and the romantic Gabriele d'Annunzio, under the title 'Italia Irridenta'. Miss Sugg was also a great frequenter of Choir School gatherings and a friend to many exchoristers.

At the school the end of the war saw the biggest change of all—the end of an epoch. Sir Frederick Bridge retired on December 31, 1918, after forty-three years at the Abbey. He was succeeded by Sydney Hugo Nicholson, later Sir

Sydney, who remained at the Abbey until Christmas 1927 and left to found his Royal School of Church Music. The present writer knew him at St Michael's College, Tenbury, in the first years of the Second World War, and knows the enthusiasm which he aroused in others with his indefatigable capacity for organization. He was an innovator with all the implications of the word; and, during his years of office, held considerable disciplinary powers within the school, especially as there were many day boys who were introduced into the school so that services could be sung all the year round. Also in the summer term of 1918 the experiment of having non-singers was begun, but within three years was found undesirable.

It was Nicholson who, with the great help of Mr J. Russell Perry, began another side of the school life which has remained and without which it would be impossible to make a portrait of him. This was his deep belief in the Scout Movement of his friend Lord Baden-Powell of Gilwell, O.M. A Wolf Cub Pack was founded in 1928.

The bias of all special occasions in the post-war Abbey was towards the Memorial Service; but there were returning some of the pageants, such as the Installation of the Knights of the Bath on May 24, 1924. An innovation due to Nicholson was the successful Cathedral Choirs Festival, which sang in the Abbey and this conception was to lead him three years later to found his own school of church music. Sir Frederick Bridge had died on May 26, 1925, and a memorial tablet was dedicated to his memory.

Within the school itself is a fine new stained glass window set in the bay of the dining room, depicting Henry Purcell standing and around him, each in one pane of glass, the names of the organists and Masters of the Choristers since the Dissolution in 1540. The designer, executant and donor of this was Mr A. K. Nicholson, a brother of the organist.

Mr F. H. Goodwin, who remained until the break up of the school in 1940.

Seeing the approach of war, the Dean and Chapter made arrangements with the authorities of Christ's Hospital for the boys to share that school's fine buildings at Horsham in Sussex, and accordingly they were evacuated there in time for the autumn term of 1939.

The threat of invasion however, coupled with the fact that it was extremely difficult to maintain within the framework of a normal Public School the choral practices which an organist of Westminster Abbey requires, led to the disbanding of the Abbey Choir and School. It was a pleasure to many of the old boys to hear that Miss Weston, who had given many years of her life to their welfare, was remembered gratefully by the Dean and Chapter.

It is curious that the '40s have always been critical for the Abbey choir. In 1540 Henry VIII dissolved the Monastery: in the 1640's the break-up was complete, and although the '45 Rebellion did not affect the school, the 1840's were bad and led to the overdue formation of a separate establishment. The year 1940 led to a break up and a blitz which might have been final.

The third Dissolution took place in 1940, the last boys leaving at Christmas. Those old enough went to their big schools: five of the younger ones went to the Choir School of New College, Oxford; six to Magdalen; and two to King's College, Cambridge. Dr Bullock left the Abbey in the same year; and Dr William Neil McKie, who was serving overseas with the R.A.F., was appointed to succeed him.

In the early months of 1943 the Pro-Precentor, Dr Jocelyn Perkins, and the deputy organist, Dr O. H. Peasgood, gathered together a temporary choir from schools in London and Middlesex, so that boys might be heard on Sundays, festivals and special days. Easter Sunday

1943 was the first occasion on which they functioned as a choir for a whole day's services. They did not attend school at the Abbey, although thirteen joined when it reopened.

When the school reopened there was a race for time, and Dr McKie had a difficult task. The decorators came in on New Year's Day, 1947, the first voice trial was held on January 10th and the Battle of Britain Window was unveiled by King George VI on May 21st. On November 20th, Her Majesty the Queen, then H.R.H. the Princess Elizabeth, was married to H.R.H. the Duke of Edinburgh, K.G.

One of the first things to exercise the mind of Mr Thompson was the provision of adequate playing fields. The time-honoured pitches at Vincent Square had disappeared under a balloon barrage site and the ground was repulsive. The railings had gone with those of Dean's Yard into the melting pot. Journeys had to be made to Raynes Park for a little over a year and it was there that the football and cricket teams were born. Then Vincent Square was opened: and there was a great thrill of appreciation at its proximity and splendour. Within five minutes—trotting by way of the former disreputable area, much of it now bombed and re-erected in concrete and towering stone—players can go from school to ground.

A further great joy was the permission from His Grace the Lord Archbishop of Canterbury to use the grounds of Lambeth Palace. This was a boon to set beside Vincent Square which can be used only at certain times.

One of the greatest uses of Lambeth comes on Saturday evenings when Scouts and Cubs can go down and lay trails, light fires and cook: and it is a pleasure to get away and relax.

The school work is the same as in other preparatory schools, and the time spent on services and rehearsals—and after all that is the real reason for the school's existence—is more than balanced by small forms, which never have more than eleven boys in one classroom, and by the long terms. The result is that the boys do very well in the competitive examinations and, being used to working and playing hard, find no lack of energy when they go on. The one general comment when older boys return is that the food is never as good as it used to be at the Choir School, where its planning and preparation has been in the same capable hands for the past five years.

The school today is divided into two houses, named after Blow and Purcell, and there is very keen rivalry in House Matches which are played for challenge cups. The boys still swim in the neighbouring Marsham Street baths or go to Dolphin Square. Cricket and Football fixtures are numerous; but the Football, Athletic and Cricket Matches with St Paul's Cathedral are the most keenly appreciated; and the Jackson Cup, which goes to the winner of the majority of the events, is still the crown.

The acting of plays is a great feature of the present school, which since 1947 has presented *As You Like It*; *Julius Caesar* in the ancient courtyard outside the Jerusalem Chamber; *The Merchant of Venice* in the great Hall of Westminster School, and *A Midsummer Night's Dream* in the Abbey Garden against a background of flowers and a bombed building. The Festival of Britain prevented a production in 1951, as there was a festival of music in the Abbey which lasted a fortnight and was quite unforgettable, as was the magnificent scene when they sang at the Dedication of the Royal Festival Hall on the South Bank. A visit to the Exhibition was one of the highlights of the year.

Many have been the visits of foreign royalties and notables, especially to the Unknown Warrior's Grave: but of all the occasions in the Abbey, no one then at the school will ever forget the last visit of His Majesty King George VI to the Maundy Service in 1951 and that of Her Majesty the Queen in the following year.

The necessary licence for the re-opening of the school was granted after his personal inspection by the Minister of Education.

Outings are continued as before: to the Old Vic; to The Open Air Theatre; to the plays at Westminster School, now understandable in English. Sometimes on a wet Wednesday afternoon there is an excursion to a News Theatre or a Cartoon Programme. Very soon after the re-opening a talking film projector was bought and film shows are given on Saturday evenings several times a term during the autumn and spring.

Usually, once or twice a term, a longer outing to Epping Forest or Wimbledon Common is possible and a regular Exeat of four or five days makes a break at the beginning or middle of November. Since the school does not disperse for Christmas, this break is particularly welcome.

Christmas is a particularly happy time, with the school changed and the boys decorating their own dormitories according to taste. On Christmas Eve after Evensong the boys go round with the Gentlemen of the Choir to sing carols at Westminster Hospital, and refreshments are provided. When the boys have gone to bed, the staff decorate the passage and the main downstairs rooms; desks are stacked away and table tennis is set up in the schoolroom and in the gym, while the billiard table is more used than ever. The meals are something to be believed and remembered. On Christmas night there is a party at which the Dean, resplendent in a hat made for him by one of the boys, is the guest of honour.

On their return on Christmas Eve from singing at the hospital the boys go in procession round the house, everyone in the school coming to watch, until they go down into the dining room and in front of a crib a huge candle is lit which will burn all over Christmas. This is lit by the youngest boy in the school. Nowadays the youngest boys go home before Christmas, but there is no doubt that everyone who goes would like to have the best of both worlds, and envies those who stay.

There is an Exeat on Boxing Day after the Carol Service so that boys can go out with their parents. On the 27th, after another Carol Service, there is a party given by Field Marshal the Viscount Montgomery of Alamein, K.G., who provides a tea and a conjuror and, whenever possible, comes in person. After the war, he presented a badge to be worn by the senior chorister: and he has on many occasions taken three or four boys out at a time to the Athenaeum to lunch and then to the Royal Tournament, to the Trooping the Colour Ceremony and to the circus. His car with its pennant and striking windscreen is a great attraction.

A feature that strikes everybody who comes to the school today is that the boys talk naturally with guests. Here, consideration and respect for other people's feelings gives access to the Headmaster over any troubles, small or big.

And so, as the footsteps of the choristers go forward past the coronation of Elizabeth II and into the future, it remains only to wish and to hope for those who come after as happy a time at the school as the boys of today enjoy.

Chapter Twenty

THE CORONATION OF ELIZABETH
THE SECOND

And so Elizabeth II was crowned.

We had begun rehearsals in St Margaret's, Westminster, on Tuesday May 5th, exactly three weeks earlier. From the school thirty boys had been chosen; the remaining six probationers attending all the rehearsals except those of the Earl Marshal and having seats in the triforium during the Service.

Most of the living composers of the choral works were present and were consulted repeatedly. Dr, now Sir William McKie, was Director of the Coronation Music and his sub-conductors were Dr John Dykes Bower of St Paul's Cathedral and Dr William H. Harris of St George's Chapel, Windsor. All choristers were expected to be note-perfect before these final rehearsals.

Rather unexpectedly the practices did not upset the curriculum of the school, mainly because there were no Abbey services and therefore there was considerable spare time in the afternoons. The atmosphere even more closely resembled that of an ordinary preparatory school, and there was a much appreciated long holiday at Easter. There were successful athletics meetings against St Paul's Cathedral and Westminster Underschool.

Nor did work suffer, and one of the boys carried off the top Open Scholarship to a well known Public School during the period of the greatest musical activity. Crowds were avoided, and swimming was postponed but otherwise the routine was normal. The boys appeared in television, sang in recorded programmes on the wireless, were photographed and stared at, yet they became neither bored nor over-excited.

It was perhaps fitting that they should sing Evensong at 3 p.m. on Saturdays in Lent in St Margaret's, Westminster, and that rehearsals should be held there, because so many of their earliest Masters and predecessors lay buried around and beneath them. It was a matter for regret that one of the most distinguished living ex-Abbey choristers, Dr E. Stanley Roper, who was to have had a part in the directorate, had been forced to resign from this and from the Chapel Royal through ill-health. Another ex-Abbey boy present was Mr Herbert Dawson, the Organist of St Margaret's.

There were four rehearsals for boys' voices only, three for full choir and, on Tuesday May 26th, a full-scale one in the Abbey for choir and orchestra. An innovation was the inviting of forty ladies representing the Commonwealth to sing in the choir.

Not long before the Day the boys spent a full afternoon and evening in Lambeth Palace Grounds, lighting fires for cooking and erecting a rope runway. The Archbishop, walking alone in his garden, came over like any squire in whose grounds Scouts or Cubs were camping, and chatted with us. When he asked if the youngest had yet learned their Walton *Te Deum*, he was offered an excerpt but with mock horror preferred to wait. Two days after the coronation he met the boys in the same grounds playing cricket and congratulated them.

On the Saturday in the lull between the Earl Marshal's rehearsals of May 27 and 29, and the coronation of June 2, the boys spent the evening in Dean's Yard building a trestle bridge and following an elaborate trail, oblivious of the sightseers who flowed in and out of the Yard at all hours of the day.

On May 26 boys and staff were invited to tea at the newly-restored Deanery, which had been badly damaged in the blitz of 1940. After a most satisfying meal in the refectory, the visitors were shown round by the Dean and Mrs Don and taken out on to the leads of the cloisters where all were fascinated by the carved stone heads and the unusual views of the Abbey. In fact so enjoyable was the occasion that the boys were most reluctant to leave. One serious questioner, hearing that former Deans of Westminster had also been Bishops of Rochester as well, and knowing the great part the Dean has in a coronation, was overheard to ask, 'Mr Dean, is the Dean of Westminster more important than a Bishop?' The reply came with equal seriousness, 'Oh yes: much more important.'

A frequent visitor to the school was the Viscount Montgomery of Alamein who came to change into his Garter robes, and who posed for the boys on the doorstep with his page carrying his coronet. The page stayed at the school and was the centre of a barrage of questions. The Field Marshal also provided a tea which was much enjoyed, and at lunch one day told the boys that his *George* had belonged to Lord Roberts.

The details of the great ceremony were worked out with the most meticulous care and there cannot have been a coronation more punctiliously prepared. After one of the rehearsals the choir stewards went into the Abbey and studied plans for the seating. Each place was numbered and each steward had a blueprint. It was apparently unavoidable that many of the choir could not see the floor of the Abbey.

The splendour of the Earl Marshal's rehearsal, on Friday May 29, was astonishing. The Duchess of Norfolk represented the Queen and every phase of the service was gone through with the peers and Knights of the various Orders of Chivalry in their robes and mantles. The blue of the hangings and the gold of the massive central carpet made a perfect background for the riot of colours. The Earl Marshal used a portable microphone for comments on positioning and timing.

On the eve we were privileged to go into the Jerusalem Chamber and see the Regalia at close range as it lay on the long table and while Yeomen Warders of the Tower pointed out details to us.

The boys went to bed early and were awakened at 5 a.m. when the news of the climbing of Everest spread like wildfire and added to the excitement which was too intense to be noisy. All ate a good breakfast and found that sandwiches had already been put into cassock pockets. They robed, as previously, in the Song School, the top twenty-two remaining there and the rest going to their places with decani choir. The Headmaster and the present writer were stewards wearing scarlet cassocks and blue arm bands with the Abbey arms in yellow. The other choristers robed in Westminster School's gymnasium, the gentlemen in the Chapter House and the forty ladies in the Museum.

The Processional Choir was lucky in that it was not required to be in the Abbey until 9.15. Meanwhile cantoris choir lined up in the East Cloister where it was very cold. However, only a short time elapsed before the signal was given and, the men leading, we moved into the Abbey, across the *Theatre* before a blazon of the peerage. Everything was incredibly orderly and we saw decani moving into position across the gulf from us. Mr Eugene Cruft, father of two former Abbey choristers, was acting as Secretary to the orchestra which was already assembled in the organ loft under the leadership of Mr Paul Beard. Their names read like a roll call of British instrumentalists and their playing under the baton of Sir Adrian Boult would have been reason enough for getting up at five o'clock in the morning.

At 9.30 the Regalia was carried in procession from the high altar by the Abbey clergy and by the Headmaster of Westminster and the Master of the Queen's Scholars, preceded by the Abbey and Chapel Royal choirs singing the Litany to the setting of Thomas Tallis. Amid a great hush they moved to the West Door where the Regalia was handed over to the great Officers of State who were to bear it before the Queen. The choir then went to their places in the front of decani choir.

While the great congregation waited, the magnificent orchestra played more than twenty items by English composers including music for the separate processions. That of the Princes and Princesses of the Blood was led by H.R.H. the Princess Royal, who was most reminiscent of her mother, the late Queen Mary. This was stirring indeed. So too was the entry of Her Majesty Queen Elizabeth the Queen Mother and H.R.H. the Princess Margaret.

So we came perceiving yet imperceptibly to the fanfares and the wonder of the Queen's procession, a tide of surpassing loveliness with Her Majesty like a ninth wave.

Parry's anthem *I was glad* was sung, the vivats of the Queen's Scholars sounding as the Queen was passing under the organ loft.

The recognition proved most moving with the Queen seeming a lonely figure as she stood and then curtsied to her people while the Archbishop with superb delivery proclaimed her to the four corners. The choir were to cry out only at the western presentation and certainly did not fail of their duty.

Without music followed the Oath and the Presenting of the Holy Bible, after which began the Communion Service with the Introit by Dr Herbert Howells, *Behold O God our Defender* and the Gradual by Dr William H. Harris, *Let my prayer come up into Thy Presence*. The Creed was sung to Vaughan Williams' setting with the Abbey choir singing certain phrases alone.

Then four Knights of the Garter took from the Heralds the wavering golden canopy for the Queen's Anointing while *Come Holy Ghost* was sung. When the Archbishop had prayed with his hand on the Ampulla, *Zadok the Priest*, whose words have been used for at least a thousand years, were sung to the familiar music of Handel. This ended amid a great and oppressive silence as the Queen was anointed, the Spurs and Sword presented and, for the first time in history, the Armills were put on. Then the Dean of Westminster with the Mistress of the Robes put on the Queen the Robe Royal or Pall of cloth of gold with the Stole Royal, the Orb was brought and returned to the altar, the Ring was placed on the Queen's fourth finger, the exquisite Sceptres with the Cross and with the Dove were presented, and then, at last the Crown was brought and in the supreme moment, placed upon the Queen's head.

Immediately after the fanfares and the great shouts while the peers and peeresses put on their coronets and the Kings of Arms their crowns, we could hear the distant guns of the Tower. After the Archbishop's prayer in the hushed silence the choir sang Sir George Dyson's *Confortare*.

The Enthroning with its subsequent Homage brought the Queen and the ceremonies surrounding her nearer to us: and the choir sang sixteenth-century John Redford's *Rejoice in the Lord*, Dr Healey Willan of Canada's *O Lord our Governour* and S. S. Wesley's *Thou wilt keep him in perfect peace*. Many regretted the omission of Byrd's *I will not leave you comfortless* and Gibbons' *O clap your hands*, but the Homage had been shortened to save fatigue. At the end there was a great fanfare and cries of *God save Queen Elizabeth. Long live Queen Elizabeth. May the Queen live for ever*.

The whole congregation then sang the Old Hundreth with Dr Vaughan Williams' setting and with John Dowland's faux-bourdon in verse four and a triumphant trumpet descant in verse three.

Then came the central part of the Communion. The whole service seemed so much deeper in its meaning and atmosphere than anything the majority present had ever experienced that some of the music which had sounded splendid in St Margaret's seemed to shrink and to be inadequate, though this certainly did not apply to the moment when, after Vaughan Williams' Sanctus, his lovely *O taste and see* was sung pianissimo by three Abbey boys unaccompanied, alternating with the Abbey men during the Queen's and the Duke's communion.

The last choral work, Sir William Walton's *Te Deum*, seemed fitting to the occasion and although somewhat startling in its apparent brassiness persuaded that it was in the grand manner and on a suitable scale. And so in a service that was at once superbly intricate and touchingly humble, Queen Elizabeth was crowned.

When the Queen had gone, the congregation was marshalled out of the Abbey. A microphone voice announced which sections were to move and there was no confusion.

The choir on the cantoris, or north, side of the Abbey had had to cross in full view between the throne and the altar. It appeared that at the previous coronation cantoris had not been able to get out until six o'clock and several of the gentlemen had been afraid of a repetition. Decani could get out and into the cloisters without attracting much attention. It was therefore the cause of a muted cheer when, after the service was over, the voice announced, 'The choir southside may now move'.

Refreshment buffets were ready in the cloisters for the boys; but we returned to the school and were already having boiled eggs for tea by the time the State Coach which had been waiting just outside (the school doorway providing a shelter for the grooms and postillions from the pelting rain) rumbled out into the Sanctuary. As it disappeared under the archway into the rain and the crowds for the great procession home, Dean's Yard was suddenly and devastatingly empty. It was all over.

But if you have ever sat in the Abbey and dreamed, if by degrees the grey shadows have begun to move and to stir with colour, if the banners and blazons, the shining armour and the gold, come to complete the white and scarlet of the choir so that the whole place is filled with the cry, Here is Mowbray, here is Bohun, here is Beaufort, Warwick and Westmorland, Lancaster, Richmond, yea and much more than these, here is Plantagenet, then you will know, beyond the trivialities, the truth and will have understood the sacring and the crowning of the Queen.

INDEX

260

INDEX

Chapter Clerk: *see* Westminster Abbey

Chapter Minutes: *see* Westminster Abbey

Charles I, 96, 101, 102, 104

Charles II, 96, 98, 102, 119, 122-3, 128, 131

Charles V, Emperor, 22, 29

Charlotte, Queen, 146

Chaucer, Geoffrey, 23

Chester Cathedral, 87, 230

Chester, Colonel, 133, 152

Chesterfield, Philip Dormer, Earl of, 138

Chiffinch, Thomas, 126

Chiswick, 84, 93

Choir Schools' Association, 242-3

Choral Service of the United Churche, The, 193

Christian, Alice and Thomas, 133

Christian, William, 133

Christie, Manson and Woods, 152

Christmas Bells, 216

Christ's Hospital, 247

Chronicles of England, The, 24

Church House, *see* Westminster Abbey

Church, James, 112, 113

Church, William, 41, 42, 43

Clapham, 188

Clarke, 131

Clarke (Chorister), 189

Clarke, John, 92, 96, 102

Clavering, 161

Clement, A. F., 187-8

Clement, Arthur, 188

Clement, Horace, 188

Clementi, 164

Coates, Albert, 243

Coborne, Lancelot, 101

Coks, 35

Colebrook, Elizabeth, 146

Colet, Dean, 76

Collard, 230

Collingwood, Laurence, 238, 243

Committee of Lords and Commons, The, 103, 113

Communist Manifesto, The, 173

Convocation, 212

Cooke, Benjamin, 143, 145, 146, 149, 164, 181

Cooke, Robert, 172, 175, 178

Cooper, 188

Cork (Eire), 170

Corfe, Arthur Thomas, 164

Corny, Thomas, 126

Cornyshe (Cornyssh), family, 19-23, 25, 35, 49-50, 63, 64

Court, Cecil Martin, 215

Covent Garden, Shop in, 149

Covent Garden, Theatre Royal, 144, 145, 149

Coward, James, 180, 181

Coxe, Bishop A. Cleveland, 193-4

Cranmer, Thomas, Archbishop of Canterbury, 52, 57

Cranwell, Mr, 88

Cretoff, Roger, 28

Cricket, 207, 208, 209, 228, 248, 249, 253

Croft, William, 139, 143, 219

Cromwell, Oliver, 110

Cromwell, Thomas, 37

Croppe, Thomas, 42

Crosdill, John, 145, 146, 174

Crotch, 154

Croyland, 173

Crucifix, Robert, 151

Cruft, Eugene, 255

Cumbe, Brother Peter, 15

Cumberland, George, Duke of, 141, 160, 161

Cunningham, 181

Cunningham, Mr, 218

Curiosities of London, 141

Daily Telegraph, The, 219, 238

Dalzell, 232

Dams, Rev. V., 241, 242

Dams, Rev. W. B., 187, 237, 241

Daniell-Bainbridge, Rev., 236

Davies, Frances, 164

Davis, Edmond & John, 181

Dawlish, Devon, 148

Dawson, Herbert, 234, 236, 238, 253

Day, Bishop, 57

Day, Thomas, 102, 104, 105

Dean's Yard, 13, 14, 188, 190, 191, 199, 229, 233, 239, 241, 248, 253, 259

Declaration of Indulgence, The, 134

Denbigh, 25

Denmark, The Queen of, 239

Devonshire, The Earl of, 97

Dickens, Charles, 199, 200, 209, 229

Diodorus Siculus, 25

262

INDEX

INDEX

INDEX